DIRECTOR

to go

....Dennis Chominsky

Prentice Hall PTR, Upper Saddle River, NJ 07458

Editorial/Production Supervision: Mary Sudul
Acquisitions Editor: Tim Moore
Editorial Assistant: Julie Okulicz
Manufacturing Buyer: Alexis Heydt/Maura Goldstaub
Art Director: Gail Cocker-Bogusz
Interior Series Design: Rosemarie Votta
Cover Design: Scott Weiss
Cover Design Direction: Jerry Votta

The publisher offers discounts on this book when ordered in bulk quantities.
For more information, contact

Corporate Sales Department,
Prentice Hall PTR
One Lake Street
Upper Saddle River, NJ 07458
Phone: 800-382-3419; FAX: 201-236-714
E-mail (Internet): corpsales@prenhall.com

Printed in the United States of America

10 9 8 7 6 5 4 3 2 1

ISBN 0-13-013782-0

Prentice-Hall International (UK) Limited, London
Prentice-Hall of Australia Pty. Limited, Sydney
Prentice-Hall Canada Inc., Toronto
Prentice-Hall Hispanoamericana, S.A., Mexico
Prentice-Hall of India Private Limited, New Delhi
Prentice-Hall of Japan, Inc., Tokyo
Simon & Schuster Asia Pte. Ltd., Singapore
Editora Prentice-Hall do Brasil, Ltda., Rio de Janeiro

**This book is dedicated to
Dad, Mom, John Paul, and Diana.
Thanks for getting me here safely.**

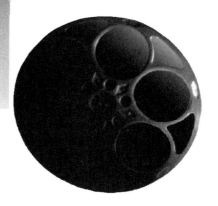

CONTENTS

CHAPTER 3

BUILDING BETTER NAVIGATIONAL TOOLS WITH INTERACTIVE APPLICATIONS 57

CHAPTER 4

DIVING INTO DIRECTOR WITH LINGO 85

CHAPTER 5

CREATING KILLER VISUAL EFFECTS 129

CHAPTER 6

ADDING LIFE THROUGH ANIMATION AND LAYERING 155

CHAPTER 7

TECHNIQUES EVERY DEVELOPER CAN USE 197

CHAPTER 8

AVOIDING AUDIO AND VIDEO NIGHTMARES 243

CHAPTER 9

IT'S ALL FINISHED ... NOW DELIVER IT 295

CHAPTER 10

SHOCK IT FOR THE WEB 333

CHAPTER 11

INTRODUCTION

In today's world of ever changing technologies, one thing remains constant—people need to communicate. Over the past few decades, people have become partially immune to static presentations. With the types of special effects used in the movies and on television, the average person's attention span has gotten shorter and shorter while the search for more exciting methods of communicating information grows. Computers have enabled most of us to evolve from the old dog-and-pony shows to something maybe a bit more exciting ... the still-image electronic slide show. Over the past few years, however, the need to elevate beyond this linear slide show has open the doors for technology to deliver new and effective types of presentations.

Enter the *true* multimedia presentation, incorporating a variety of media formats into an exciting and interactive platform. Macromedia Director allows users to create and display some of the best multimedia applications seen anywhere. Its unique ability to custom design virtually any type of presentation (or movie as Macromedia calls it) and incorporate just about every type of digital file available allows you to present your message in a way that can take on whole new level of style and creativity.

Macromedia Director is an innovative program combining the most powerful tools in a single package for producing and designing the high-quality professional interactive applications and digital presentations. No other software package on the market allows you to use a combination of graphics, images, video, text and animations with the flexibility and interactivity to develop virtually any type of application you need to deliver. If you are developing applications to distribute over the Internet, have no fear. Many of the limitations of interactivity and integration have been eliminated via Shockwave, Macromedia's solution for the explosion of the Web and the demand for pushing it's boundaries. Director has truly become the industry standard among programs for creating and distributing interactive applications with its award-winning power, performance, and productivity.

Due to the vast capabilities available within Director, I will only be able to touch on a small amount of the true flexibility and power of this program. I will cover some of the more advanced features and real-life examples for those users who know the basics of Director and are looking to increase their knowledge of the program. Once you have conquered the basics and have a good handle on how Director works, let your imagination run wild with whatever you want to create. This book is written to demonstrate just how easy it is to begin putting together high-powered presentations and interactive multimedia movies. Take the time to experiment on your own. Use the examples presented in this book as just that ... *examples*. What you should get out of each situation presented in this book are ideas that will get you started in the right direction for putting together your own creative programs and the know-how to build the types of projects you use to just admire. Remember, be patient. Miracles may happen overnight, programming complex interactive applications does not. This book tries to cut through the fluff and focus on the essentials.

WHO SHOULD READ THIS BOOK

This book is written for people who are already designing multimedia applications and want to continue developing their interactive programming abilities to bring their skills up to the next level. This book is intended toward users who:

◆ Are In A Hurry—programmers who want and need information fast.

◆ Already Know The Basics—this is not an introduction to Director book.

◆ Expect Real Insight—the examples are from real projects. The Notes, Tips, and Warnings will really give you the perspective you are looking for in a book.

◆ Want To Improve The Quality Of Their Work—serious individuals who take pride in developing new applications while learning every step of the way.

Through the course of this book, I will introduce different features programmers have been integrating into their applications today. It would be great to fill up a book with the best and wildest programming scripts that have ever been developed, but if they don't warrant any practical use, then I have wasted your time.

HOW THIS BOOK IS WRITTEN

This book is laid out in a way that focuses on some very specific topics within Director. You can use this book as a quick reference, jump right in and get the answer you need type of book. There are a few sections that do apply a bit more of a basic overtone. The reason for this is that with a program as powerful and dynamic as Director, with the ability to incorporate so many different media types, you need to understand how to put together and use the examples presented throughout the course of this book and look at the bigger picture. By analyzing the examples in this book and formulating your own versions when creating your projects, you will begin to expand the capabilities you can offer to your clients and pick from a multitude of tools to incorporate in your next Director piece.

Each chapter contains a variety of icons indicating points of interest that will help you while developing your applications. These icons include:

Notes contain information that will make understanding the point being discussed more clear and include any related information that fulfills the topic being discussed.

Tips are suggestions that can save you time and energy while developing your program. Some tips contain recommendations about other topics that will help develop your skills.

These are cautions. I highly recommend you read them to make yourself aware of possible problems or pitfalls you may encounter while programming.

WHAT YOU WILL NEED

I will assume that if you are flipping through the pages of this book, you are interested in using Director or are already a Director programmer. My recommendation to get the best bang from this book is to own or have access to Director so that you can walk through the procedures step by step while working in front of your computer. This book covers some topics for version 6.0, some for 6.5 and even for 7.0. Most topics cover material that applies to all these versions. When information is pertinent to only one version, I have listed which version these features fall under.

The next, and most obvious, thing you will need is a computer. Whether you work on Macintosh or Windows, just about all of the features apply to both platforms. Keep in mind that your original Director movies are cross-platform. Read Chapters 2 and 9 to learn more about working with cross-platform issues. Which ever system you choose, load it up with as much memory as possible. This will make your authoring time more enjoyable, leaving you more time to be creative and not waiting for your computer to process information.

The last thing you will need is either the Director Multimedia Studio package or other third-party programs. These are not necessarily required, but will be essential when building your multimedia applications. You can use just about any type of graphics, animation, audio or video software to create files that you can import into Director so that you can begin developing your next Director movie.

GOING BEYOND THE BOOK

One thing that makes this book unique is that you can take it beyond the text and images printed on this page. If you need to contact me regarding the topics covered in this book or have suggestions and ideas that you would like to see in the next edition, let me know. I have learned while writing this book that the more you learn about a program, the more you still have to go. If you want to ask a question or show off some of the neat things you have created using Director, email me at **dennis@pfsnewmedia.com.** If you prefer snail mail, send me a letter or CD with samples of your work to:

Prentice Hall
Attn: Dennis Chominsky
One Lake Street
Upper Saddle River, NJ 07458

OUTLOOK TOWARD THE FUTURE

Technology is moving faster than some of us can keep up with. Or is it that people today are pushing manufacturers for more features and greater performance out of their software? Whatever the case may be, software developers are constantly striving to improve on the current versions of software in distribution.

I asked a number of my friends and colleagues for their opinion regarding the future of multimedia and the role Director will play in it. A friend and fellow multimedia developer, Eric Mueller summed up the majority of responses I received with his comments, "The future of Director and the interactive industry as a whole is very bright indeed. New, rich forms of media are continually being developed, allowing developers freedom never before experienced. Through support from these new types of media, developers will finally be free to focus more on content, rather than code ... Additionally, Director has and continues to become highly extensible, allowing developers to not only build their own authoring tools, but extend Director's own environment in ways undoubtedly never imagined by even Director's original authors."

I must agree. I think the information age is going to grow even more than we can imagine. People want more value, more content, more excitement out of the information around them. I think Director will be one route people will use to provide that information in a more dynamic way. Take a look at the internet and how it has developed so far. At first, people used it only to transfer files, pass along basic information (usually in text format), and was accessed only by a select few. Today, I see more sites containing useful information while presenting it in a much more interesting way. Director has the ability to provide the end user with the interactive capabilities desired for personalizing how that information is found while providing all the flare that catches people's attention. Video, audio, and animation are becoming more commonplace on the Web. The future indeed looks very bright for developers who can take advantage of this need for content-rich information and provide it in a way that will leave the user wanting more.

EXPANDING THE APPLICATIONS

As Director makes programming easier, more people will begin adopting it's power and performance. Its flexibility allows for such a wide array of users to begin programming whatever type of application they need. There will definitely be more:

◆ Complete Websites—including Director's animation, interactivity, and high-performance digital media capabilities.

◆ Corporate Presentation—a shift from the over-indulged PowerPoint presentation to something with more impact.

◆ DVD Home Movies—adding the extra features and interactive controls that make DVDs a better product than its linear cronies.

◆ Enhanced CD—all music CDs released from the record companies will have interactive games, bios, and possibly even concert footage clips to go along with the music tracks.

◆ Kiosks—the trend for information kiosks will be popping up everywhere, in schools, in restaurants, and maybe even on sidewalk corners.

All of these things exists right now in some fashion, but will continue to increase at a rapid growth rate as Macromedia introduces more features and easier ways for developers to put these types of applications together.

TO SUM IT UP

This book tells it like it is. Real-life examples. Real-life applications. With the way technology is changing daily, more people will be using Director because of its flexibility when developing applications that will suit their specific needs. The great part about Director is its versatility. It's hard to stop at the basics. More and more, developers are pushing the limits of technology and creativity, putting together some of the most amazing multimedia applications. Once again, I encourage you to read this book, use it as a stepping stone, and then let your creativity take it one step further. Remember, your only limitations are the ones you let stand in your way. Happy programming.

ACKNOWLEDGEMENTS

Believe it or not, writing a book takes more people than I would have ever imagined. This book goes out to all the people who, throughout my life, believed in me and gave me the opportunity to fulfill my dreams. Thanks to everyone who has helped me get to where I am. To all my family and friends, I could not have done it without your support. Special thanks to Jason Miletsky, because without him, I would not have had the opportunity to write this book. Thanks to the rest of the PFS New Media staff for keeping the business going when I had to leave at 5 o'clock: Mariana, Jerges, Mike, Val, Jill, and Bill.

I would like to thank some other people who have, in some way, contributed directly or indirectly to this book, including Phil Pfisterer, Darlene Pepper, Richelle Wangelin, Eric Mueller, Joseph Graiff, Trevor Crafts, and Jay Thompson.

A special thank you goes to the team who made the ordeal all worthwhile: Tim Moore, Jim Markham, Bart Blanken, and all the others at Prentice Hall. Thanks to all of the people who graciously donated their software, including Leona Lapez at Macromedia, Steve Perlman at Visible Light, Shannon Bruce at Media Labs, Colin Adams at Indigo Rose Software Design, and Alison Baxter @ StatMedia.

To the people who put up with me during my time of stress, especially Tara King (for all those nights watching TV alone on the couch while I typed ... thank you), Brad Shalit (living with a roommate who could never hang out), and Rebecca Cochrane (for making sense out of all those figure numbers and templates). To Joe, Ruben, Dinger, Andrea and the rest of my friends, I'm available for that beer now. And, of course, my nocturnal buddy, Monty, who kept me company every night.

WHAT'S NEW
WITH DIRECTOR

Programs need to be constantly updated to keep up with the growing demands of users and innovative technological advances. For those of you who have worked with (or are still working with) Director 5.0, Macromedia has made some tremendous improvements with Version 6 to really improve the way you work and decrease the time it takes you to develop a project. Since then, Macromedia has made incredible headway with Director with the introduction of Version 7, which allows for more web-based applications to be created. This chapter will cover some of the key improvements made in Version 6 and how those, and other features, were improved on for Version 7.

DIRECTOR 6.0

BETTER FILE SUPPORT

Director now supports more file formats, especially when developing for cross-platform applications. Whether you are developing your program on a Windows system or on a Macintosh system, Director is able to recognize many more file types on both systems. These cross-platform graphic file formats include:

- ◆ BMP
- ◆ GIF
- ◆ JPEG

◆   LRG (images saved in xRes)

◆   Photoshop 3.0

◆   MacPaint

◆   PNG

◆   TIFF

◆   PICT

This list contains only image file formats. There are additional sound and digital video file formats that also work on both platforms.

EDITING SPRITES OUTSIDE OF DIRECTOR

Director has introduced a feature called Launch and Edit, which consists of the ability to select the particular application you prefer to work with while making changes to your elements within your movie. Being that most developers have a specific program in which they prefer to work in, Director now has the ability to allow you to make changes to your already imported sprites inside of Director while making the changes in another program. If you are one of those developers who is used to customizing images using programs such as Photoshop, you can select Photoshop to be the default application used for editing sprites instead of Director's internal Paint window. This very useful feature allows you to work in a program that you are more comfortable working with and offers you the ability to use programs with more features than Director's internal editing applications while it automatically updates the newly edited files and images into your cast and your score. This saves you tremendous amounts of time from having to go through the old method, which generally involved:

1. Exporting a file from Director.
2. Launching it in the editing program.
3. Making the appropriate changes.
4. Saving the new file.
5. Returning to Director.
6. Re-importing the file.
7. Finally editing the updated changes into every single area where you used that cast member.

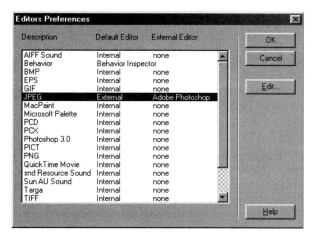

Figure 1-1   Selecting an external editing application.

Version 6 allows you to independently specify which external editing application you wish to use for each file type (Figure 1-1). See Chapter 5 for complete details on working with Launch and Edit capabilities.

MAJOR SPRITE IMPROVEMENTS

Working with sprites is the main ingredient used for building a Director movie. There have been a number of improvements made to make working with sprites much easier. These features include:

◆   More sprite channels.

◆   How sprites are displayed in the score.

◆   Accessing sprite information directly from the stage.

There are now 128 sprite channels for you to work with. Besides having the ability to add more layers to any given frame, these additional channels allow you to separate your sprites and organize them on specific channels. This comes in handy when you want to apply Lingo commands to certain channels for applying specific features (such as turning visibles on and off). By dedicating specific channels for those sprites, you will not have to worry about other sprites placed in the same channels at a later portion of your movie acquiring those unwanted characteristics.

One of the most useful feature improvements comes in the way sprites are displayed and function in the score. When a sprite is created in the score, it is now represented as a single object, covering the complete duration of the sprite (Figure 1-2). In prior versions, sprites were displayed as a series of individual frames covering the selected area. Each frame displayed only the cast member number, which made viewing a score containing several sprites very difficult to read (Figure 1-3). Having the sprite displayed as a single object makes viewing and editing a sprite much easier. You can set the information displayed for that sprite by changing what is displayed using sprite labels. To change the information displayed for sprites in the score:

1. Open the View menu.
2. Select Sprite Labels.
3. Select the type of information you want to display in your sprite from the popup menu (Figure 1-4).

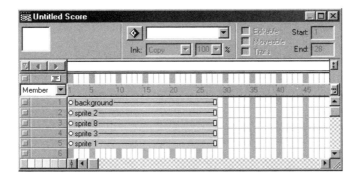

Figure 1-2   Sprites displayed in score as single objects.

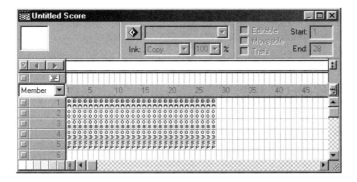

Figure 1-3   Earlier versions of the score were more difficult to view.

Figure 1-4   Sprite labels popup menu.

Changing the information with sprite labels affects the way sprites are displayed for the entire score, not just a selected sprite.

As a developer, you may prefer to work directly on the stage. Director 6 introduced a feature called Sprite Overlay (Figure 1-5). This window contains a great deal of useful sprite information condensed into a small window:

◆ The name of the sprite for easy identification.

◆ Which cast it is from.

◆ The type of file (bitmap, field, etc.).

◆ Sprite channel number.

◆ Bounding box coordinates on the stage (distance in pixels—top left corner from left side of stage, top left corner from top of stage, bottom right corner from left side of stage, bottom right corner from top of stage).

◆ Ink effects applied to sprite.

◆ Transparency level of sprite.

◆ Behavior and script information.

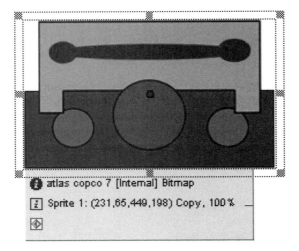

Figure 1-5   Sprite overlay window.

 Choose Sprite Overlay: Settings from the View menu to open the Overlay Settings window. Here you can select when to display the Sprite Overlay window.

The three icons in the Sprite Overlay window are quick buttons to access even more useful information directly from the stage.

1. Click the blue icon to open the Cast Members Properties window.
2. Click the red icon to open the Sprite Properties window.
3. Click the green icon to open the Behavior Inspector window.

 Use the slider on the right side of the Overlay window to alter the transparency level of the window (Figure 1-6).

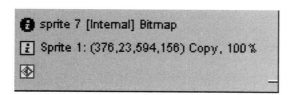

Figure 1-6   Transparency level for sprite overlay window.

WORKING WITH KEYFRAMES

Keyframes are used to set position and other relevant information when animating sprites using the tweening method. Director 6 introduced the ability to access keyframes from both the score and the stage. Director will automatically add and set keyframes and tween the necessary frames directly on the stage. To automatically set keyframes from the stage:

1. Drag a cast member to the stage.
2. Move the sprite on the stage either at its starting position or ending position.
3. Click on the opposite frame in the score than the position set in Step 2. (If you set the starting position on the stage, click on the last frame in the score and vice versa.)
4. Drag the sprite on the stage to its new position, automatically creating a new keyframe.

Select any frame in between the first and last frame for Step 3 to create a keyframe somewhere in between the sprite's end points. Now you can directly manipulate that point on the stage to curve your sprite's motion path.

INCORPORATING 3D OBJECTS FROM EXTREME 3D

Director is designed to work as a two-dimensional (2D) animation program. You do not have the ability to move a camera to change the viewing angle of your stage the same way you can with other three-dimensional (3D) animation programs, such as Infini-D and 3D Studio Max. However, you now have the ability to import 3D modeled objects from Extreme 3D, which offers full manipulation to rotate the object in Director (Figure 1-7).

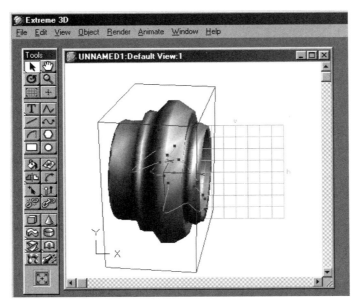

Figure 1-7   Object imported from Extreme 3D.

 You must save your objects in the .3DMF (3D MetaFile) format to access this capability. You must have the QuickDraw3D Xtra for Director installed on the user's system. To download the latest version of the QD3D Xtra for Director, check out www.macromedia.com.

INTERACTIVITY USING BEHAVIORS

By far the best improvement added to Director in Version 6 was the implementation of behaviors. Behaviors are a shortcut method to adding interactive functions to your movie without needing to write Lingo codes. These behaviors are preprogrammed templates, represented as cast members, with all of the Lingo written into them behind the scenes. They can be applied to either frames or sprites, depending on the nature of the behavior. All you need to do is add in the final specific parameters, instructing Director exactly what you want it to do when it encounters one of these commands. Chapter 3 goes into great detail about working with and customizing behaviors. To add the desired functionality to your movie using behaviors:

1. Select Behavior Library from the Xtras menu. A cast of behavior templates appears (Figure 1-8).

2. Drag the desired behavior to the appropriate frame or sprite.

3. Enter the required information in the Behavior Parameters window (if applicable: Figure 1-9).

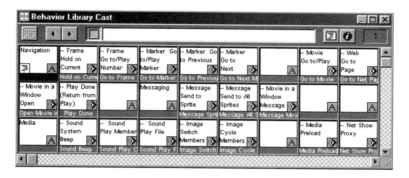

Figure 1-8   Behavior Library Cast (Version 6.5).

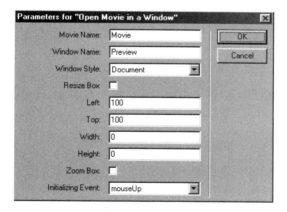

Figure 1-9   Parameters window for selected behavior.

Some behaviors are completely functional as is and will not display a Parameters window when applied. Other behaviors will display its own Parameters window containing the choices for the specific information it requires in order to complete the function properly.

BEHAVIOR INSPECTOR

The Behavior Inspector is a simple-to-use window that allows you to create and manipulate behaviors without using Lingo. The Behavior Inspector window is set up in a convenient way to allow you to quickly and easily edit the functionality of any given behavior (Figure 1-10). The Behavior Inspector window offers you three main areas where you can build new behaviors or customize existing behaviors.

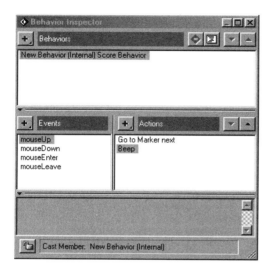

Figure 1-10   The Behavior Inspector window.

 See Chapter 3 for a complete explanation of how to work with behaviors for adding basic interactivity to your movie without typing lines of Lingo commands.

EXPANDING DIRECTOR ONTO THE INTERNET

One of the main directions Macromedia is heading toward is seamless integration for all users to develop and play back content via the Web. Director 6 makes implementing play-only and interactive movies very easy. Shockwave is Macromedia's compression format for converting useful applications into a workable file size that can easily be distributed and downloaded over standard modem connections. In previous versions, you

Figure 1-11   Director and Shockwave movie icons.

had to use Afterburner, a separate application for creating shocked media. Now, Director includes this compression engine right within the program.

Shockwave movies can be compressed tremendously without loosing any quality. Shocked movies are represented with a .DCR file extension as opposed to the standard .DIR extension (Figure 1-11). For more information about using Shockwave for your Director movies, check out Chapter 8, Shock It for the Web.

You can save your files using Shockwave even if you plan on distributing them on disk, instead of the internet. Being that Shockwave movies are compressed, they will generally take a bit longer to launch while they are decompressing.

BENEFITS OF USING SHOCKWAVE AUDIO

Incorporating more advanced features than static text and images has become a growing challenge for web developers. Programs like Director not only make it fun, but really do most of the work for you in order to get the project in the form that you need. Shockwave for Audio is one of the features added into Version 6 of Director. These files are indicated by a .SWA file extension. This allows you to package your audio files in a compact file format that can easily take files too large to play over the Internet and turn them into files that can stream sound with almost no download time. You can com-

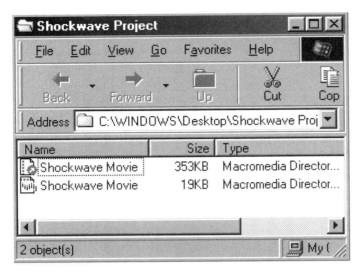

*Figure 1-12   Comparing file sizes of Director (.DIR) and Shockwave for
                Audio (.SWA) files.*

press these audio movies down tremendously, from 176 to 1. Notice the file size difference between the original Director file and the Shockwave movie (Figure 1-12). This
also means that by compressing these files, you are also saving lots of extra disk space.

**Just like your regular Director movies, you can distribute
Shockwave for Audio files over the Internet or on fixed media
disks.**

USING MEDIA FROM THE INTERNET

Being that Director has become more web driven (just like the rest of the planet), you
can incorporate files in your movie that are accessible from the Web. This means that
you can link to media files located on the Internet just as you would any other type of
external file. Director allows you to choose any file from any URL. Make sure you have
Link to External File selected in the Media popup menu at the bottom of the Import
window (Figure 1-13).

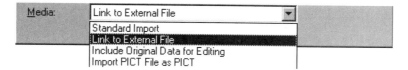

Figure 1-13   Link to External File Option in the Import window.

 You must be connected to the Internet every time you run your movie if you choose to link media from a specific URL. The only information that is stored as part of the movie is the link from the cast member (where the external file exists). Director imports these files as needed every time you play the movie.

DIRECTOR 6.5

Not as major as the jump from Version 5.0 to Version 6.0, Macromedia released Director 6.5, which added several useful features, including such things as improvements to the way Windows systems handle the mixing of sound files and overall application fixes.

SUPPORTING QUICKTIME 3.0

One of the long-awaited advancements for multimedia was the introduction of Quick-Time 3 (QT3). Director 6.5 has the capability of incorporating the features and benefits of working with the newest release of QT3. Both Windows and Macintosh systems support QT3 with the use of the QT3 Asset Xtra that comes standard with the 6.5 upgrade of Director. New technical features that benefit Director developers include the ability to rotate and scale movies, set starting and ending points for QuickTime digital media, and use MPEG video and audio files without any third-party decoders. To access the QuickTime Xtras Properties window:

1. Select a digital media file cast member or sprite.
2. Select Media Elements from the Insert menu.
3. Choose QuickTime 3 from the popup menu (Figure 1-14).

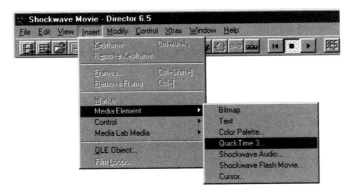

Figure 1-14   Importing QuickTime 3 files from the Media Elements popup menu.

Covering all of the specific feature enhancements added to QuickTime 3 goes beyond the scope of this book. To learn more about the capabilities available with QT3, check out Apple's website at www.apple.com.

MPEG digital video files work with QT3 only on Macintosh systems.

UPGRADING YOUR POWERPOINT PRESENTATIONS

For those users who are still designing their presentations in PowerPoint, but need the added features found in Director, there is finally an answer. Director now has the ability to import entire PowerPoint presentations, retaining all of the graphics and interactive controls without having to redesign from scratch. Director brings in the file as a complete presentation, importing all of the graphics and text as separate cast members and building the score that recreates (as close as possible) the original presentation with mouse clicks, transitions, and text-build layering effects (Figure 1-15). Once your presentation is in Director, you can add the extra animation and interactive elements unavailable in PowerPoint. Chapter 11, Enhancing Your Movie, contains a step-by-step description on how to save your PowerPoint file and bring it into Director quickly and easily.

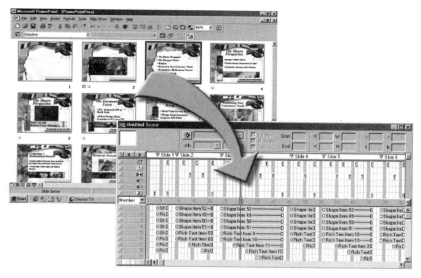

*Figure 1-15   PowerPoint files can be brought into Director automatically building the
Score and Cast (see Color Figure 1).*

WEB-BASED ENHANCEMENTS

Director 6.5 is moving even closer to advanced web-based integration. You now have
the ability to save your movie as a Java application, one of the more complex Internet
programming functions. Using the Save As, Java will create a Java applet that can play
your Director movie using any Java-enabled browser. You can even have Director write
the source HTML code that is needed to embed the applet into one of your web pages.
There is good news for those of you who program using behaviors. The Behavior
Library in Version 6.5 has been optimized to support the codes used for Java applets.

**Embed Java scripts directly into you Lingo commands to gain
extra features and added benefits.**

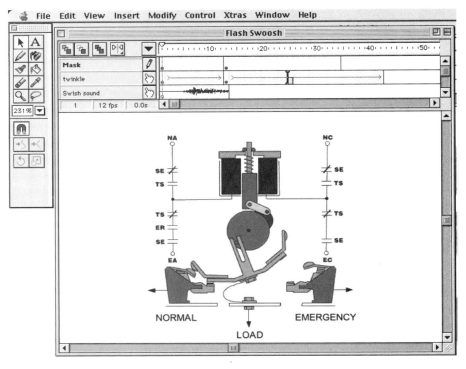

Figure 1-16   Movies created in Macromedia Flash can be integrated into Director (see Color Figure 2).

Now, other Macromedia products are being designed to allow files to be integrated into Director. Flash, a vector-based 2D-animation program, can be imported directly into the cast (Figure 1-16). Flash animations function like digital video files and take on similar characteristics. These animations can be set to play once or loop infinitely. Version 6.5 allows you to have full control over your animation through Lingo commands. Chapter 8 touches on how to import and use Flash animations in Director.

DIRECTOR 7.0

Recently, Macromedia introduced the next generation of Director, Version 7.0. As with 6.5, Director is attracting a whole new audience of developers and users. There have been a number of significant improvements with this release; several features have been added and many functions have been improved on. The most significant changes have been in the targeted direction Director is taking. The name of the new product says it all … Director: Shockwave Internet Studio. Macromedia has incorporated many new enhancements that allow you to develop your movies for both stand-alone media platforms and the internet. The real power of this new and improved version of Director will appear as soon as you begin to build your movie.

IF YOU NEED MORE LAYERS

When you first open the score in Version 7.0, you will not notice any radical changes from Version 6.5. As you begin to look around, you will notice that a few additional functions are now available. You can now add up to 1,000 sprite channels to your score for truly limitless layering capabilities. Most (if not all) of your movies will require far less sprite channels than the system default of 150 channels. You can select the number of sprite channels used in a particular movie to help optimize it for playback. To change the number of score channels available:

1. Select Movie from the Modify menu.
2. Select Properties from the Movie popup menu.
3. Enter the desired number of sprite channels to be available for the current movie (Figure 1-17).

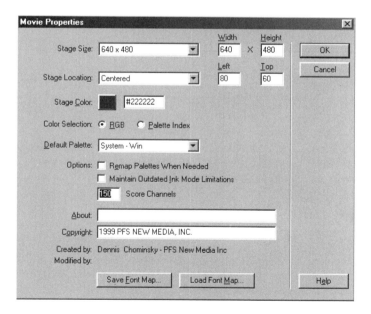

*Figure 1-17   Enter the number of desired sprite channels in the Movie
Properties window.*

MATCHING THE RIGHT COLORS

One problem that faces graphic designers and animators is trying to get the images to look their best. A problem often arises when you need to match a specific color for an image, such as a company's logo. Director has taken the guesswork out of finding the exact color. You can now enter the RGB values to create the exact color you need for anything that requires a specific color. To enter a RGB value in the Paint window or any other area where you can modify colors:

1. Click and hold down the mouse button (left button for Windows) on any color swatch in Director. The color menu window appears (Figure 1-18).

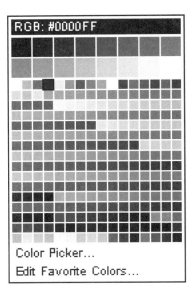

Figure 1-18   Color swatch selection.

2. Click on Color Picker on the bottom of the window.

3. Enter the desired RGB values using numbers ranging from 0 to 255 for each field (Figure 1-19).

For quicker access, you can create and save custom color palettes and color swatches from the Color Picker window that displays your most often used colors in the color menu window.

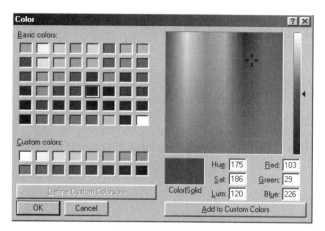

Figure 1-19   Using the Color Picker to enter RGB values (see Color Figure 3).

EMBEDDING FONTS FOR ACCURATE TEXT DISPLAY

Typically, programs that allow you to select font types for text you add to your movie require that the end user have the same fonts installed on their system. If the same font is not present, the system will substitute a font close to the structure of the one required. Many times it does not select a suitable font and the text in your movie is displayed incorrectly (Figure 1-20). Version 7 allows you to embed fonts that you plan on using in your movie so that the fonts you used are properly displayed, even if they are not installed on the user's system. Embedded fonts are compressed to keep the overall file size of your movie down to a minimum, generally adding only 14 to 25K to the file.

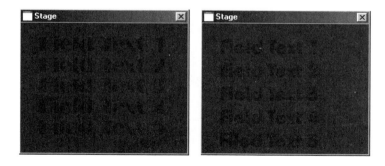

Figure 1-20   Comparison of fonts being displayed incorrectly.

By law, you cannot copy or distribute fonts. Distributing applications using embedded fonts is legal because the fonts are only available within the Director movie.

To embed fonts into a Director movie:

1. Select Media Element from the Insert menu.

2. Select Font from the popup menu. The Font Cast Members Properties window will appear.

3. Select one of the system fonts already installed on your computer from the Original Font pulldown menu.

4. Optional: You can include bitmapped versions of your font for smaller sized text that should make it look better than the standard anti-aliased outlined fonts. Enter the point size(s) that you want to also include when embedding fonts (Figure 1-21).

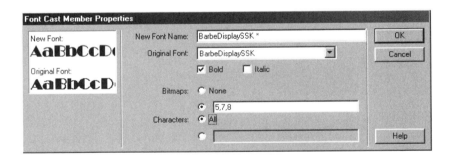

Figure 1-21   Predetermined bitmapped fonts can be included within your movie for better display.

Enter the font name followed by an asterisk when embedding fonts (Times*). This will use the embedded font for all text displayed in the movie, saving you the time and hassle of setting the font for all the text used throughout the entire movie. These fonts are now displayed as cast members and can be applied with the same parameters to other text cast members and sprites (Figure 1-22).

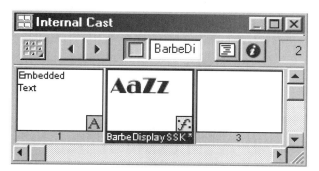

Figure 1-22   Embedded fonts displayed as cast members.

IMPROVED BEHAVIOR AND OBJECT LIBRARIES

One of the most powerful features added to Director in the release of Version 6 was the availability of behaviors, preprogrammed cast members that allow basic interactive functions to occur without using Lingo. Version 7 has improved and added to the way you can add interactivity and other controls to your movie by using the Drag-and-Drop icon from the Library palette. Your movies can now contain more advanced functionality without the need to type in strings of Lingo commands. To learn more about using behaviors, check out Chapter 3, Building Better Navigational Tools with Interactive Applications.

WORKING WITH ALPHA CHANNELS

If you work with 32-bit graphics, Director 7.0 allows you to import graphics with alpha channels. For those of you who do not know what they are, alpha channels allow you to have a clean cutout of an object, including its transparency levels, and manipulate it independently over any background image (Figure 1-23). For those of you who know the benefit of working with alpha channels, this feature will really improve the quality of your images. If you design your elements in third-party programs, such as Photoshop, you can save the images with an alpha channel and import them into Director the same way you import all the rest of your images.

Take a look at Chapter 3 for more information about working with images that have alpha channels, the benefits of alpha channels, and creating masks (a separate file used to simulate an alpha channel). Alpha channels only work with 32-bit graphics. If you import an image at any bit depth lower than 32 bit, Director will automatically strip out the alpha channel.

Figure 1-23   Alpha channels used for object layering.

There are third-party programs available for those of you who
want to work with alpha channels, but are still working on
Version 6.5 or below. Check out the section in Chapter 4 dealing
with AlphaMania and Photocaster by Media Labs, Inc.

TWISTING AND TURNING SPRITES

One of my favorite simple-yet-useful features added to Director in Version 7 has been the
ability to rotate or skew sprites (Figure 1-24). Before this release, you would actually
have to create and import many slightly altered images and animate the movements using

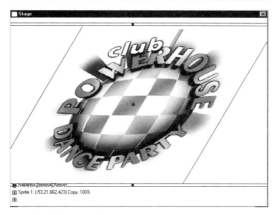

Figure 1-24   Sprite rotation and skew.

multiple cast members. In the score, you can use keyframes to set the points where you want the sprites to begin rotating or skewing. Chapter 4 covers many examples of how to use the rotate and skew functions effectively in your next multimedia project.

The cursor icon changes depending on where you position the mouse once you select the Rotate and Skew button. Director will operate as the rotation function when the cursor is placed within the bounding box of the sprite. It will operate with the skew function once you drag the cursor outside of the sprite's bounding box. The appropriate cursor icon should be displayed.

CREATING VECTOR GRAPHICS INSIDE OF DIRECTOR

Throw away Freehand and Illustrator (just a figure of speech). Director has now added the ability to create and manipulate vector-based graphics. This is a great way to draw simple shapes and lines to create dazzling effects. Use the pen tool to add points to create irregular shapes, then manipulate them into the exact shape you want using Bezier handles (Figure 1-25). Designing your application with vector graphics is beneficial for several reasons:

◆ Vector graphics are clean-looking images. All images are anti-aliased for smooth-looking edges.

◆ Vector images can be resized infinitely without distorting or pixelating like bit-mapped images would (Figure 1-26).

◆ Vector graphics are extremely small in file size, even when compared to the images created using Director Paint.

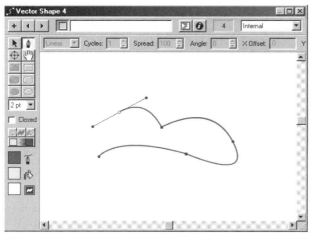

Figure 1-25   Bezier handles for manipulating vector-based images.

Figure 1-26   Comparison of enlarged vector and bitmapped images. Vector images resize without pixelizing.

7.0 AND THE WEB

As previously mentioned, Director 7.0 is geared toward making interactive applications more powerful and posting them on the Web much easier. One of the new features actually demonstrates the synergy with the Web by allowing you to import HTML documents into Director. Director understands most standard HTML tags, including tables. Any tags that it does not recognize, Director will just ignore. Therefore, it is very important to double-check that the formatting appears correctly. See Chapter 10, Shock It for the Web, to find out more information about creating Director movies for the Internet.

CREATING COLOR PALETTES FOR THE WEB

Images created with an 8-bit color depth are limited to a set of 256 specified colors in a palette (system or custom) attached to all or part of your movie. If the colors in the object you design do not fall within the colors of the active color palette, the playback system will try to interpret or substitute the closest color from one in the current palette. This can cause your images to be displayed incorrectly and look terrible. Chapter 2 describes how to map all of your 8-bit images to a palette that contains the colors needed to make your images look the best they can (colorwise) in any browser.

TESTING MOVIES IN A BROWSER

Director movies can be designed to run on the web. This means before you put your movie online for the public to view, you will want to test it to make sure the movie functions and displays the way you want it to appear (Figure 1-27). You do not need to save your movie as a Shockwave movie to test it in a browser. Director automatically creates a temporary Shockwave file (.DCR) and necessary HTML code in order to open your movie in your browser. If you have multiple browsers installed on your system, you can specify a particular browser as the default browser. See chapter 10 to answer all of your questions about how to use Director for the web.

Be sure to test your movie on several browsers and different sized monitors (if possible). Web pages may appear slightly different on various monitors and browsers. Shockwave movies are compatible with the following browsers:

◆   Netscape Navigator 3.0 and higher for Windows and Macintosh.

◆   Microsoft Internet Explorer 3.0 or higher for Windows.

◆   Microsoft Internet Explorer 4.0 or higher for Macintosh.

◆   Browsers compatible with Netscape 3.0 plug-ins (i.e., AOL).

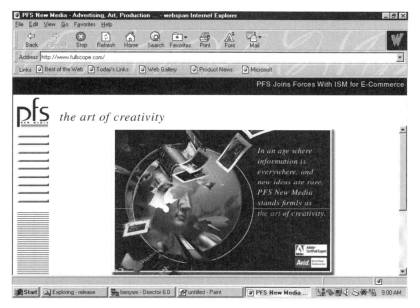

Figure 1-27   Test the appearance of your movie in a browser.

PLAYING SHOCKWAVE MOVIES WITHOUT A NET

With Director 7.0, you can save the applications you create as a Shockwave movie and play them independent of a browser. This allows you to bundle your movies in a compressed format (smaller file size) for distribution on low-storage media platforms like floppy disks. These files will take longer to open than the same movie saved as a projector because Shockwave files need to be decompressed.

All Shockwave movies display a progress bar indicating how much of the file has been downloaded or decompressed (Figure 1-28).

Figure 1-28   Shockwave download progress bar (see Color Figure 4).

SUMMARY

There are many new and exciting changes being made to Director. The best part is that Macromedia is making what used to be a very cumbersome programming oriented application and designing it to be more user friendly with time-saving features and easier-to-view displays. If you have been using Director for years, you will love the changes added to the new versions. If you are new to Director, jumping in and building advanced applications is easier than ever before.

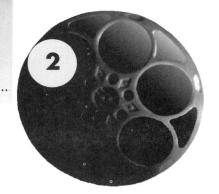

c h a p t e r ②

PREPLANNING PROJECTS FROM THE GROUND UP

Your client calls you and says he wants to talk about putting together a CD-ROM for his company. Before you can begin designing the CD-ROM, you need to have some questions answered first. Otherwise, you will spend an ungodly amount of time halfway through the project fixing or completely changing things that could have been avoided from the beginning. Once you begin designing interactive applications for other people, you really need to get down to detail and find out exactly how they intend to use the program. Some of the questions in this chapter should help make your multimedia programming a more pleasurable and profitable experience. Use these suggestions as guidelines to tailor your own list of questions for developing interactive programs.

Many of these questions are applicable beyond the scope of Director. They might expand into other types of multimedia projects, but nonetheless hold true for designing Director movies.

DEFINING THE PROJECT

Question #1: What type of project is this? (Make sure Director is the right application for your client's needs.)

Getting the best possible insight will help in your approach to putting this project together the best possible way. Is it for training? Promotional purposes? Sales? All these different applications can determine what types of features you may want to include or exclude. If the program is going to be used by a select group of people who will be involved with the development of the project from the very beginning, than you can probably consider using some more advanced interactive features. These features include hidden links that only the user knows the location of, so he or she does not have to go searching aimlessly for these hotspots during the middle of an important presentation. If the program you are going to be designing is to be used by novice computer users, you will most likely want to make the navigational system as simple and easy to follow as possible. Another consideration might be to offer an interactive help section accessible through a Help button, which is available from virtually every section of the program (Figure 2-1). Throughout the course of this book, we will demonstrate examples from real programs that incorporate many of these features. Make sure that the end result of what you produce is in line with the requirements set forth by the scope of the project.

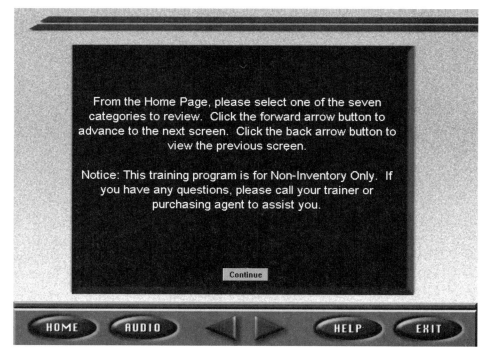

Figure 2-1   Help Button available on every screen (see Color Figure 5).

STRATEGY: HOW TO APPROACH THE PROJECT

Where to begin? The first thing that you should do is sit down with a client and try to determine the overall content and focus of the program. This will help to decide what types of media you will be working with, what content you will have to include, and how you can begin to lay this project out. One thing you must realize is that every multimedia project that comes your way is going to be different. Gather as much information as possible from the client. If the client can, have them put together an outline of the general topics that the project will encompass. If they are supplying you with any types of artwork or other relevant files, try to get them as early as possible. Having these files in your possession will help you visualize the look of the project and start developing the layout. Once you have as much of the materials as they can provide (which 9 out of 10 times will either be not enough information or excessively too much), begin to sketch out a schematic or flow chart (Figure 2-2). You will begin to see what headings will be included, what topics you will need to expand on, and how the interactive navigational structure will function.

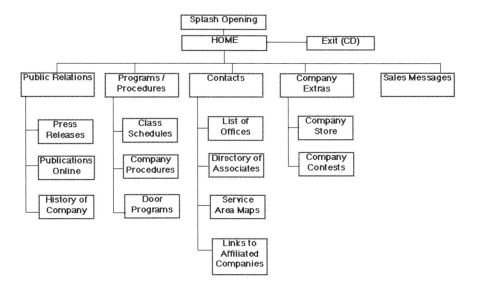

Figure 2-2   Schematic drawings and flow charts help lay out the structure of the project.

Depending on the nature of your project, the exact format shown in Figure 2-2 will not always apply, but the general concept should give you a good head start. Begin by working from the top down, generally from some type of Main Menu or Home Page. Every section added will have a strong foundation and can begin growing from the Home screen.

As you can see from the schematic drawing, having the Home screen as your foundation does not mean your actual program must begin with the Home screen. Splash screens or opening movie clips usually make for an interesting opening for your project.

Once you have all of the main topic headings and subsections mapped out on paper, you will quickly see the correlation between what you have sketched out and what you will begin to set up in Director. The score is where you will begin to compile all of your elements to bring life to your movie. One of the most powerful features about Director is that the score works in a nonlinear fashion. Figure 2-3 illustrates how you can set up your score. Notice how Section 1 is not placed at the beginning of the score. You can begin to program your content in any order you wish. You can have your ending be the second group of sprites in your score timeline. For those programmers who tend to rush through projects, Director's nonlinear capabilities can be a drawback. Sound confused? That is exactly my point. The fact that your score does not have to be designed in a linear fashion means that, if you are not careful, you might accidentally link the wrong sections of your movie or spend a great deal of time hunting around for the section you need. Without that visual flow chart to look back on and reference once in a while, all those sprites filling hundreds of frames across multiple channels intertwined and linking in every direction can be very cumbersome for even experienced programmers. You might wonder why you wouldn't program in a purely linear manner. There are two reasons:

1. In real-life scenarios, clients tend to add things at the last minute and change their minds from time to time.

2. Nonlinear capabilities allow you to build your program in any order you choose. You may not have all your materials together for the beginning sections, but you can build other sections without wasting any time.

We will get into more specifics about actually building interactive presentations and designing the navigational tools available through Director in the next chapter.

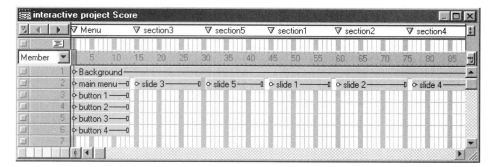

Figure 2-3   The order of sections in the score does not necessarily determine the playback order.

DEFINING YOUR TARGET AUDIENCE

Question #2: Who will be using this program?

Your target audience is going to vary for just about every Director project you build. This is where Director really delivers. Its versatility and flexibility allows programmers to design just about any type of interactive application clients can dream up. Macromedia Director is continually upgrading and improving its capabilities as developers need more options and features. As technology changes, Director is there with new enhancements to help deliver the types of applications you need, whether it's a stand-alone presentation or an outrageous shocked file for the Web.

How you develop your application will depend on how you classify the intended audience. If the users are computer savvy, you will have the opportunity to work with more advanced features and interactions. If the target audience consists of novice computer users, you will have to concentrate on making the navigational controls and layout as clear and simple to use as possible. If the company you are producing this project for is conservative, bright flashy colors and animations probably won't appeal to the client. Focus all aspects of the project to the client's needs and demands while always keeping in mind the end user of the program.

THE 3Ss: SCRIPTS, SCHEMATICS, AND STORYBOARDS

Question #3: What will be the content of the program?

The most beneficial tools for any programmer to develop and use are the script, storyboard, and schematic flowchart.

◆ The script basically tells the story of your program in a textual manner. Just like in the movies, a script is used to describe each section, list any audio or video files required, and provide a basis for any text that will appear onscreen or be read by a voiceover talent (Figure 2-4).

Screen / Page	Text	Audio / Video
Home / Main Menu	Welcome to the Training Program. Please click you mouse on one of the buttons along the bottom of the screen to advance to the next section.	Custom Music V/O reading text SFX on Button Clicks
Screen 1	History. Our company was started over 5 years ago, with the dream of becoming a large production company.	Music Continues V/O reading text Video Clip 001
Screen 2	Today, with over 1,000 employees, XYZ Inc. has locations in over 24 countries world wide.	V/O reading text Video Clip 002
Screen 3	XYZ has become a leader in the industry for producing one of the industries leading widgets. With a record of 7 out of ten major awards under our belts, XYZ has been the choice of Fortune 500 companies for the past two years.	Awards Music Clip V/O reading text Video Clip 003
Screen 4	Closing Graphic. XYZ Inc. sees itself becoming one of the worlds most leading technology companies in the world. By expanding our markets into new territories, we can provide job opportunities to over 100 nations.	V/O reading text Visionary Music Video Clip 004

Figure 2-4   Typical multimedia script format.

◆ Storyboards are used when developing just about any type of visual image presentation that tells a story or flows from one section to another (whether it is for print or video). Each main screen, or change in scenery, is sketched out by the artist or designer to help other people involved in the project visualize the way each scene is going to look (Figure 2-5). For Multimedia, storyboards help you design the layout of each screen (placement of images and navigational elements, font styles, and color schemes).

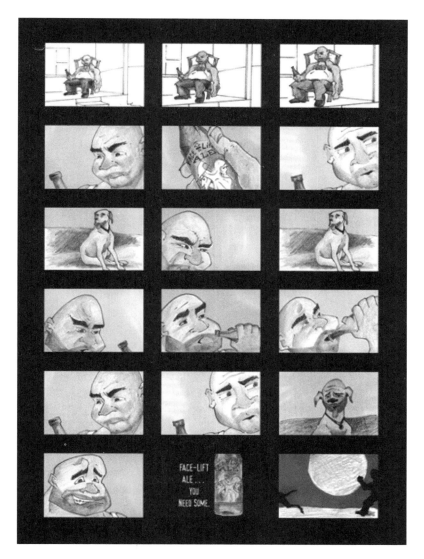

Figure 2-5   Sample storyboard layouts (see Color Figure 6).

◆   Schematics and flowcharts are the best way to sketch out the navigational structure of a program and make sure that each of the sections is properly connected. With this map sketched out on paper or in a computer document, you will be able to see if you are missing any sections or whether any links or connections will not be able to work as initially planned.

Always make navigational elements reversible. Too often, users tend to click around without realizing where they are going. Having either a back button or at least a Return to Home button allows the user to quickly and safely get to where he or she belongs.

Use these three forms (and any other materials you create) for clients to look at, approve, and sign-off on. This way, you will save yourself the trouble of redoing a lot of work if and when the client changes his or her mind. Once they sign-off and approve the script and storyboard designs, any changes at that point can generally be billed at an additional fee.

WORKING WITHIN THE BOUNDARIES OF SYSTEM REQUIREMENTS

Question #4: What type of system will this program be designed for?

System Requirement Limitation is often referred to as trying to determine the lowest common denominator. What this means is listing the minimum computer specifications (both hardware and software) that are required to run the application you are designing. The optimal scenario is to find out what types of computers your client or end user plans on running these programs on. If they have a slew of Pentiums, fully loaded, and only a few 486s with barely enough memory to remember that it's a computer, you are faced with two choices:

1. Develop the program to meet the specs of the low-end systems.
2. Recommend to your client that you design the application for the high-end systems (for better performance and superior images) and not run it on the slower systems.

As you program your Director movies, many factors will come into play as far as what types of media you can use and how it will play back:

◆ The CPU (central processing unit)—clocked as the speed in which your computer can compute data and other types of information.

◆ RAM—the system's memory, which will play a vital role in how fast files load and how smoothly they run. This is especially true when it comes to digital video and audio files.

◆ Sound Cards—required for each computer in order to hear any sound files added to the movie.

◆ Graphic Excelerator Cards—beneficial for better graphic and video display.

◆ Monitors—high-resolution monitors will be required to run applications set for resolutions of 800x600 or 1024x768. (See Chapter 5 for more detailed information regarding resolution and color depth.)

 Generally, the more power (processor speed, memory, etc.), the less problems you will encounter when authoring with more complex features.

To go into a bit more detail on monitors, the screen resolution will have a significant impact on the color display, size, and overall look of your movie. The standard resolution of multimedia projects was to design your movies to run at 640 pixels (width) by 480 pixels (height). Today, with the advent of higher resolution monitors and LCD (liquid crystal display) displays on laptops, it has become common to develop applications at much higher resolutions. All of these factors need to be determined before creating any images for your project. To change the screen resolution (Figure 2-6):

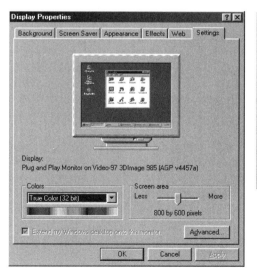 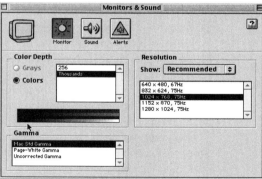

Figure 2-6   Windows and Macintosh screens for setting monitor displays.

For a PC system:

1. Select Settings from the Start menu (Windows 95/98/NT).
2. Select Control Panel.
3. Double-click on Display.
4. Choose Settings in the Display Properties window.

For Macintosh users:

1. Select Control Panels from the Apple menu.
2. Choose Monitors and Sound.
3. From the Display window, select which resolution you want your system to display.

 The make and model of your computer monitor and the video card installed in your computer will determine what settings and resolutions are available on your particular system.

PC, MACINTOSH, OR BOTH

Question #5: How would you like your project delivered?

The first issue that will determine what files you will be able to author and design with is to figure out which platform the application will be created for. Macintosh? PC? Others? What type of operating system? If it is on a PC, is it for Windows 3.1, Windows 95/98, or NT? Will it be for multiple operating systems? More importantly, will it be for cross-platform use? Do you want your end users to have the ability to run this program on both a Macintosh and a PC-compatible system?

Designing a CD-ROM seems easy at first. The biggest pitfall for developers is to overlook these basic questions or, even worse, assume that they know what the client wants. Perhaps after working with a client on several projects, these questions will soon become irrelevant. Remember, each platform and operating system will determine a number of things, especially which types of files will work on which types of systems.

GATHERING THE FILES

Question #6: Are files going to be provided by the client?

Many times you will not be the only person working on a project from start to finish. There may have been design work done prior to this project that your client would like to implement into this new Director piece. The client might also have a logo that needs to be included (hopefully they can supply it to you in electronic format). Whatever the case may be, it is important to communicate with all parties involved to find out:

1. How they will be saving the files (PICT, TIFF, BMP)?
2. What type of media will they be providing, containing all of these files (CD-R, Zip, Jaz)?

CHOOSE YOUR WEAPON: SELECTING THE APPROPRIATE FILE TYPES

The thing that makes Director such the number one choice of developers is that it can develop for many different applications and situations. You can author one movie and then play it back on either a Macintosh or a PC. This is possible because Director handles so many different types of file formats. Whether you are using PICT, GIF, TARGA, or TIFF files, you can import virtually any standard type of bitmapped or vector-based image into Director. Director also works with digital video and audio files, including AIFF, WAV, AVI, and QuickTime. Therefore, it is extremely important to know which files are cross-platform and which ones are system specific.

Use programs like Flash to create vector-based graphics and animations to import into Director (Figure 2-7).

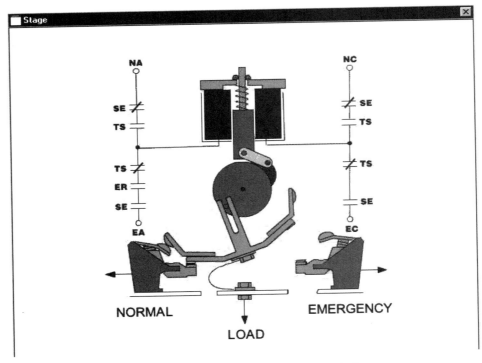

Figure 2-7   *Single frame from a vector-based image created in Flash.*

PREPARE TO TEST, TEST, AND RE-TEST

I cannot emphasize enough that you must get into the habit of testing early in the production process and test often. This philosophy holds true even more so for those of you designing more complex programs. The higher the degree of complexity, the more often you need to test your program to ensure accurate results. No matter how good of a programmer you think you are, it is never fun to assume that you have laid out all of your cards in the proper order, when … BAM! The program doesn't work. Every time you make a significant change to a portion of your Director movie is generally a good time to take a few moments and make sure that what you have designed is functioning the exact way you intended it to play.

Give your program what I call the "Grandma Test." Find a person who has little knowledge about computers and let them run through your application. If they can get through the majority of your application without struggling, then you know the average person will have no problem using your program.

CUSTOMIZED SETTINGS

You will have to make some decisions and set up your project from the very beginning once you finally begin to build your Director movie. Depending on the client's request, you will have to set your stage dimensions. Most stand-alone applications used to be set at 640 by 480 pixels. Today, with higher screen resolutions and more applications being developed for the Web, there really are no standard sizes. That is why it is so important to communicate with your client and establish these settings to begin designing your program. To set the size of your movie's stage:

1. Select Movie from the Modify menu.
2. Select Properties from the popup menu. The Movie Properties window will appear (Figure 2-8).
3. Enter the numeric values in the first field to set the dimensions for the current stage.

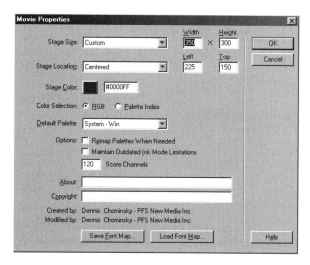

Figure 2-8   Movie Properties window.

You can change the size of your stage at a later time. However, changing the size may affect the placement of your sprites on the stage as to whether they are even displayed at all.

    The first field contains a pulldown menu with preset sizes most often used for Director movies (Figure 2-9). If one of these settings does not meet your requirements, there are the individual fields to the right in which you can enter your own custom values for the height and width of your viewing area. You will notice that as soon as you enter a number in these fields that is not equivalent to one of the presets, the text in the dropdown menu automatically switches to a custom setting.

    The next set of field entries is the stage location. With the same layout as the stage size, you can choose from one of the preset locations or numerically enter your own custom setting. I highly recommend that if you do not need to alter the screen location of your viewing area, leave it in the centered position. Depending on the stage size you set and the display settings of the end user's system, you run the risk of having one or more of the edges hidden off screen (Figure 2-10). By leaving it set for a centered location, no matter what size monitor the user is watching your program on, the image will appear centered in the middle of their screen.

    The next setting involves choosing a color palette for the display of your images. We will go into more detail about palettes later in this chapter. The last important setting in this window that you will use on a regular basis is the stage color. This is what determines the background color of the viewing area. To change the stage color:

1. Click on the Stage Color color swatch located in the Movie Properties window. A color palette will appear (Figure 2-11).

2. Select the color you wish to display in the background of your movie.

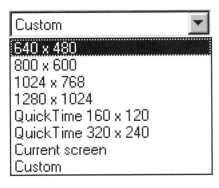

Figure 2-9   Movie Properties Stage Size pulldown menu.

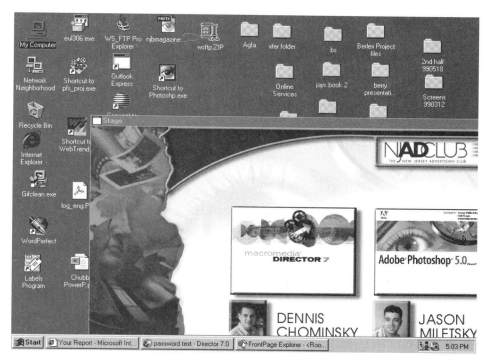

Figure 2-10   Image being cut off when not properly centered for current monitor settings.

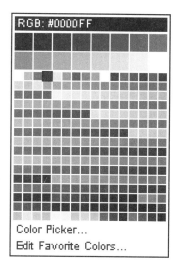

Figure 2-11   Color palette.

For those users who set their monitor resolution higher than the size of the stage viewing area of their program, you can select an option in Director to fill the outside of your application with the same color that you have chosen for the stage background color. This way there is a consistent color scheme to blend with your project and the viewer will not be distracted by any of the desktop windows open while viewing the movie. You can select this option to cover the desktop around the stage's viewing area when you are ready to finalize your movie and make a projector (see Chapter 7). To choose this option:

1. Select Create Projector from the File menu. The Create Projector dialog box will appear.
2. Click on the Options button. The Projector's Option dialog box appears.
3. Click on the Full Screen radio button under options (Figure 2-12).
4. Click OK.

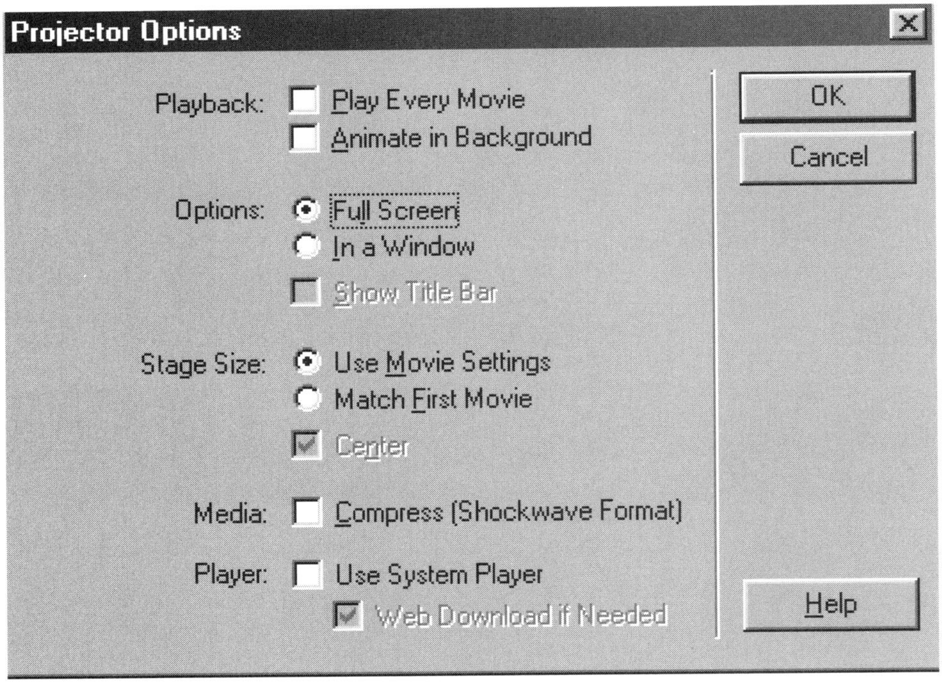

Figure 2-12   *Full screen setting for projectors.*

Once you save your project and create a projector, any time you launch your movie it will play back with the screen fully covered. If the resolution of your monitor is the same as the program you made, your movie will play back filling up the entire screen. If the resolution of your monitor is set higher than the size of your Director application, your movie will play back in a window and the rest of the desktop will be filled with whatever color you have selected as the stage color (Figure 2-13).

Figure 2-13   Background color fills screen around smaller image size (see Color Figure 7).

UTILIZING THIRD-PARTY PROGRAMS

What really makes Director Multimedia Studio (Version 6.x) a complete package is that it comes bundled with all the tools necessary to put together interactive multimedia applications. Director 6.5 and below come complete with xRes for designing graphics, Xtreme 3D for modeling three-dimensional objects, and either Sound Forge (Windows) or Sound Edit 16 (Macintosh) for audio editing. Director 7.0 bundles graphic and other programs geared toward website creation. Between these bundled software programs and the features inherent inside Director, you can design some really high-end and creative projects. But to design some intense programs that will wow your viewer and offer you features not included with the studio packages, you will need to start utilizing some other third-party programs on the market. There are a few programs that no multimedia developer should live without.

Keep one thing in mind before you go out and blow your whole budget on these software programs. Just because you buy the best programs doesn't mean you can create the best images and files.

Most multimedia software programs, including Director, take a little bit of talent and a whole lot of time to become even remotely proficient with them. Some of the third-party software and hardware packages that I reference throughout the course of this book include:

1. Adobe Photoshop—for creating and editing bitmapped graphics and layered images.
2. Avid Media Composer and Adobe Premiere—for creating and editing digital audio and video clips.
3. Terran Interactive Media Cleaner Pro—for compressing and formatting digital audio and video files.
4. 3D Studio Max and Infini-D—for creating three-dimensional graphics and animations.

There are really hundreds of different programs available to create the elements you need to build your project. This again is what makes Director such a powerful and sophisticated program. It has the ability to work with files from just about any multimedia program out there.

BE A NEAT FREAK: MANAGE YOUR MOVIE

One of the best techniques to save you time and aggravation is to keep your cast members neat and organized from the beginning. There are several different things you can do to make the search for a particular cast member more efficient. Many developers waste time doing redundant steps or searching for a particular cast member through thousands of others because they did not break up and organize their project. Remember each cast can hold up to 32,000 cast members. Do you have the time to constantly search and scroll through 32,000 cast members every time you need to find an image? Take the time in your preplanning stage to organize the types of files you will be using and whether or not you will be able to use these files again in another project. The following are a few suggestions that you can do so that you can devote more time toward building your movie than hunting for lost cast members:

1. Name each cast member.
2. Group all similar cast members together.
3. Place cast members from each section into groups.
4. Work with multiple casts.
5. Build external casts of common images that can be used for other projects.

DO NOT NAME FILES JOHN DOE

If you follow any one of the aforementioned organizational techniques, I suggest that you name each cast member. Do not just leave them numbered. When you use Lingo to refer to a particular cast member (such as swap sprite with cast member such and such). Name each one with a name that identifies what image it relates to or what purpose that cast member fulfils. A proper naming convention might look like:

◆ Home button
◆ FAQ button
◆ Background image
◆ Play loop script

A not-so-effective method might be:

◆ Button
◆ Button 2
◆ Untitled
◆ Script 1

Developing an accurate naming convention will not only make finding cast members easier in the cast, but will assure working with the right sprites in the score (Figure 2-14).

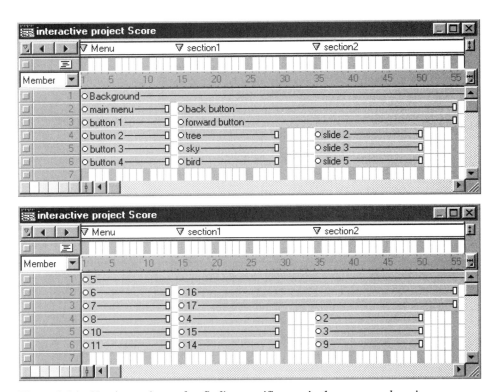

Figure 2-14   Naming sprites makes finding specific ones in the score much easier.

IMAGES TO THE LEFT, BEHAVIORS TO THE RIGHT

Another method to help organize your cast members is to group similar items together. If you import graphics that will be used as buttons for an interactive interface, keep them all in line. Keep all of your behaviors and scripts grouped together (Figure 2-15). If you haphazardly place them all over throughout one cast, it takes time scrolling through the cast to find the one you are looking to use. In addition to placing similar cast members alongside each other, try to group cast members used for each section of your movie as its own distinctive area of the cast. For instance, divide your cast up into distinctive areas for each part of your movie that is designated by a new marker (Figure 2-16). Cast members used within the same section of your movie should be grouped together in the cast. Leave a few blank cast member windows in between each marked section to visually separate each section in the cast.

Figure 2-15   Organizing similar cast members in groups for easy accessibility.

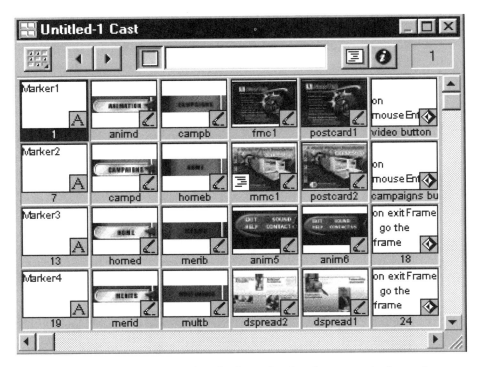

Figure 2-16   Organizing cast members by the section that they appear in the movie.

 Add a text cast member before each group of cast members to identify the name of each section for easy recognition (Figure 2-17).

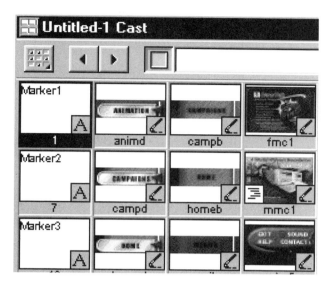

Figure 2-17   Using a text cast member to identify the sections or groupings of the cast members.

TIMESAVING WITH MULTIPLE CASTS

Setting up multiple casts may seem to be overkill at first, but once you start working on large multimedia projects with thousands of files, you will really appreciate the ease of searching for the right files without the hassle of combing through unnecessary cast members. There is no need to try scrolling down through hundreds of cast members trying to find a digital video clip among all the other graphics, behaviors, scripts, sound files, and text fields. By separating the cast members into categories, it becomes very easy to find a particular file (Figure 2-18).

There are many other reasons to divide your elements into separate casts. One of the most useful advantages is that you can create and save these external casts as virtual libraries for use in other projects. If there are certain elements that you seem to use over and over again in other projects, you can save yourself the hassle of importing these elements for every project. Depending on what types of projects you create, you may want to save separate casts for the following categories:

- Logos and images
- Customized behaviors and scripts
- Buttons and navigational elements
- Sound clips
- Digital video files
- Transitions and effects

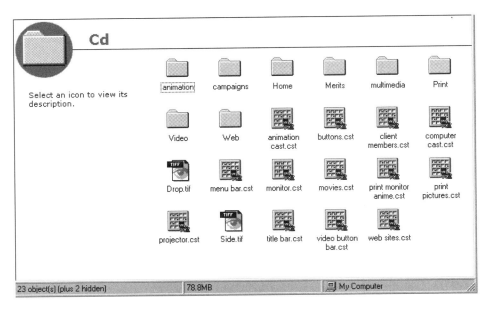

Figure 2-18   Dividing cast members into distinct multiple casts (see Color Figure 8).

External cast members work just like other types of external files; they are just linked files. This means that you must keep the external cast with the Director movie (whether in .dir or projector format).

USING LINKED EXTERNAL CASTS

Is this a project for a client that may have different applications for this material in the future? Are there certain files that you seem to use over and over in different projects? If so, you may be wasting time by constantly searching for and importing these files into new casts for every project. If you plan on using the cast members across several Director movies, you would opt for linking the external cast to each particular movie. To link an external cast to the current movie:

1. Select Movie from the Modify menu.
2. Choose Cast from the popup menu. A Movie Cast window appears showing a list of all the casts associated with this particular movie.
3. Click the link button at the bottom of the window to link an external cast (Figure 2-19).

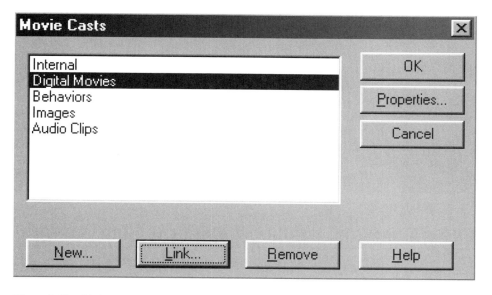

Figure 2-19   Link to external cast.

4. Use the standard file system to find your external cast and select it. Now your external cast has been added to the Movie cast window.

5. Click OK.

To see which casts are available for your current movie, click on the Choose Cast button on the current cast window (Figure 2-20).

Figure 2-20   Pulldown menu displays list of all casts linked to current movie.

USING UNLINKED EXTERNAL CASTS

When you bring in an unlinked external cast into a movie and try to drag a cast member to the score or stage, you will be prompted with a dialog box asking if you would like to link this cast to the current movie. If you prefer not to link the entire external cast to the movie, you must then copy the cast member(s) that you wish to use into an internal cast.

USING UNLINKED EXTERNAL CASTS AS LIBRARIES

You don't need to link every cast to a particular movie. One great example is to consider creating your own cast library. To create an external cast to be used as a library, simply type the word "library" as the last word when you name and save your cast. Director will interpret this cast as a library (just like Director's internal libraries).

Director automatically copies the cast member to an internal cast in your current movie when you drag a cast member out from the external cast library to the stage or score. Basically, you can use this "library" of cast members as a pool or holding area for items such as buttons and behaviors that you will use on a regular basis in other movies.

Remember when distributing and packaging your movie either on a disk, CD, or the Internet, you must include the external cast file. For more information on packaging your movies see Chapter 8.

LEAVE A PAPER TRAIL

No one likes to do paper work. However, keeping a notebook on hand to document any important procedures or scripts that you produce will come in handy the next time you need to recreate the same happening. Nothing is more frustrating than trying to replicate or figure out how and why you did something a certain way. This will become your own personal database of information, full of tips and tricks you have learned and utilized. This personalized reference guide will come in handy the next time you are trying to troubleshoot a situation that you previously had worked out in a project several months ago.

Have documentation to back up what steps were taken to perform certain programming tasks, especially when working with a team of people on a project. This way, if you or another team member is unable to continue, someone else can easily figure out where to pick up from.

REPURPOSING MEDIA FOR MULTIMEDIA PROJECTS

If you are working on a project where the client may want to use the images and designs you create in a broader campaign of other media types (print, video, web), you should consider developing your images so that they can be repurposed for more than one medium. Designing your images to be used for various media purposes from the beginning is more efficient than creating new content for each phase of the project. It is easy to design an image at 300 dpi (usual print resolution) and scale it down to 72 dpi (standard video and CD-ROM resolution). It is quite impossible to convert an image in the other direction. Therefore, planning ahead and asking the client ahead of time could save you the trouble of doing the work twice. Instead, you will come out looking like a hero producing a multiproduct campaign with a consistent look and feel, all by doing the initial work once.

SUMMARY

This chapter discusses a number of techniques you can use to help manage a new multimedia project. The best steps when preplanning any project are to ask a lot of questions in the beginning and continue to ask questions throughout the entire process of your development. No one likes to work with someone watching your every move over your shoulder, but periodic progress and approval phases will keep your project on target. Taking the time to prepare all of your materials instead of trying to rush into things can save you an enormous amount of time in the long run. Get organized. Ask questions. Be patient.

chapter 3

BUILDING BETTER NAVIGATIONAL TOOLS WITH INTERACTIVE APPLICATIONS

Technology fascinates us, especially when it comes to CD-ROMs, kiosks, and the Internet. What makes these things so interesting is the ability to interact with them. The real strength of Director is its ability to make your movies interactive. No matter what style designs you create, and no matter what type of content you include, developing applications with Director offers the user the choice of how, where, and when to maneuver around the program.

CONTROLLING THE SPEED OF YOUR MOVIE

Before you can begin setting interactive controls, you will need to know how your movie will play. To control how your movie will play, you will need to add commands for Director to acknowledge so that your movie will perform the way you intended it to play. The tempo settings are primarily used to adjust the rate of how fast or slow sprites are displayed and animated during playback.

The type of system you are running your program on will also affect the playback performance of your movie. The amount of RAM you have, the type of hard drive, and the speed of your processor will determine how smoothly your Director movie runs. If your computer cannot play the movie at its intended rate, Director automatically slows down the tempo during playback in order to play every frame. The opposite effect occurs when Director plays digital audio and video files. Because it cannot change the speed at which the digital media files were created, Director begins to randomly drop frames in order to complete the duration time of the file. For example, a 5-second video clip created at 30 frames per second will inevitably drop a few frames on a slower machine in order to have Director play the movie in exactly 5 seconds. Therefore, the tempo setting does not have any bearing on how digital audio and video files play. The playback rate for these files is determined when they are created. Check out Chapter 8 to find out more about working with digital audio and video files.

USING THE WAIT FEATURE

Although the Wait option is not technically an interactive command, it is another useful feature that adds more control to the playback performance of your movie. To set up a wait command:

1. Double-click any frame in the Tempo channel of your score.
2. The Frame Properties: Tempo dialog box appears (Figure 3-1).
3. Select Wait to have the playback head pause on that particular frame for the amount of time you choose. When the playback head enters that frame, it will hold on that frame for the set time, and then continue playing the rest of your movie.

Figure 3-1   Frame properties: Tempo dialog box.

LONG WAIT TIMES FOR PRESENTATIONS

You can use the Wait slider to set a pause duration from anywhere between 1 second to 60 seconds. For a presentation that requires more than a 60-second pause, you can be creative with when, where, and how many Wait commands you use. If you need to set a longer pause interval than 1 minute and will not have access to the mouse or keyboard during the presentation:

1. Add a Wait command on the last frame of the sprite.
2. Set the value to the maximum (60 seconds).
3. Add a second Wait command to the previous frame of that same sprite.
4. Enter the value for this pause interval.
5. Repeat Steps 3 and 4 as necessary (Figure 3-2).

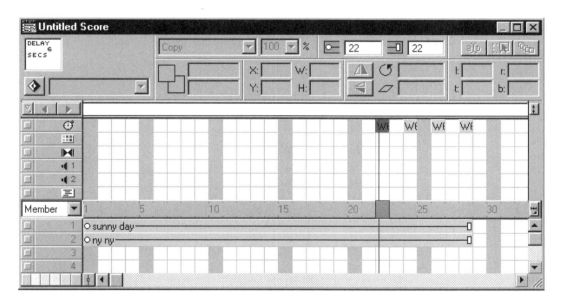

Figure 3-2   *A score containing multiple wait commands.*

Your movie will now play until it comes across the first Wait command in the score. It will pause on that frame for that given duration, then continue to play until it enters the next frame with a wait command.

ADDING BASIC INTERACTION

The easiest type of interaction you can add to your movie is the ability to advance to the next screen with the click of the mouse or key press. This type of interactivity is useful when creating Director movies that will be used during presentations. Use Director's `Wait for Mouse Click` or `Key Press` feature to hold on a particular frame indefinitely until the user chooses to go on. To set up this function:

1. Double-click the Tempo channel in the frame where you want to add this control. (Typically, add it to the last frame of a sprite before a new image appears or other event takes place.)

2. Click the `Wait For Mouse Click or Key Press` radio button in the Frame Properties: Tempo dialog box to activate the command.

3. Click OK.

4. Rewind and play your movie. The playback head will hold in the frame that you set the `Wait For Mouse Click or Key Press` command. To signify that your movie is still in play mode, the cursor turns into a blinking arrow pointing down to let the user know that Director is waiting for a command to continue on with the program (Figure 3-3).

Figure 3-3   The cursor changes to a blinking arrow while waiting for a mouse click.

5. Click the mouse or any key on the keyboard to advance to the next frame of the movie.

6. Repeat Steps 4 and 5 to add this command to any other frames.

You are now *interacting* with your movie. If you want to add this control to every screen of a slideshow presentation, use copy and paste.

1. Create the first `Wait For Mouse Click or Key Press` command.

2. Single-click on that frame to highlight it.

3. Use the Copy Sprite feature located under the Edit menu or use the keyboard shortcuts (Control-C for Windows; Command-C for Macintosh).

4. Click the next frame where you want this command.

5. Use the Paste Sprite feature in the Edit menu or use the keyboard shortcuts (Control-V for Windows; Command-V for Macintosh).

6. Repeat Steps 4 and 5 to add this command to any other frames.

DIRECTOR: A NONLINEAR WORLD

The best way to approach any new Director project is to plan ahead. But don't panic if you realize at the last minute that you forgot to include a section or need to change the order of the sequence. Depending on the complexity of your program, it may only involve changing a few commands as opposed to completely renovating your entire score. Working in a nonlinear fashion means that you do not have to have sections next to each other in order for them to play sequentially. Director uses a feature called Markers to allow the playback head to maneuver around the score to different sections of your movie.

JUMPING AROUND WITH MARKERS

Markers are the key ingredient used for navigation to identify specific sections of your movie. Using Lingo scripts or behaviors, Director responds to these commands and brings the playback head to the area defined by these markers. To add a new marker, click in the markers channel. To delete a marker, drag it out of the channel.

Example: To set markers in the score in order to jump to different sections of the score:

1. Add the sprites for the first section of your movie to the score starting on Frame 1.

2. Add the sprites for the additional section to the score starting on Frames 30, 60, 90, etc.

3. Add a Marker to Frame 1 and name it "Menu."

4. Add a Marker to Frame 30 and name it "Section2."

5. Add a Marker to the first frame of each sprite series that you have added to the score and name each one appropriately (Figure 3-4).

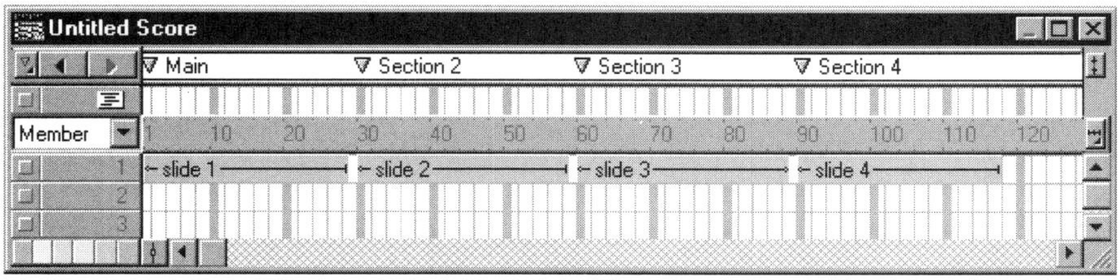

Figure 3-4 Naming each marker to identify a new section of the score.

These markers will designate the "jump to" area for Director when you begin adding interactive commands using behaviors or Lingo scripts to the movie. To leave one section and navigate with markers to a new area, add the following frame or sprite script:

```
on mouse up
      go to marker "nameofmarker"
end
```

Marker names must always be put in quotation marks.

NAMING MARKERS

It is crucial that you take the time to name each marker you add to the score. Because Director uses markers as navigational reference points, they need to be labeled so that the playback head can locate the precise frame when a command is given. Things to keep in mind when naming markers:

1. Keep it limited to a one-word alphanumeric name with no spaces.

2. Exact spelling counts.

3. Markers are not case sensitive (i.e., menu, MENU, Menu, mENU, mEnU).

ADDING COMMENTS TO MARKERS

Because Director recommends working with one-word names for markers, it can get confusing as to what each section is named and why. Using the Markers window, you can add descriptive comments for each marker to remind you of the purpose and function of that marker. The Markers window is especially helpful when:

1. Other programmers will be assisting you on the project. It will help them understand where these markers navigate to and from.

2. You have been working on multiple projects at the same time.

3. Provides a refresher when updating a project that has not been worked on in some time.

To use the Markers window:

1. Add markers to your score and name them.
2. Open the Markers window from under the Window menu.

   OR

   Click the Markers Menu button in the score to open a menu with two choices. Select Markers to open the Markers window (Figure 3-5).

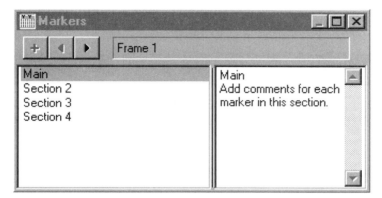

Figure 3-5   Markers window.

3. In the left-hand column, select from a list of markers already in your score.
4. Click in the right-hand column and hit the return key to start a new line.
5. Type in any useful text comment.

Do not type over the marker name in the right-hand window, as it will change the name of your marker. Make sure to hit return to move down to the next line.

NEXT, PREVIOUS, AND REPEAT WITH MARKERS

In your Director movie, you will often need controls to cycle to the next section or return to the previous section (Figure 3-6). Relative Markers allow you to navigate forward or backward one section at a time in relation to where the playback head is, without writing custom Lingo commands for each section (Figure 3-7). The user can jump from one section to the next in either direction by simply applying the following commands to the navigational sprites:

Figure 3-6   Next and Previous buttons for navigation.

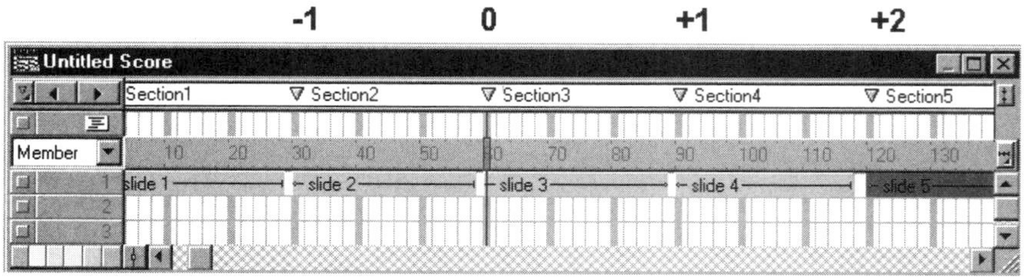

Figure 3-7   Relative markers illustrated for simplifying Next and Previous navigation.

To jump to the next section designated by a marker:

```
on mouseUp
    go to marker (1)
end
```

To jump to the previous section designated by a marker:

```
on mouseUp
    go to marker (-1)
end
```

To jump back to the beginning of the same section designated by a marker:

```
on mouseUp
    go to marker (0)
end
```

The Return to Beginning of Current Section, or Repeat button, is very useful in training type applications where the user would benefit from repeating the information before continuing on to the next section (Figure 3-8).

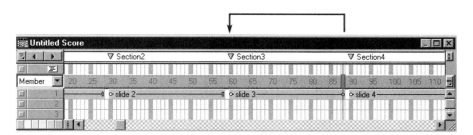

Figure 3-8   The Repeat button allows viewer to replay the current section of the movie designated by a marker.

MAKING SENSE OF BEHAVIORS

For those people who wish to create interactive multimedia applications without having to dedicate their lives to learning how to program codes in some nonhuman type of language, you can relax now. Since the introduction of behaviors with the release of Version 6, Director has taken most of the work out of manually typing lines of commands in order to implement simple interactive events. Behaviors are simply a way to add functionality to your movie through a series of drag and drop cast members with specific commands that apply the Lingo scripts for you behind the scenes. All you have to do is enter the specific information you want the behavior to perform. When that specified event occurs, the behavior triggers Director to perform a certain function, such as navigating the Playback head to a different frame or altering the sprite that contains the behavior.

Behaviors can be attached to sprites or frames. Sprites can have as many behaviors as needed, whereas frames can only contain one behavior.

USING THE BEHAVIOR LIBRARY

Director has taken a number of the most often used commands and created behaviors for them. These behaviors reside in the Behavior Library as a cast of commands ready to be applied to the sprites in your score.

To access the Behavior Library for Version 6:

1. Click on the Xtras menu.
2. Select Behavior Library. (Figure 3-9).

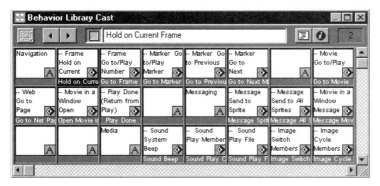

Figure 3-9   Behavior Library (Version 6).

To access the Behavior Library for Version 7:

1. Click on the Window menu.
2. Select Library Palette (Figure 3-10). The Library Palette shows all of the behaviors available for that specific Library.

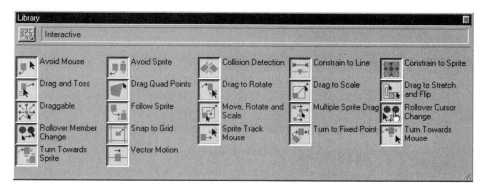

Figure 3-10   Library Palette (Version 7).

3. Click on the Library List icon to select one of the different Behavior Libraries from the popup menu (Figure 3-11).

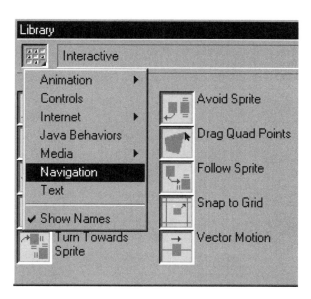

Figure 3-11   Library List button menu.

A cast of behaviors appears for Version 6. A panel of behavior icons appears for Version 7. Drag and Drop the behavior on to the appropriate sprite or frame. It's that easy. Depending on the behavior and the type of action you are trying to achieve will determine whether you drag them onto a sprite or place them on a frame in the script channel. Director automatically adds a copy of that behavior to the current cast so you can customize its specific function without changing the original template. Some of the premade Behaviors include Go To commands, Open commands, Message commands, and Media Control commands. To apply a behavior from the library:

1. Open the Behavior Library.
2. Drag a behavior to the appropriate sprite or frame in your score.
3. Enter the desired parameters for the dialog box that appears (Figure 3-12).

Figure 3-12   Behavior Library parameters window.

Each dialog box contains a different set of parameters depending on which behavior is selected.

CUSTOMIZING BEHAVIORS

These templated Behaviors are a great time-saver for basic interactive programming. However, there will be many times when you will want to modify the command without getting in over your head with Lingo. Use the Behavior Inspector to create your own or modify existing behaviors for interactive commands.

To modify an existing Behavior template:

1. Select a sprite or frame that you want to apply the custom behavior.
2. Open the Behavior Library (Version 6) or Library Palette (Version 7).

3. Open the Behavior Inspector window by clicking on the Behavior Inspector icon (diamond-shaped button) in the score.

Or

Select Inspectors from the Window menu. Choose Behavior from the submenu (Figure 3-13).

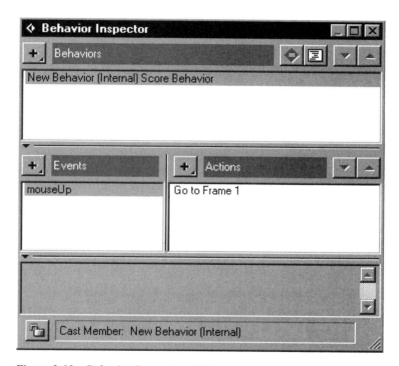

Figure 3-13   Behavior Inspector window.

4. Click on the Plus sign in the top of the Behavior Inspector window.

5. Pick from one of the template behaviors in the Library.

6. Highlight the event that you want to alter.

7. Select a new action or alter the existing one.

If you are using one of the included behaviors from the Library, Director automatically places a copy of that behavior into the movie's cast. This will prevent you from accidentally changing the characteristics of the template behavior.

ADDING COMMENTS TO BEHAVIORS

You can add comments to remind yourself or another developer about the purpose or function of a particular behavior. Type an `on getBehaviorDescription` handler in the script of the behavior to add a description in the bottom pane of the Behavior Inspector (Figure 3-14).

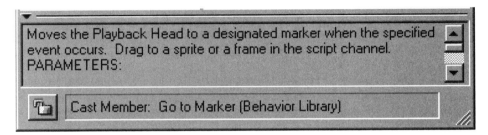

Figure 3-14   Description of behavior in bottom of the Behavior Inspector window.

```
on getBehaviorDescription
        return "Type in the behavior comment here."
end
```

SAVING CUSTOM BEHAVIORS

Once you have customized a behavior in Director 6 that you plan to use again in this or any other projects, save it to the Behavior Library.

1. Drag the new behavior you have created using the Behavior Inspector from your cast to the Behavior Library Cast (Figure 3-15).

2. Place the behavior into an unoccupied cast member window.

3. Close the window.

4. A prompt will appear asking if you want to save the changes you have made to the Behavior Library.

5. Click Save.

The next time you open the Behavior Library, either in this movie or a new one, those custom behavior templates that you created will appear in the cast member window that you placed it in. It will maintain all of the event and action characteristics you selected. All you will have to do is supply Director with the new specifications for the sprite or frame to which you are applying the custom behavior.

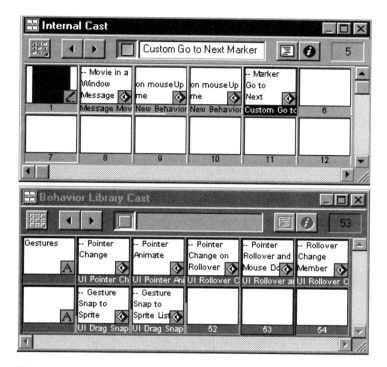

Figure 3-15   Adding customized behaviors to the Behavior Library cast.

SETTING THE DEFAULT EDITOR

The Behavior Inspector is the default window that appears if you want to make changes to an existing behavior. For those users who prefer to edit behaviors using Lingo, you can change the default setting to work in the Script window.

1. Choose Preferences from the File menu.
2. Select Editor. The Editors Preferences window appears (Figure 3-16).
3. Click Behavior.
4. Click the Edit button. A dialog box appears asking you to select the default editor for behaviors.
5. Click the radio button to select which method you would prefer to use to edit behaviors.
6. Click OK.

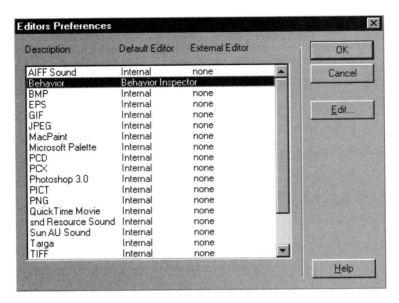

Figure 3-16   Editors Preferences window.

BUILDING INTERACTIVE APPLICATIONS USING BEHAVIORS

Customizing behaviors can allow you to create some pretty intricate interactive programs, complete with navigational links and controls for different media types. The following example will show you how to apply behaviors to create an entire interactive project. Before you begin adding any interactive behaviors or scripts, build your timeline by placing all of the necessary sprites in their proper location in the score. Using a typical interactive screen as an example (Figure 3-17), you will learn how to:

1. Apply behaviors to create sprite rollover properties.

2. Apply behaviors to create sprite navigational links.

3. Apply behaviors to frame scripts.

4. Duplicate behaviors to apply to different sprites.

5. Customize and save behavior templates.

Figure 3-17　Typical interactive multimedia interface (see Color Figure 9).

CONTROLLING PLAYBACK WITH BEHAVIORS

One of the most common commands used in any multimedia program is to have the playback head hold on a particular frame waiting for the user to choose from one of the interactive selections available on the screen. To add this Hold on Current Frame Behavior:

1. Add a sprite to your score.
2. Open the Behavior Library window (Version 6) or Library Palette (Version 7).
3. Drag the `Hold on Current Frame` behavior to the script channel of your score and place it on the last frame of the sprite (Figure 3-18).

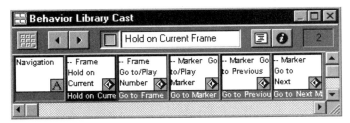

Figure 3-18   Hold On Current Frame Behavior for Version 6 and Version 7.

4. Rewind and play your movie. Notice how the playback head stops in the frame with the behavior script while the Director movie remains in play mode.

This type of command would be used on any frame from which the user will have choices available to navigate. This command will keep the Director movie waiting in that frame until the user makes a choice of which step to take next. This command will be used more frequently as you add more interactive elements to your movie.

CREATING ROLLOVERS WITH THE BEHAVIOR INSPECTOR

Most multimedia applications incorporate some type of user interactions to show responsiveness to the movements of the mouse. Set each button on the interface to change characteristics when the mouse moves into that sprite's area.

1. Import all of the graphic elements you need. (See Chapter 5 for more information on designing elements for interactive programs.)
2. Select the sprite that you want to apply rollover properties.
3. Open the Behavior Inspector from the Window menu.

4. Use the rotating triangle to open the windows on the Behavior Inspector.

5. Click on the Plus sign in the top left corner of the window to add a new Behavior.

6. Select New Behavior and name it (i.e., "Rollover").

7. Click on the Plus sign in the Event column. Select a command from the most commonly used events in the popup menu.

8. Choose `mouseEnter`. This command will tell Director to perform whichever action we set for this sprite when the mouse enters within the proximity of the sprite. The bounding box area determines the proximity of the sprite (Figure 3-19).

9. Click on the Plus sign in the Actions column.

10. Select Sprite from the popup menu.

11. Choose Change Cast Member from the Sprite submenu.

12. Enter the name of the cast member that you want to display when your mouse enters the area of the original sprite.

13. Rewind and playback your movie.

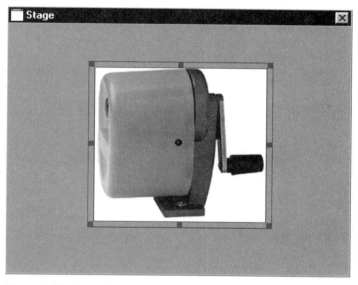

Figure 3-19   Bounding box of sprite.

Notice that a new behavior named "Rollover" was automatically added to your cast.

Now when you play the movie, the original sprite will change to the new sprite you selected when the mouse rolls over the area of the original sprite. Because we only set a command to change the sprite when the mouse enters the area, the new sprite will remain displayed for the remainder of the movie. You must set the commands for the second part of a rollover, which is to change back to the original cast member as the mouse leaves the vicinity of that sprite. To set the reverse command:

1. With the original sprite still selected, open the Behavior Inspector window.

2. Make sure "Rollover" is the behavior listed in the top of the dialog box.

3. In the Events column, select mouseLeave from the popup menu.

4. In the Actions column, select Sprite from the popup menu.

5. Choose Change Cast Member from the Sprite submenu.

6. Enter the name of the original cast member to be displayed when your mouse leaves the area of the rolled-over sprite.

7. Rewind and play your movie. Notice the sprites changing when you move the mouse in and out of the area set for the original sprite (Figure 3-20).

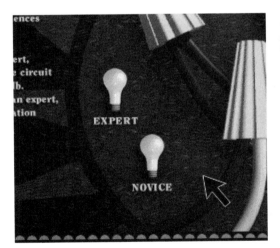 

Figure 3-20   Sprite changes appearance as mouse "rolls over" that sprite.

SPRITE NAVIGATION WITH BEHAVIORS

Writing codes to perform a specific navigational function when the user clicks a button is a task that every developer of interactive applications has to incorporate into his program. Using behaviors reduces the time needed and eliminates most of the typographical errors common with this interactive necessity. To make sprites have navigational characteristics using behaviors:

1. Select the sprite you want to use as a navigational control element (Figure 3-21).
2. Open the Behavior Inspector.
3. Add a New Behavior and name it (i.e., "button click").
4. In the Events column, select mouseUp from the popup menu.
5. In the Actions column, select Navigation from the popup menu.
6. Choose Go to Frame from the Navigation submenu.
7. Specify the frame number where you want the playback head to go when the mouse button is clicked and released. (For this example we want the History Section going to Frame 74; Figure 3-22.)

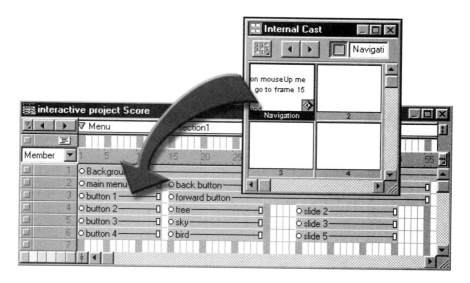

Figure 3-21   Navigational behavior being applied to selected sprite.

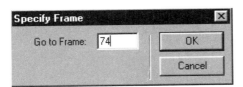

Figure 3-22   Specify frame in the Go To Frame window.

ADDING BEHAVIORS TO OTHER SPRITES

Now that you have created one link using behaviors, use that template to add navigational functionality to all of the other sprites in your movie that require the same type of command. Use the behavior that you created for the first button and apply it to the rest of the navigational buttons.

Hold the Alt key (Windows) or the Option key (Macintosh) and drag a cast member to an open panel in the cast to make an exact copy of a cast member.

1. Take the behavior cast member you just created in the previous section and copy it. Make as many copies of that behavior as you need to assign one to each button on the interface (Figure 3-23).

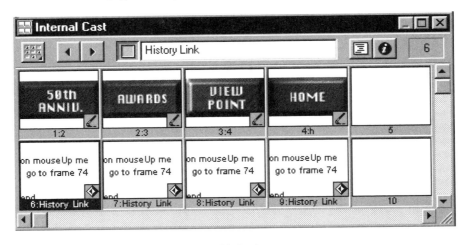

Figure 3-23   Cast with multiple copies of behavior.

2. Rename them according to which link they will be applied (Figure 3-24).

3. Drag each new behavior cast member to its respective button.

4. Open the inspector window for each sprite.

5. Change the frame number variable in the Specify Frame dialog box for where you want that sprite to jump (Figure 3-25).

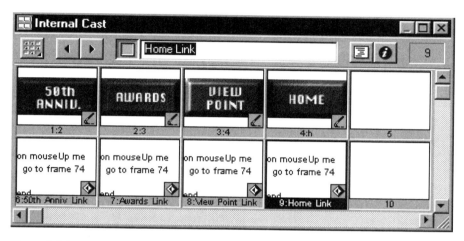

Figure 3-24   Renaming behaviors for specific tasks.

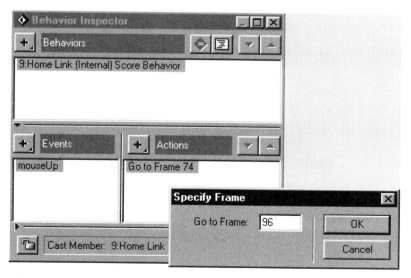

Figure 3-25   Customizing behavior to link to a new frame number.

If you are using any type of interactivity, you will want to use a wait command or a hold on current frame script so that the user has ample time to make a selection without having the playback head leave that main section. This way the user gets a chance to make a selection.

FRAME NAVIGATION WITH BEHAVIORS

Not all Behaviors have to be applied to sprites. There are many examples where you can apply Behaviors directly to the script channel to enhance the navigational routing of your score. You can set the playback head to jump to particular frames, go to markers, or go to net pages (see Chapter 8 for web-related activities). For example, a new section needs to be added to an existing project. The potential time and errors that can occur by moving sprites around in your score can be very costly. Instead, use a frame script to navigate to the new section and then continue back to the next required section (Figure 3-26).

1. Open the Behavior Library.
2. Drag the Behavior Cast Member Go To Marker to the script channel (Figure 3-27).
3. Set the Destination Frame, Event, and Play Mode in the Parameters for "Go To Marker" dialog box (Figure 3-28).

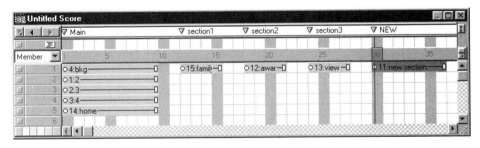

Figure 3-26   New section added to score.

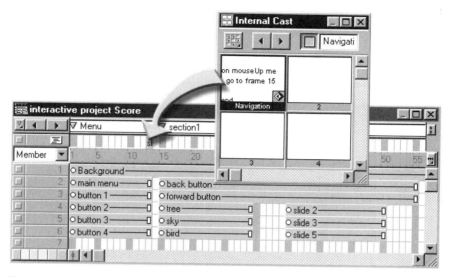

Figure 3-27   Navigational behavior being applied to script channel of score.

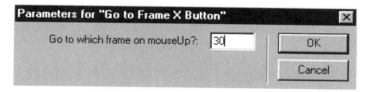

Figure 3-28   Parameters for "Go To Marker" dialog box.

4. Rewind and play back your movie. The playback head should jump from the frame where you placed the behavior to the frame number that you designated. You can use this quick function to return the user automatically back to the previous section.

I QUIT

The most important navigational element you can include in your movie is a quit or exit feature. Unless your projector is set to automatically quit, the user will be stuck eternally inside your application without some type of exit command. The only alternative would be to force quit or reboot the system. You can use the Behavior Inspector to add this functionality to any sprite or frame:

1. Select the sprite or frame where you want to add this feature (Figure 3-29).

Figure 3-29   Interface showing example of an Exit button (see Color Figure 10).

2. Open the Behavior Inspector.

3. Click on the Behavior popup button.

4. Select New Behavior from the popup menu and name it.

5. Click on the Event popup button.

6. Select one event from the events list to execute the function.

7. Click on the Action popup button.

8. Select Exit from the menu list (Figure 3-30).

Now, when you perform that function (i.e., exit on mouseUp), the application will quit, returning the user to the Windows or Macintosh desktop.

OR

Try your luck at adding a Lingo script. The quit command is the shortest and simplest command. Enter the following text depending on the type of script being applied:
For a frame script:

```
on exitFrame
     quit
end
```

Figure 3-30   *Setting the behavior to exit the application.*

For a sprite script:

```
on mouseUp
     quit
end
```

You can add different handlers to perform the action with any
event you choose (exitFrame, mouseEnter, etc.).

SUMMARY

The examples listed earlier cover just some of the basic navigational controls that you can, and probably will, apply to every project you create. You can see how working with behaviors makes programming your Director movie fast, easy, and clean. There are obviously many more examples I could have covered. Scan through some of the other chapters in this book to see how to use some of the other behaviors for different types of scenarios. If this has been your first experience working with behaviors, I'll bet you love it. Build a library or cast of your own personalized custom behaviors to save you the time and hassle of doing the work all over again. I hope these shortcuts help.

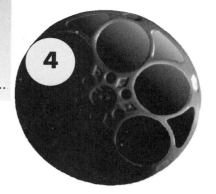

chapter 4

DIVING INTO

DIRECTOR

WITH LINGO

To add more powerful features to your interactive multimedia applications, you will need to use Lingo, Director's scripting language. For those of you who have gotten by without experimenting with Lingo, don't wait any longer. Lingo is the brains behind your movie, allowing you to create interactive buttons, text fields, menus, and other movie controls. It can determine how your movie will function as the user interacts with the program. Without Lingo, you probably would not have the ability to set up any type of complex navigational layout that the user can interact with. As you will see, Lingo allows you to program choices for the end user to determine how and where he proceeds through the program. As you learn the capabilities involved with programming with Lingo, you will begin to see the sheer power and flexibility available to you when designing multimedia applications in Director.

HOW DOES LINGO WORK?

Lingo is written as a set of phrases called scripts (yet another theatrical metaphor) in the script window. These scripts provide you with the ability to control the playback of your movie in one of the following ways:

1. Keep the playback head in position on a particular frame.
2. Jump to a different section of the score.
3. Change the properties of any sprite.
4. Respond to the user's interactions with the program.

85

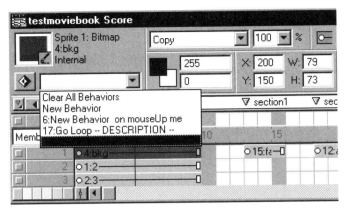

Figure 4-1   Creating new Lingo script.

To open a new Script window:

1. Click on the empty pulldown menu in the score window (Figure 4-1).
2. Click on New Script. A new script window appears with some text already in it but it has no functionality yet.

   OR

3. Double-click on a frame in the Script channel.

   OR

4. Single-click on the script channel and begin typing.

UNDERSTANDING LINGO HANDLERS

The codes on exitFrame (or some variation) and end must appear in every script. This text that is being added is part of a group of phrases that make up an instructional phrase called handlers. These handlers are what give Director its ability to perform specific tasks. Every handler in Lingo must begin with an on command and end with an end command.

 Handlers must be written in the exact structure that Lingo needs in order for Director to understand the command and perform the function.

If you are not sure of the exact Lingo code but have a good idea of the function you are trying to accomplish, Director provides a categorized list of Lingo commands in the script window (Figure 4-2).

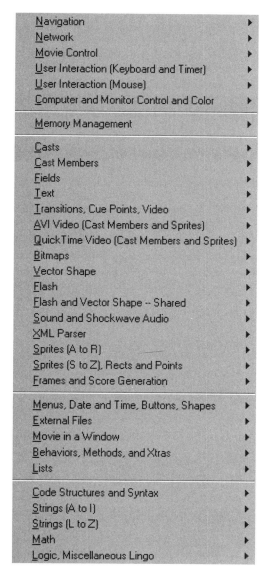

Figure 4-2   Category list of Lingo commands.

1. Open the Script window.

2. Select the Lingo command List.

3. Roll your mouse down each category to display a submenu of Lingo commands.

4. Depending on which script command you select, Director adds the proper language to the script window. Director will either highlight or give you instructions on what required information is needed to function correctly.

5. Type in the necessary information (Figure 4-3).

Figure 4-3   Director indicates where to type required information when using Lingo commands from category list.

Lingo is not as complicated as it first appears. Break down each line and decipher what is being said. On exitFrame tells Director to perform the function as soon as the playback head exits the current frame. The on mouseUp command performs the same task as most other handlers, instructing Director to activate a function or perform a given task when the specified event occurs.

THE MOST COMMON SCRIPT

The go to the Frame command tells the playback head to keep looping the current frame. In essence, this command acts as a pause command, yet keeps all of the sprites located in that frame active. The play head reads this instruction or script and continues to play that same frame over and over, thereby keeping the movie in play mode while waiting for some other type of user interaction. This script performs exactly like the behavior Hold on current frame that we applied in an example earlier. To use this script:

1. Double-click on a frame in the script channel where you want to place this function.

2. Type out the string of commands to match the following:

```
on exitFrame
    go to the frame
end
```

3. Close the Script window.

4. Rewind and play your movie. The playback head should stop when it reaches the frame where you placed the script.

Be very careful where you put this script. If you place it in a frame that also contains a transition, that transition will infinitely be looping and you will have no way out. Unless you are looking for that particular effect in your Director movie (which I hope that no one will ever use), make sure not to place a transition on any frame that has a `go to the Frame` script in the score.

Use the `go to the frame` command instead of entering a specific frame number so that if you slide the sprites around in the score, the function will still operate correctly. Having a specific frame number entered in the script will require you to make changes to that script every time you shift things around in the score in order for your movie to play back correctly.

GO TO ANOTHER LOCATION

The second most common Lingo commands used for navigation are the Go To (a specific frame number) and Go To (a specific marker). These commands allow you to jump around to different sections of the movie to take advantage of Director being able to work in a nonlinear environment. Apply these commands as either frame scripts or as sprite scripts. Set up the same type of navigational links that you did earlier using behaviors. To program the commands on the interactive menu screen using Lingo:

1. Add markers to the first frame of each section in your score and name them (Figure 4-4).

2. Select a sprite or frame on which to apply the navigational command.

3. Click on the Script pulldown menu in the score.

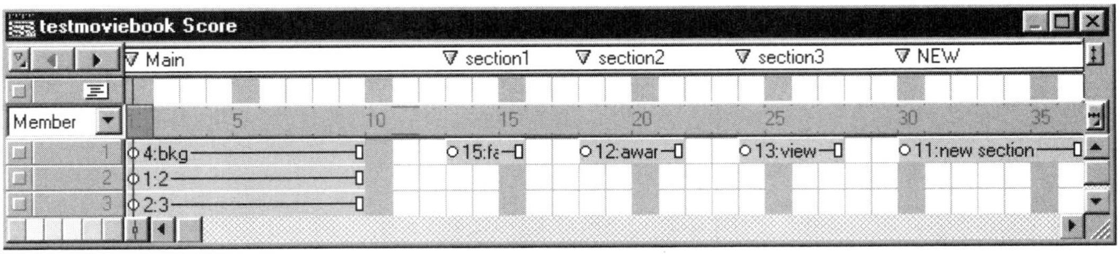

Figure 4-4   Score with markers indicating various sections of movie.

4. Select New Script and name it.

5. In the Script window, enter one of the following scripts (Director automatically adds the beginning and end handlers):

```
on mouseUp
   go to "Section1"
   -- goes to the marker name
end
```

　OR

```
on mouseUp
   go to frame 2
   -- goes to the frame number
end
```

6. Repeat Steps 2 through 5 for each button that you want to function as a button that links to a different portion of the score.

7. Rewind and play the movie.

When you click on the sprite containing the script, the playback head will automatically jump to that marker named Section1. You can also go to a specific frame by using the command `go to frame #`. This command will perform the same function as the Go To Marker command but with one disadvantage.

During the course of developing your program, if you add and remove any frames, not to mention rearrange certain portions of your script, the command "go to frame #" will not take you to that same section any longer (Figure 4-5).

> By using the command `Go To Marker`, Director will always be able to jump to that exact frame location, no matter where you move that section to or how many frames have been added to or deleted from the score.

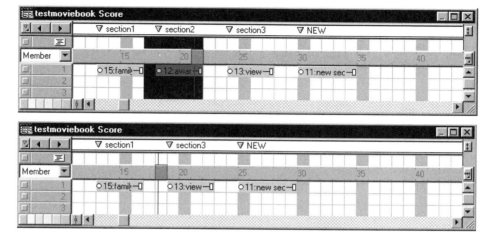

Figure 4-5   Comparison of scores—indicating how frame numbering is altered when deleting frames.

Marker names must be put in quotation marks and spelled exactly the same as they appear in the marker channel.

WORKING WITH CONSTANT IMAGES

Markers and Go To commands do not always have to send the user to a different section of the program. If you are designing a program where only one aspect of the screen changes when you click a button, add markers to a continuous section of the original sprites in the score (Figure 4-6). To accomplish this task:

1. Copy all the sprites from one frame of the main section except the script (the last frame contains a `Go to the Frame` command that we do not want in this new section).

2. Paste them into the frame directly after the main section.

   OR

3. Extend all of the sprites from the last frame leaving the script commands in Frame 28 (Figure 4-7).

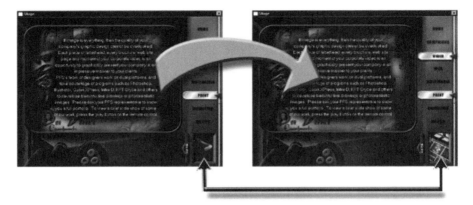

Figure 4-6   *Interface of an application where only one aspect within the entire image changes.*

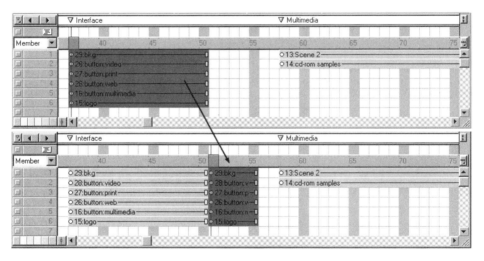

Figure 4-7   *Copying a section of sprites and adding them directly after that section to extend the images.*

4. Add a marker above Frame 29 and name it (i.e., animation).

5. In the same sprite channel, replace the logo image with a film loop (Figure 4-8).

6. Add a `Wait for Cue Point` option to allow the animation to finish playing.

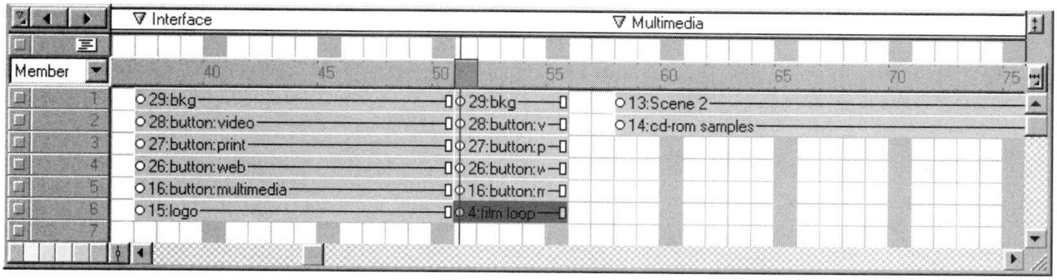

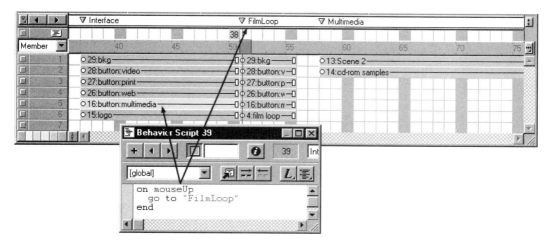

Figure 4-8 **Replacing only one sprite in the newly extended section for the image that will be changing.**

7. Add a frame script command:

```
on exitFrame
    go to "multimedia"
end
```

8. Add markers and film loops for each new section (Figure 4-9).

Figure 4-9 **Script applied to sprite navigates to new section added in score.**

9. Rewind and play the movie.

The playback head should play through the movie up until Frame 28. The script command in Frame 28 keeps the playback head looping in this frame waiting for the user to make a selection from one of the interactive buttons. When the user selects the Multimedia button, Director sends the playback head into Frame 29. As soon as the playback head enters this frame, the film loop begins to play. When it is finished playing, Director automatically sends the playback head down to the section marker labeled "multimedia." This entire process gives the user the illusion that they have stayed within the original section and executed an animation before jumping into a whole new area of the program.

LOOPING SECTIONS

There may be situations when you want to keep the playback head within a particular section of your movie, waiting for the user to make a selection from one of the interactive elements on screen. Normally you would add a `go to the frame` command. If the project required animations to be continuously playing, one way to do this while keeping the playback head within the current section is to add a loop feature. The command `go loop` tells Director when the playback head reaches this command (usually set as a script in the last frame of a given section) to go back to the marker in the beginning of the current section and play it over again (Figure 4-10). The playback head will continuously loop until an interactive selection is made by the user. To add the loop command:

1. Add a marker to the first frame of any given segment.
2. Add all necessary sprites and animate them as desired.
3. Double-click on the script channel in the last frame of the current section to open the script window.

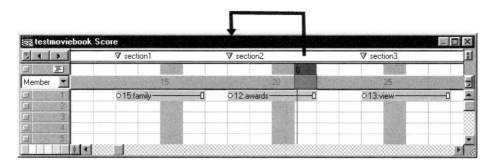

Figure 4-10　Go Loop script applied to continuous loop section identified by markers.

4. Type the command:

```
on exitFrame
    go loop
end
```

5. Rewind and play back your movie.

Notice how the playback head automatically returns to the frame with the marker and continues to play the current section over again.

PLAYING OTHER DIRECTOR MOVIES

Director has the ability to open other .dir movies from your current movie. You can use this feature to make your movie function as if it is simply navigating to another section of the current movie. The advantages include:

1. If you want to demonstrate the complex programming that you designed in another application, you do not need to reprogram the entire movie.
2. You can keep the file size of your current movie down, so that it will not overload the system's memory.
3. Each movie may have been built with different requirements, such as bit depth and color palettes. By calling up a seperate movie entirely, it plays under its own custom parameters originally set when the program was developed. You may store the target movie anywhere on your system. The Open dialog box will prompt you to select a file, setting the path where the behavior can find this file on your system (Figure 4-11).

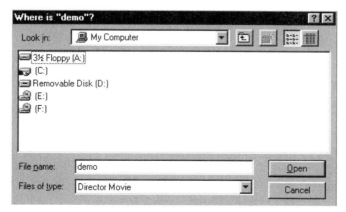

Figure 4-11   Open dialog box.

Linking other Director movies is a great way to design promotional products or compilation programs of past works. Advertising and marketing firms use this feature all the time, designing demo CDs to showcase their work of past projects. Students and independent developers can use this technique to create interactive resumes to highlight projects they have produced.

For this example, use image buttons to "link to" or open other Director movies. To implement opening another movie from within Director:

1. Open the main Director movie.

2. Determine the event that will play another Director movie. This can include most navigational sprite scripts or frame scripts, such as on mouseDown or on exit-Frame.

3. Add the Lingo command to the sprite script for the event that you chose. For this example, type:

```
on mouseDown
    play movie "name of new movie"
end
```

OR

Use the Behavior Library:

A. Open the Library Palette.

B. Select Controls from the Library List popup menu (Figure 4-12).

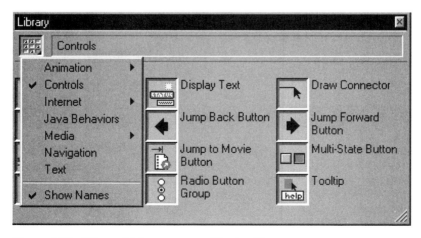

Figure 4-12   Library List popup menu (Version 7).

C. Drag the "jump to movie" behavior onto the desired sprite.

D. Select the file name from the Open dialog box.

OR

Use the Behavior Inspector:

A. Open the Behavior Inspector.

B. Select New Behavior and name it.

C. Select mouseUp from the Event column.

D. Select Navigation from the Action column.

E. Select Go To Movie... (Figure 4-13).

F. Enter the name or path of the Director movie you want to navigate to in the Specify Movie dialog box.

4. In the new movie, add a frame or sprite navigational link back to the original movie. Enter the same Lingo or use the same behavior, putting the original movie name in place of the new movie name.

5. Rewind and play back your movie.

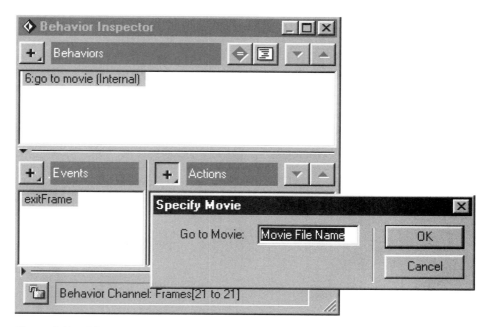

Figure 4-13   "Go To Movie..." action selected in Behavior Inspector.

AUTOMATIC RETURNS TO A DIRECTOR MOVIE

A common feature when jumping to or playing another Director movie is to have it automatically return to the original movie. This feature is known as branching. To return back to the original movie, use the movie script Lingo `play done`. This allows the user to automatically return to the original movie without adding any additional buttons. As long as the new movie does not contain any `mouseUp` handlers in any sprites, frames, or cast members, the user will be able to click the mouse anywhere on the screen to end the current movie. To add this movie script:

1. Select Script from the Window menu or use the keyboard shortcut Control-0 (Windows) or Command-0 (Macintosh).

2. Enter the following Lingo (Figure 4-14):

```
on mouseUp
    play done
end
```

3. Save the new movie.

4. Rewind and play the original Director movie. When you link to the new movie, click the mouse button to automatically return to the original movie.

Jump to movie, play movie, and branching are all techniques used to give the illusion that the playback head is instantaneously navigating to a different section of the score within the same movie as opposed to having the user close the current movie in order to play the new one. You can also branch to a specific frame of the new movie, instead of the default first frame (Figure 4-15), by entering the command:

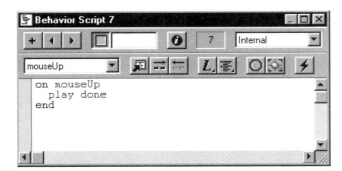

Figure 4-14   "Play Done" Lingo script.

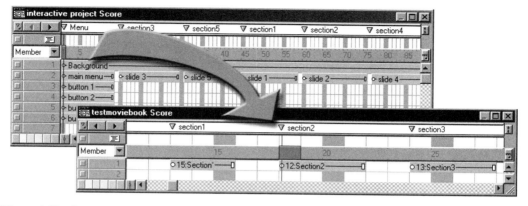

Figure 4-15   Branching to a specific section of a movie instead of the first frame.

```
on mouseUp
    play frame "section2" of movie "newmovie"
end
```

INTERACTIVE CHANGING CURSORS

To help the user maneuver more successfully through your program, have the cursor change form to signify different events taking place. Just like on the Web, the cursor changes from the traditional arrow to the finger-pointing icon to let the user know that he is over an area of the screen that will link him to another section of the program (Figure 4-16). You can apply changing cursors to text and images in Director for roll-overs, hyperlinks, and button clicks.

To change cursors for a rollover effect:

1. Click on the sprite that is being rolled over.
2. Open the Behavior Inspector window.
3. Create a new Behavior and name it (i.e., "Rollover").
4. In the Event column, choose `on mouseEnter`.
5. In the Action column, choose Change Cursor.
6. Choose one from the list of the system default cursors.
7. Go back and choose mouseLeave in the Event column.
8. In the Action column, choose Change Cursor.
9. Choose Arrow from the list to return the cursor back to its original state.

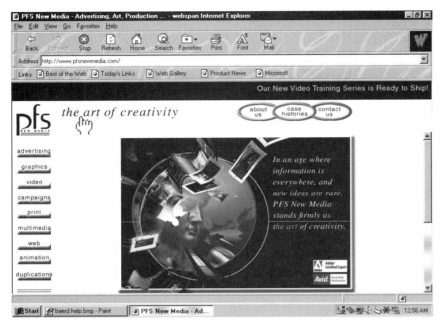

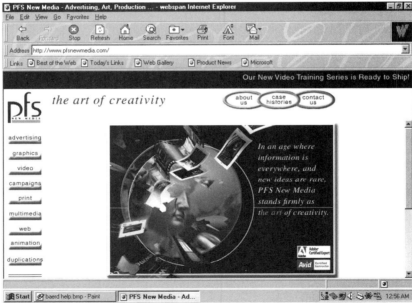

Figure 4-16   Website rollover area indicated by changing cursor (see Color Figure 11).

10. Close the Behavior Inspector window.

11. Rewind and play your movie. The cursor should change as you roll your mouse over the sprite you have selected. You can apply this behavior to any other sprite that you wish to take on this characteristic.

Some of the most common default system cursors for Director 6 and later:

arrow	0
hour glass or watch	4
no cursor (hidden)	200
help	254
hand	260
pointing finger	280
magnifying glass: zoom in	302
magnifying glass: zoom out	303

To learn how to create and implement custom cursors, see the section "Designing Custom Cursors" in Chapter 5, Designing Killer Effects.

LINGO CONDITIONS: TRUE OR FALSE

As you start adding more complex features to your Director movie, you will need to start relying on Lingo commands more often. One common feature is to have Director check to see if a certain condition exists at the current time. Director looks at this command as to whether the condition exists or does not exist.

1. To instruct Director that a particular condition exists, set the condition equal to True.

2. To instruct Director that a particular condition does not exist, set the condition equal to False.

A value of 1 can be used instead of typing the word True. A value of 0 indicates a False statement.

Example: If you want to make a sprite invisible during a particular section, set the visibility to False or 0 (Figure 4-17):

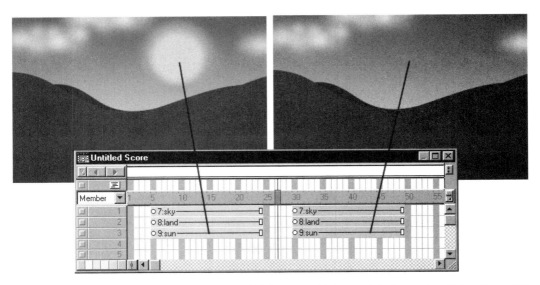

Figure 4-17 *Sprite "sun" visibility set to true on left image and false on right image (see Color Figure 12).*

```
on enterFrame
        set the visibility of sprite (which channel) = False
end
```

If you want to give the user the ability to drag a sprite around the screen while playing the movie, set the equation equal to True or 1:

```
on startMovie
        set the moveableSprite of sprite 1 = 1
end
```

ONE SPRITE, TWO FUNCTIONS

A feature that will be helpful in the development of your application is to add the programming capability to use a single sprite as a toggle switch. A common example is to pause your movie. Click the sprite once to pause the movie. Click that sprite again to resume playback from where you left off (Figure 4-18).

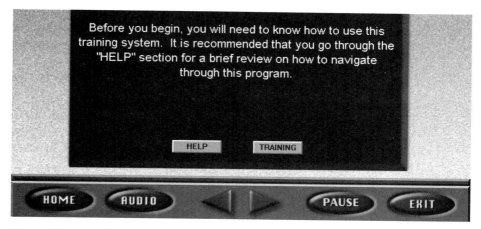

Figure 4-18   Interface showing a pause/play toggle button.

1. Select the sprite that will operate the pause/playback feature.
2. Open a Score script and type:

```
on mouseDown
   if the pauseState = True then
      go to the frame + 1
   else
      pause
   end if
end
```

 PauseState is a common Lingo command used to test the pause value of the movie. The value returns as True when the movie is in a pause mode. Otherwise, it will return a False value.

CAN SCRIPTS MAKE DECISIONS?

You can use a series of Lingo commands to allow your movie to interpret the conditions of a particular section of the movie in order to determine the appropriate action and response. Use the `if`, `then`, and `else` elements to have Director check whether certain conditions are active or present for your movie at a given time. How it works:

1. Lingo checks to see whether the condition of the first statement exists by using the `if` command.

2. If that condition does indeed exist, Lingo responds with the proper action set in the `then` statement.

3. If the condition of that statement does not exist, then Lingo will execute the alternative action set by the `else` statement.

Example: In Chapter 7, we cover how to use buttons to raise and lower the volume of your movie. This action is dependent on what the condition of the movie is at the current time (Figure 4-19). To raise the volume:

Figure 4-19   Audio controls to adjust volume.

```
on mouseUp
     if soundLevel = 0 then
         set sound = 1
     else
     if soundLevel = 1 then
         set sound = 2
     end if
--Continue for each step of volume control you prefer.
end
```

IF SHORTCUTS NEEDED, THEN USE CASE

The Case statement can be used as an alternative to the `if...then` statements when you are incorporating many branches of Lingo. Instead of continuously entering the `then...else` portion of the command, use the case statement to list the possible responses to the actions of the statement. Lingo begins examining each possible condition until it comes across a statement that exists and then executes that command. The case statements can be used to create and implement many scenarios throughout your movie. A good example that can utilize the case statements is when setting up multiple choice questions for your user to answer (Figure 4-20):

```
on keyDown
     case (the key) of
          "A": go to frame "Congratulations"
          "B", "C", "D", "E":
     alert "Incorrect. Please review the material again."
     beep
     go to frame "Question1"
          end case
     end keyDown
```

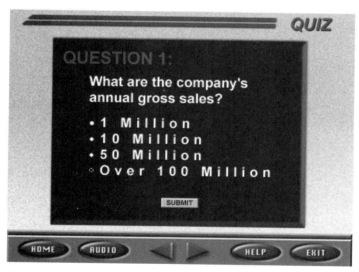

Figure 4-20   Application with multiple choice selection.

This seemingly confusing script is actually fairly simple to understand if you break down its components. Basically, the command is checking the conditions as to which key on the keyboard is pressed. If the A key is pressed, Director jumps to the section labeled with the marker "Congratulations." If any of the other keys from the multiple choice quiz were pressed (B, C, D, or E), Director puts up an alert window, beeps, and returns them to the question screen again.

This quiz method will not keep track of the number of questions the user got correct. It is merely used to check how well the user grasped the information, and if not, suggests to review the material again.

SETTING VALUES AND VARIABLES

A feature often needed in a multimedia application is to have the program calculate a value for something and continually update it as the movie plays. You can set just about any type of variable or equation in Director for this feature. By constantly changing the value of that variable, Director can keep track of items such as user input information, the score of a game, or whether or not a particular event occurred. Use the Lingo command set x = y to calculate the different values. To test commands before implementing them in your Director movie, use the Message Window (Window menu > Message).

1. The phrase "set" tells Director to make the first portion of the equation equal to the second portion of the equation.

2. The phrase "put" tells Director to display the calculation in the Message window (Figure 4-21).

Director uses the internal components of the computer to calculate time, date, and mathematical calculations.

Example 1:

1. Open the Message window.

2. Type: Set Score = 0

3. Type: Put Score and hit return.

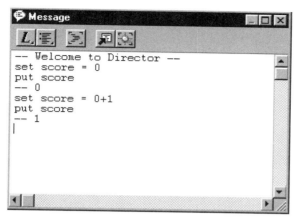

Figure 4-21   Message window demonstrating the Set/Put commands.

4. Director should display "0."

5. Then type: Set Score = 0 + 1.

6. Type: Put Score and hit return.

7. Director should now display "1" because you set the score equal to zero plus one.

Use a practical naming convention for all of your variables. As your program gets more complex, keeping track of variable with generic names is quite difficult. Use a descriptive term for the variable you are setting: `Use set myName = Dennis instead of set x = Dennis`

GLOBAL VS. LOCAL VARIABLES

According to Director, a variable is created the first time you assign a value to it. Apply variables to different equations or change the value of the variable based on the frequency of the event. Global variables are set for the duration of a movie or until it comes across a `clearGlobals` command. By declaring a variable as a global, it makes it available to every handler for the entire movie. A good example of when to use a global variable is during a program in which you want to display the user's name throughout the program (Figure 4-22).

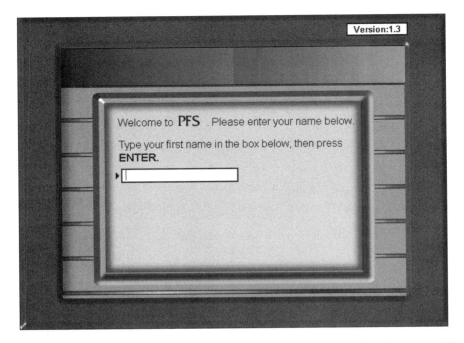

Figure 4-22   Area for user to enter his name which will be displayed in other areas of the program (see Color Figure 13).

```
global gName
put "Dennis" into gName
```

This statement is telling Director to make the variable gName global and make it have the value of Dennis. You can change the value of the variable later on in the movie without changing the global variable.

```
on nameChange
    global gName
    put "Jason" into gName
end
```

To help you quickly identify which items are global variables, put the letter "g" before each global variable.

You can also use global variables to keep track of whether that person has gone through a particular section of the movie already. This is the best way to have Director achieve this interactive record-keeping task during the course of the movie.

> **This function will only work during one session of the program. If the user quits and restarts the program, the values are not saved from the last session.**

```
on startMovie
     global gSection1, gSection2, gSection3
     set gSection1 = False
     set gSection2 = False
     set gSection3 = False
end
```

Each of these statements tell Director to set the variable for each section equal to false, meaning that the user has not gone through any of these sections. To check whether or not a user has entered a screen, use an `if...then` statement to determine the conditions of the movie. If the user has entered a particular section, you can change the look of the button sprite for that section to let the user know that he has already gone through that section (Figure 4-23).

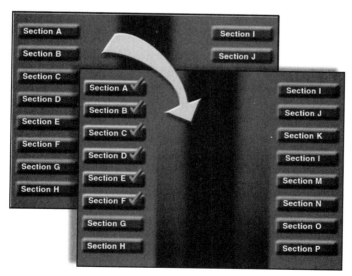

Figure 4-23   *Check marks on buttons indicate which section the user has completed (see Color Figure 14).*

```
on displayChecks
      - checking on main menu whether use had entered a section
      global gSection1, gSection2, gSection3
      if gSection1 = True then set the visibility of sprite 7 to true
      if gSection2 = True then set the visibility of sprite 8 to true
      if gSection3 = True then set the visibility of sprite 9 to true
            --where sprites 7, 8, 9 are check marks that are
            positioned over the buttons to their respective sections.
      updateStage
end
```

On the first frame of each section (this script is for Section 1), add:

```
on enterFrame
      global gSection 1
      set gSection1 = True
end
```

When the user goes back to the main menu, Director will look to see if any of the variables have changed, indicating that a user has entered that particular section:

```
on enterFrame
      displayChecks
end
```

As the user goes through each section of the program and returns to the main menu screen, Director does a quick check through the Lingo commands to see if any sections have been visited. If any of the Lingo commands are set to true for a given section, Director is now instructed to display a sprite of a check mark over the button linking to that section. This way the user can quickly see which topics he has covered during this session of the program.

To effectively set the global variables for the entire movie, assign your global variables before the actual movie begins by using the on `prepareMovie` handler.

Use global variables sparingly. They get loaded into the memory from the start of the movie and remain there until the end. Too many globals can greatly reduce the performance of your program.

Unless the handler contains the phrase "global," all other variables are automatically set as Local variables. Local variables exist only while a specific handler is running and do not save their value. Once Lingo encounters an `end` command, the variable is no longer valid. Use local variables when you only want to set the variable for a short time, not the entire movie. The basic layout for local variables is:

```
set (variable) = (value)
set backgroundColor = Red
```

This type of command tells Director to replace any local variable with the value set in this equation.

LISTS

Lists are a type of variable that are used to keep track of several items at a time. Lists generally contain various types of variables, such as strings, integers, constants, and other lists. There are many different applications where lists can be used. The following are just a small sampling of common list applications:

```
set myList = [#MainMenu, #Section1, #Section2, #Section3]
```

Symbols in Lingo always follow a specific format: A pound sign (#), followed by an alphabetical character, and then any combination of alphanumeric characters.

ADVANCED TECHNIQUE: TRACKING SECTIONS

A commonly requested feature, especially in developing a training or educational program, is the ability for the program to track which sections the user has already completed and offer them the ability to go back and review those sections. Use the list feature to set up this function:

Use the following Lingo command as a frame script:

```
on recordLocation
    global locList, currentLabel
      -- declaring global variable
    if voidP (locList) then set locList = [ ]
      --checks contents of list, otherwise creates empty list
    put the frameLabel into currentLabel
    if not getOne (locList, the frameLabel) then
        append locList, the frameLabel
      --checks the list and adds current frame name to list
    end if

end
```

Use the following Lingo command to sprite, such as a Review Button:

```
on goBack
    global locList, currentLabel
    set previousSection = getOne (locList, currentLabel) - 1
      --local variable of locList minus 1
    if previousSection >=1 then
  go frame getAt (locList, previousSection)
      --moves the playback head to the previous section
    end if
end
```

The getAt command in a linear list returns the value of the given position.

Depending on the circumstances of your movie, you may be able to implement a simple command to jump back to the last sprite that was clicked with the mouse. The clickOn command is a function that keeps track of which sprite channel was most recently clicked on. You can apply this command as a navigational tool:

```
on exitFrame
    if the clockOn = (channel#) then
        go to "markerName"
    end if
end
```

This command tells Director that if a particular channel number was clicked on last, set its value to true and perform the given action. If no sprite was clicked on or the background image was the target of the last mouse click, the `clickOn` command returns a value of zero.

CREATING POPUP MENUS/ DROPDOWN LISTS

A very common feature to implement into your interactive applications is the use of popup menus and dropdown lists. These have been very popular on the Web and can add to the amount of interactive choices available to the user. Version 7 added a new behavior, which allows you to add this feature into your Director movie very quickly and easily. You can add the content from a text field, marker names, or movie name. Director will automatically navigate to those markers or movies if selected from a popup menu. To build a menu/list:

1. Open the Field Text window from the Window menu (Figure 4-24).

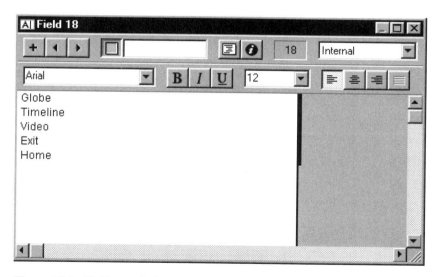

Figure 4-24   Field text window.

2. Type in the text to be used in the dropdown menu.
3. Close the window when you are finished entering all of the desired text.
4. Place the field text cast member onto the stage (Figure 4-25).

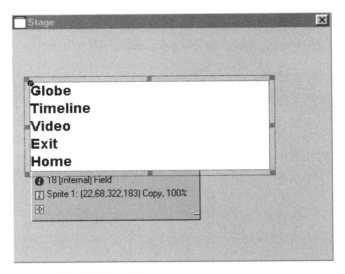

Figure 4-25   Field text list on stage.

5. Open the Library Palette from the Windows menu.

6. Select Control from the Library List popup menu.

7. Drag the Dropdown Behavior onto the Field Text sprite (Figure 4-26).

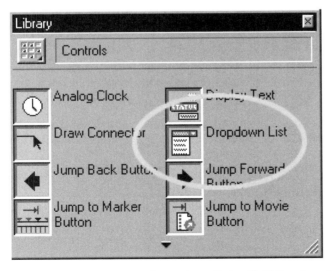

Figure 4-26   Dropdown Behavior is applied to Field Text from Library List (Version 7).

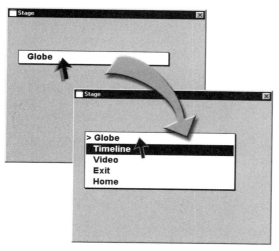

Figure 4-27   *Clicking and holding mouse over the field reveals the rest of the words in the dropdown menu.*

8. Rewind and play the movie. Only the first entry should be visible.
9. Click and hold the mouse key on the text field to display the entire list (Figure 4-27).

You can use the items in a popup menu as navigational choices that link to different sections of a movie (Figure 4-28). To implement this feature:

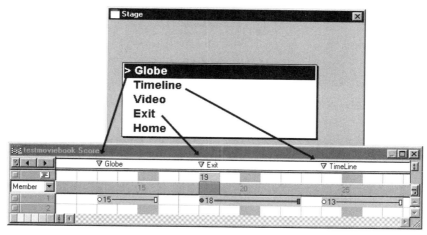

Figure 4-28   *Names in dropdown menu coincide with marker names for navigational purposes.*

1. Add all the necessary sprites to your score for each section of your movie.

2. Add markers to the first frame of each new section and name them.

3. Create a list using the Field Text option.

4. Drag the Field Text cast member to the score.

5. Open the Library palette from the Window menu.

6. Select Controls from the Library List.

7. Drag the Dropdown Behavior onto the Field Text sprite. The Parameters for "Dropdown List" window appears.

8. Name the list.

9. Set the Content of the list to "Markers in this movie."

10. Set the Purpose of this list to "Execute: go movie/go marker/do selectedLine" (Figure 4-29).

11. Click the OK button.

12. Rewind and play back your movie. Only the first field item should be displayed on your stage.

13. Click on that field to display the contents of the entire list.

14. Click and hold the mouse to highlight a selection.

15. Release the mouse over the selected item to navigate to that section of your movie.

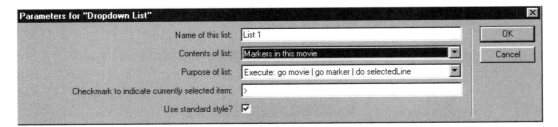

Figure 4-29   Go Marker selected as navigational command for dropdown text.

CHECKING SPRITES BOUNDING BOX WITH LINGO

One important aspect to keep in mind when applying interactive commands to sprites is that the function of the sprite is determined by the entire sprite, or area within the bounding box of that sprite (Figure 4-30). This does not change if you add ink effects, such as background transparent. The entire bounding box area is used to interact with push button or rollover commands. To determine what the actual coordinates of your bounding box are, use the Message window to display the location coordinates of the box's corners. Director provides this information as a list of the left, top, right, and bottom coordinates of the sprite's bounding box (Figure 4-31). To access this information:

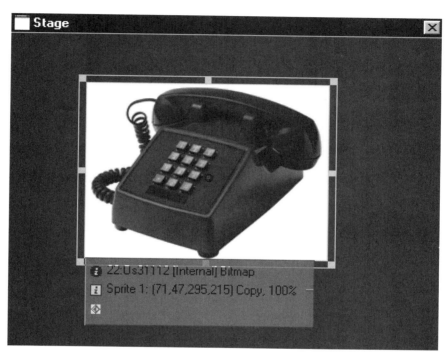

Figure 4-30   Wire framing outlines bounding box area of the sprite.

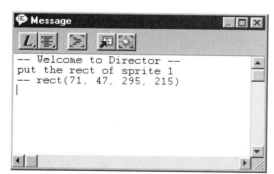

Figure 4-31   Message window displaying bounding box coordinates.

1. Open the Messaging window from the Window menu or use the keyboard short-cuts Control-M (Windows) or Command-M (Macintosh).

2. Open the score and select the sprite you want to check.

3. Enter the following text in the Messaging Window followed by hitting Enter:

```
put the rect of sprite (channelnumber)
```

For instance, to check on the sprite in Frame 10 Channel 5, move the playback head to Frame 10 and enter the command `put the rect of sprite 5`. Director will display the coordinates for each corner of the bounding box as its location on the stage.

 See Chapter 5 to learn how to minimize a sprite's bounding box area so as not to cause problems when adding interactive events to sprites in your movie.

EDITABLE TEXT

Many interactive applications will require the ability to enter text information. The ability to have user-defined entry of text information is common on forms for websites, training programs, and player profiles for games (Figure 4-32). To set up editing properties for a text cast member:

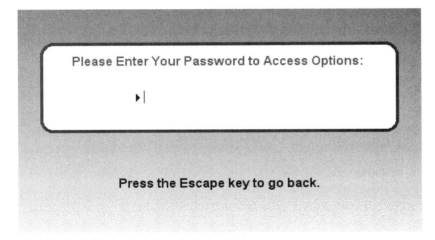

Figure 4-32   Text field can be used to enter user information.

1. Create a field cast member.
2. Select Cast Member from the Modify menu.
3. Select Properties from the popup menu.
4. Click Options.
5. To make the cast member editable, click the Editable box (Figure 4-33).

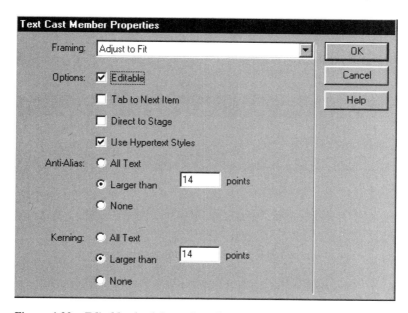

Figure 4-33   Editable check box selected in text cast member properties dialog box.

In the Text Cast Member Properties dialog box, you also have the ability to turn on and off word wrap and auto tab (which allows the user to jump from one field to the next by simply hitting the tab key on the keyboard).

Standard text cast members can only be edited in the authoring mode. Once you create a projector, standard text cast members become bitmaps. Field cast members, however, can be edited and interpreted by Lingo in both the authoring mode and as a projector.

Lingo can then check the text entered in the field by the user. The Lingo element contains or an equal sign (=) are typically used to check the string of a field entry. The contains command works by comparing whether one string contains the same information as the other string. The equal sign works by seeing if the contents of the field cast member match exactly to the string command. This method is commonly used for question-and-answer type applications. If you want your user to enter the answer and submit it by hitting the Enter key (Windows) or the Return key (Macintosh), set up the following function:

1. Create the required field cast members and name them (Figure 4-34).

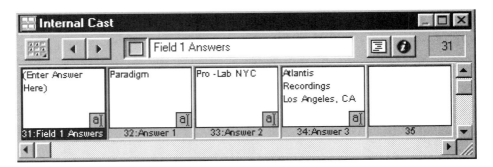

Figure 4-34   Cast members of field text answers.

2. Enter the script (sprite script or cast member script):

```
on keyDown
   if the key = RETURN then
      checkAnswer
end

on checkAnswer
   if field "question1" contains "(theCorrectAnswer)" then
     go to frame "Correct"
   else
     go to frame "Wrong"
   end if
end
```

The structure of this command can be applied to each question in your program. If the user enters the right answer (the characters entered match the string set for that particular field), then the playback head is sent to the section of the movie labeled "Correct." Otherwise, if an incorrect answer is submitted, the playback head goes to a section of the movie labeled "Wrong" (Figure 4-35).

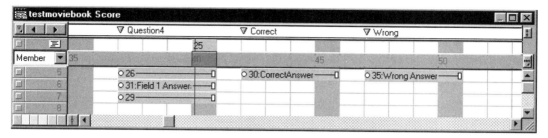

Figure 4-35   Sample score for quiz section (user input links to either Correct or Wrong marker).

You can also use the `contains` command to have Director see if the character string entered is part of the field cast member. If the answer contains several correct responses, use the following format:

1. Create the required field cast member and name it.
2. Enter the script:

```
on testAnswer
    if the field "NameofField" contains "possibleAnswer" then
        go to frame "Correct"
    else
        go to frame "Wrong"
    end if
end
```

Capitalization does not matter, but spelling does count.

ANALYZING LINGO COMMANDS AND COMMENTS

The best way to learn how to write your own Lingo commands is to study the codes of someone who knows what they are doing. Who better to learn from than the creators of Lingo—Macromedia. After applying a behavior, open the script window to analyze the precise codes used to perform this function. After all, behaviors are nothing more than shortcuts to actually writing Lingo codes. To analyze any behavior's Lingo script:

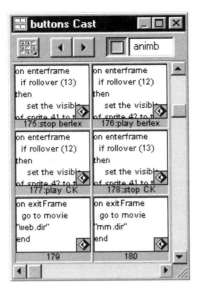

Figure 4-36   Customized behavior located in Cast window.

1. Select a behavior from the cast that has already had its parameters set (Figure 4-36).

2. Click on the Cast Member script icon in top of the cast window.

3. The automatically written Lingo script commands appear.

4. Try to break down what each handler is used for and what task each line of code is instructing Director to perform or evaluate.

Director 7.0 includes some helpful notes for developers written inside the actual codes to better explain the purpose of each line of the script.

BUILDING A HELP SECTION

Developers of most programs know there is a potential for users getting lost or not understanding how to use the program correctly. To help a user get the guidance he needs to successfully use the program, developers typically include a Help section. A typical Help application includes rollovers with text messages appearing, explaining the purpose of the function. To set up a quick, easy-to-use Help section of a program:

1. Design (and import if created outside of Director) an image to use as a Help button.

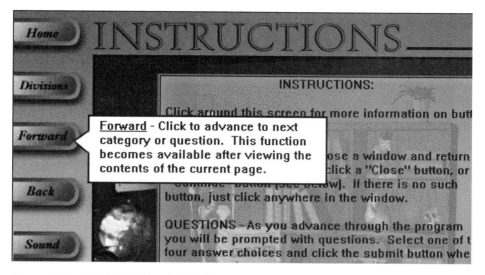

Figure 4-37   "Sticky Note" style Help boxes.

2. Add a new marker to your score and name it "Help."

3. Use a Behavior or Lingo command "go to frame (Help)" to navigate from the Main Menu to the Help section of the score.

4. Add the sprite(s) to the score for the section you are providing help.

5. Open the Paint window and create a new cast member for each item you want to label. Create a "sticky note" style Help box with text explaining the purpose of each object on the interface (Figure 4-37).

6. Create a rollover behavior for each sprite that you want to display a Help note. Use an `on mouseEnter change cast member to` (the corresponding note).

7. Add a Back button to return to the actual Main Menu. Apply the appropriate Behavior or Lingo command to navigate back to the Main Menu section of your movie.

Now if the user has any questions as to how each button functions or where that button will take him to, clicking on the Help section will provide him with the answers. Depending on the content of the program or the complexity of the material at hand, you can implement more advanced Help section capabilities:

1. If you provide access to a Help button from every screen of the application, you can add a Lingo command that will calculate the last section you were in and have the Back button in the Help section bring you back to the section you just left. (See the section "Reviewing Sections Already Visited" earlier in this chapter; Figure 4-38.)

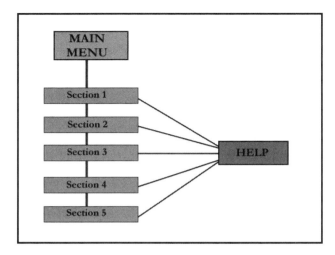

Figure 4-38   Navigation diagram detailing access to the Help section of an application.

2. Use Branching commands to link to other Director movies that play back an animation, screen-cam style demonstration. This type of application can show the user how to use a particular function or demonstrate that function in use in a real-life application. This is similar to the demonstrations used in Director's Help section. (See the section "Branching to other Director Movies" earlier in this chapter; Figure 4-39.)

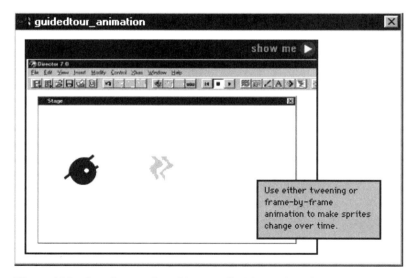

Figure 4-39   Sample page from Macromedia Director's Help section.

Do not apply navigational behaviors or scripts to the buttons and other sprites in the Help section as you do not want them to have the same interactive characteristics as they normally have in the main section of your movie.

SETTING CONSTRAINTS FOR MOVEABLE SPRITES

A common element added to interactive applications is to allow the user to move a sprite along the screen. Usually, you would not want them to place the sprite just anywhere, but rather adhere to a particular path or area of the screen. In the example in Figure 4-40, the user has the ability to drag the decoder window up and down the screen to the section that they wish to select. This function would not work properly if the user was able to drag the sprite over to the other side of the screen. It is important to set limits and constrain the horizontal positioning of this particular moveable sprite. To set up this feature:

Figure 4-40   Setting moveable sprites' horizontal or vertical constraints.

1. Create and import all necessary images.

2. Build the interface as desired.

3. Add all the required navigational links to the buttons to jump to each one's associated section of the movie.

4. Place the decoder window sprite into the highest channel of the score (Figure 4-41).

5. With that sprite still selected, click on the moveable button in the sprite tool bar of the score (Figure 4-42).

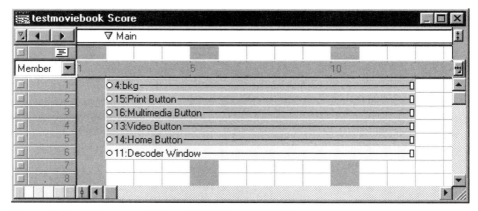

Figure 4-41   Setting moveable sprite in highest sprite channel.

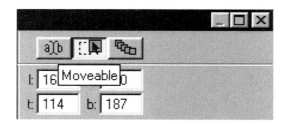

Figure 4-42   The Moveable button allows the sprite to be repositioned outside of the authoring mode.

6. Open a script window for this sprite and type:

```
on mouseUp
    set boundary = 500
        -- where number is pixel position of sprite on stage
        if the locH of sprite 3 >= boundary then
            puppetSprite (channel number), TRUE
    set the locH of sprite (channel number) = boundary
```

```
        updateStage
    end if
end
```

This command checks the horizontal position of the sprite as soon as the user lifts up the mouse button. If the sprite's registration point is set for 500, Director positions the sprite 500 pixels from the left-hand side of the screen. If the user moves the sprite to a position less than 500 pixels from the side, Director automatically places the sprite at 500.

You may also want to set a vertical constraint stating that the sprite can go no lower than a particular position. Use the same script, substituting locV for the locH command.

For Lingo users, you can set a sprite to be moveable on screen while the movie is playing by making the `moveableSprite` property to be true.

SUMMARY

The examples listed in this chapter are just the tip of the iceberg of what types of interactive features you can incorporate into a Director movie. You can see how Lingo scripts add tremendous functionality to your program. Experiment with different combinations of applications, staying within the guidelines of the commands, to formulate your own custom applications.

5

CREATING

KILLER

VISUAL

EFFECTS

We are a culture of Hollywood-style productions and million dollar effects. Every movie, T.V. show, and commercial tries to out do the previous one by adding higher budgets and more realistic visual effects. It has gotten to the point where most of us are not impressed unless the image pops off the screen and grabs us. It is our duty as developers to keep up with the changes in technology and learn how to integrate Director to design effects that would make George Lucas, James Cameron, and the entire Disney animation team jealous.

This chapter will cover a number of different styles of design elements and how to effectively implement them. There are three main points that every developer should focus on when creating a new project:

1. Quality
2. Functionality
3. Timeliness

Always remember there are many variables when working with multimedia applications that can affect the outcome of your project in the way they look and perform. In Chapter 3 we covered many of the key requirements that will ultimately determine what type of design elements you will be able to utilize or whether your Director movie will even play. If you have any questions about these important guidelines, you may want to go back and review that chapter.

LAUNCH AND EDIT

Creating multimedia programs is never easy and changes are bound to occur. Director makes these changes simple through a feature called Launch and Edit, which allows you to quickly edit your changes using the design program you prefer.

Use Launch and Edit to automatically open up your favorite bitmap image or sound editor programs directly from Director. The edit program opens with the file you selected. When you are finished making the necessary changes, Director will automatically update that file in the cast and in the score, eliminating the old process of re-importing new files, finding and replacing them in the score, and deleting old cast members.

To set up Director's list of editors:

1. Choose Preferences from the File menu.
2. Select Editors from the submenu. The Editors Preference window appears displaying a list of file types Director uses (Figure 5-1).
3. Select one of the bitmap or sound file formats, and click the Edit button.
4. Click the Scan button to display a list of applications available to edit this file on your computer.

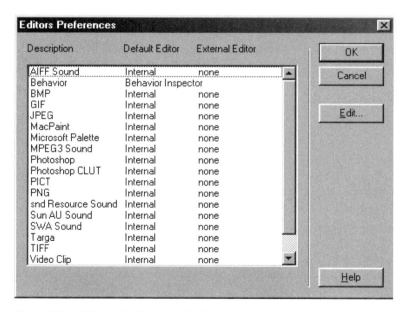

Figure 5-1   Editors Preferences window.

OR

Click the Browse button to manually search through all of your computer's files.

5. Choose an application and hit OK.

To launch a preselected editor:

1. Import files that you would prefer to change using an external editor.
2. Double-click on a bitmap or sound file cast member. The editing application should open with the file ready to be edited.
3. Edit the necessary changes.
4. Save the file and close the editing application.
5. Return to Director.
6. Click the Done button to automatically update your changes in the cast, stage, and score.

If you plan to use external editors to change your files, you must first select Include Original Data for Editing from the Media pulldown menu at the bottom of the Import window (Figure 5-2). With this option selected, Director records a copy of the original data of that file. Then, when you choose a cast member that has an external editor selected for that file format, all of that stored information is sent to the external editor. This ensures the most accurate data transfer between the programs in order to preserve the quality of your images. This additional information is not translated over into your projector or Shockwave files to eliminate any unnecessary file space.

For a quick design fix, even with external editors selected as the preferred application, you can choose to edit your image in the Paint window.

To choose the internal Paint window:

1. Single-click on the cast member you wish to alter.
2. Choose Edit Cast Member from the Edit menu.
3. Director places that cast member into the Paint window.

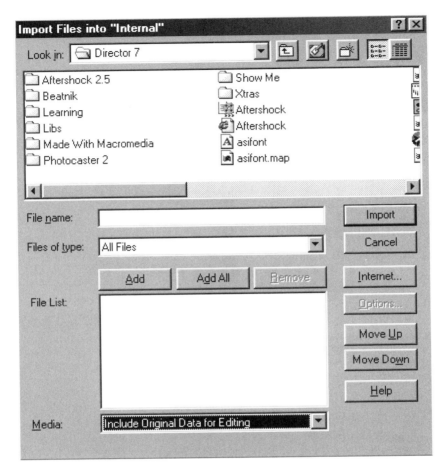

Figure 5-2   Include original data for editing during import.

DESIGNING EFFECTIVE NAVIGATIONAL ELEMENTS

As a developer, the navigational system is probably one of the first features you look at when examining any multimedia package. Is it effective? Does it impress you? Can you maneuver around the program easily and accurately? Director allows you to design your interactive links almost any way you can imagine. The creativity is up to you. Before you begin programming your Director movie, you must first design the elements that are going to be used in your application.

It is a good idea to sketch out on paper how and where you would like your navigational elements to be placed on the screen.

CREATING FLASHY BUTTON DESIGNS

My personal preference (depending on the purpose of the project) is to give the navigational elements as much life as possible. These "buttons" are what the end user will ultimately be interacting with. Make them easy to use, but don't forget that they can also be exciting. How impressed would you be if you saw a program that contained only those generic gray buttons with Arial 10 point font text in it (Figure 5-3)? Or would the interfaces in Figure 5-4 catch your attention? Even if you do not have access to any third-party design programs, you can still create some exciting buttons using Director's Paint window.

Because Director Paint does not have the same type of layering capabilities as Photoshop, it is easier to work with the outline portion of an object first and then fill in the space, as opposed to trying to put a border around a solid object.

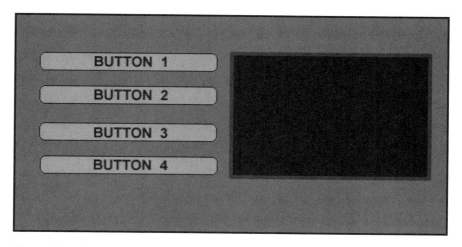

Figure 5-3   Generic interface with default gray buttons.

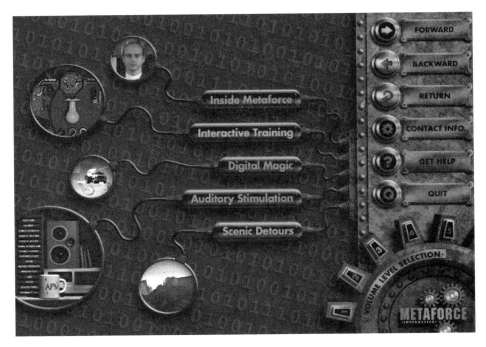

Figure 5-4   Custom interface with detailed graphic design (see Color Figure 15).

1. Open the Paint window.

2. Select a color to use as your border color in the foreground color chip. (If you are placing this object over a dark background, use a light color. If you are placing it over a light color background, use a dark color to give your object some separation to your file.)

3. Using the Hollow Oval tool, drag the shape of your button.

4. Pick a color to make the background portion of the button.

5. Use the paint can to fill in the oval.

6. Select the border color again and draw a smaller oval inside the original.

7. Using the gradient tool, select two different shades of the same color and fill the inner oval.

8. Select black as the foreground color and use the text tool to type in the name of the button.

9. Select white as the foreground color and type out the same word with the same attributes.

10. Place it slightly offset from the black text to give it a drop shadow effect. This will be used as our "up" button (Figure 5-5).

Figure 5-5   Final version of "Up" button.

11. Copy and Paste the button into a new Cast Member.

12. Repeat Steps 6 and 7 over the new cast member. This time reverse the direction of the gradient colors.

13. Type the same word using only the white color. This will be used as our "down" or "clicked" button (Figure 5-6).

Figure 5-6   Final version of "Down" button.

Use the first cast member as your stationary button. Using Behaviors, add the interactivity to change cast members on a `mouseDown` command to the second button you created. This procedure will give the illusion that the button is being depressed.

To assist in building objects in the Paint window without layers, create each element in the outside white area around the main object. Use the marquee tool set to lasso and grab your image and place it down exactly where you would like. If you put it down in the wrong area, select Undo from the Edit menu before performing any other steps.

There are no rules to creating buttons. Creating a button can be as easy as creating geometric shapes in any paint program or as complex as rendering a custom-modeled 3D object. Be creative but always keep in mind the intended audience and the scope of the project.

TRIMMING DOWN NAVIGATIONAL ELEMENTS

Director looks at the entire bounding box area of a cast member, including its background, even after you apply ink effects. If you have been experiencing strange behavior patterns with rollovers or buttons, it could be more of a graphic design issue than a navigational script problem. Notice the large white bounding area around the actual object. If you apply a rollover behavior or navigational command to this object, you will experience these interactions even within the bounding box areas of this object. If you have several navigational elements close together, the overlapping background areas may cause a different interaction than you intended. The best solution is to clean up your images.

1. Open a bitmap cast member in the Paint window.
2. Use the Erase tool to eliminate any unwanted background area (Figure 5-7).

 Hold the Shift key down to constrain the cursor to a horizontal motion in order to work with straight edges.

Figure 5-7   Comparison of unwanted background image and how to reduce it.

DESIGNING BUTTONS WITH THIRD-PARTY HELP

You do not have to be an artist to design any type of interactive controller. A simple square created in Director's Paint window is all it takes to create a button. If designing your own buttons is just not working and you cannot afford to pay a designer an hourly rate to create these elements for you, you might want to consider purchasing some third-party Xtras that have buttons already created. Some of these Xtras contain 2D and 3D animated buttons complete with sound effects and Lingo scripts. My favorite program, Instant Buttons and Controls by Statmedia, contains over 4,000 images and objects that you can use in your Director movie. They range from simple generic buttons to the wildest animated 3D buttons you have ever seen. Visit Statmedia on the Web at www.statmedia.com (Figure 5-8). The majority of third-party Xtras are easy to use and save you hours of designing and coding these buttons.

1. Open IB&C from the Xtras menu.
2. Cycle through the display of images.
3. Drag the selected button to the Stage. Notice the cast is automatically filled with each individual cast member and scripts.
4. Open the Script window (Lingo scripts already written by IB&C). You only need to enter the specific variable that will complete the Lingo commands (i.e., how and where you want these links to interact). Examples of scripts you will need to fill in may include Frame Number or Marker Name (where to link to when clicked or rolled over) (Figure 5-9).

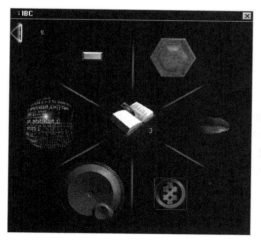 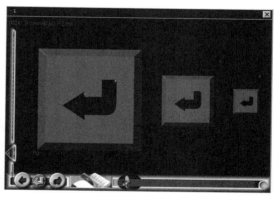

Figure 5-8   IB&C interface screens.

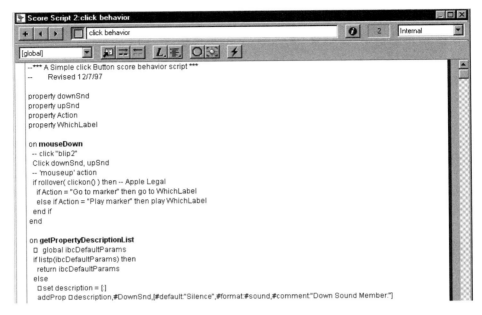

Figure 5-9   Sample script prewritten by IB&C.

CREATING ROLLOVERS WITH CHARACTER

Once you have added the basic navigational functionality to a sprite does not mean that you are through. You can stop here, but most of your projects will require a bit more flare. The desired effect we are looking for is to have a button that changes characteristics when the mouse rolls over it and also gives the impression that it is being depressed when the user clicks on that button.

1. Using any third-party graphics program, create a button (creativity is up to you).
2. Save this as your "normal" button mode.
3. Duplicate that button and change its color.
4. Save this version as your "rollover" button mode.
5. Duplicate the original button again and alter its look. You may choose to change its shadows, highlights, or completely manipulate it to make it look like it was pushed in.
6. Save this version as the "down" button mode.
7. Import all three images into Director (Figure 5-10).

Figure 5-10   Three states of a button—normal, rollover, and down (see Color Figure 16).

8. Drag the sprite labeled "normal" to the stage and place it where you want it positioned on the screen.

9. Apply the appropriate interactive behaviors. Use `mouseEnter` and `mouseLeave` commands for rollover actions and `mouseDown` and `mouseUp` commands for mouse-click actions. (A more detailed explanation on applying behaviors for rollovers and button clicks can be found in Chapter 3.)

The end result should be that the image named "normal" is visible when you play your Director movie. When the user moves the mouse into the vicinity of the button, the display changes to show the "rollover" button. When the user clicks the left mouse button down on this sprite, the display changes again to show the "down" button, giving the illusion that the sprites were interacting with the mouse movements.

Notice how all the buttons were created over a plain white background. This will be important for separating the buttons themselves from the white area when you place them over interface background.

USING SHORTCUTS TO CREATE HIGHLIGHT BUTTONS

If you did not make an alternate version of your button or navigational object when designing your images, Director has a shortcut method to give your buttons the look of actually being clicked on by highlighting (inverting their color) when the left mouse button is depressed. To set up this feature:

1. Place the sprite into your score.

2. Open the Cast Member Properties window. (Right mouse click on the sprite in Windows; hold the Control key and click the sprite for Macintosh.)

3. Select the "highlight when clicked" option available for navigational objects.

If you select this option but have not programmed any type of navigation, the object will not highlight when clicked.

COOL EXAMPLE USING ROLLOVERS

The best way to learn how to create new and exciting rollover effects is to look at other people's projects and try to emulate and vary their effects. One effect that I use involves a series of words running down the side of a screen that function as the navigational controls for the program. What is intriguing about this is that all of the text is out of focus. As you roll your mouse over each of these areas, the blurry text changes into clear words (Figure 5-11). For my company's demo CD-ROM, we incorporated the changing of blurry text with an added feature that offers the user more interactivity. We implemented a "decoder window" that as you drag it over the out-of-focus image, the clear text appears in the window. Here is how to implement this effect:

1. In the graphics program of your choice (we used Photoshop), create all of the text you need in focus.
2. Create the "decoder window" graphic with a completely white center.
3. Save each element individually.
4. Apply a Gaussian Blur (or any blur filter) of about 30% to each text image.
5. Use the `Save As` command to save each image as a different name from the original file.

Figure 5-11   Blurry text displayed as normal state and clear text displayed when cursor rolls over image.

6. Launch Director and import all of these images into the cast.

7. Drag the out-of-focus cast members onto the stage.

8. Position the out-of focus sprites into their desired locations.

9. Assign a new behavior for each sprite, choosing the in-focus sprite under the Change Cast Member action for the `mouseEnter` command. (Review the section "Creating Rollovers" from Chapter 3 if you are unsure of how to create interactive rollovers.)

10. Add to the behavior of each sprite and choose the out-of-focus sprite under the Change Cast Member for the `mouseLeave` command in the Behavior Inspector window.

11. Select the "decoder window" cast member and drag it to the score.

12. Place it in the highest channel in order to be displayed over all of the out-of-focus sprites.

13. Apply a Background Transparent Ink Effect to the "decoder window" sprite (Figure 5-12).

Figure 5-12   Decoder window used to roll over blurry sprites. Clear text appears in window.

14. With the sprite still selected, select Movable in the Sprite toolbar located at the top of the score window (Figure 5-13).

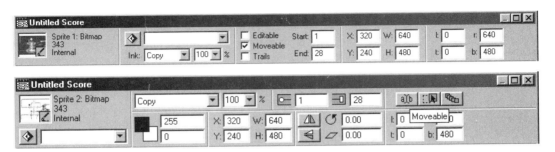

Figure 5-13   *Moveable check box in sprite tool bar.*

15. Rewind and play your movie.

As you play your movie, drag the decoder window around on the screen. The Movable command allows you to click on and drag the sprite while your movie is in play mode. The Background Transparent Ink makes the center white portion of the decoder window transparent, displaying the images beneath it. The secret to this effect is that your rollover commands are activated when the mouse comes in contact with the out-of-focus sprites. To drag the decoder window into position to "decode the hidden message," the mouse is positioned over the sprite changing the cast member to display the in-focus sprites through the window.

When creating altered versions of the same image as in the case of rollovers and click-down buttons, come up with a file naming system that will help you recognize which file you are working with by the code you use. Keep it consistent for every project you develop to decrease wasted time opening the wrong files while searching for the correct version. For buttons and other linkable objects, we use a number 1 at the end of the file name to indicate the "normal" version, a number 2 for the "down" version, and a number 3 for the "rollover" version. It's simple, easy to remember, and saves us time searching through a mess of files. In addition, by using the same file name followed by a numbering system, the computer's internal filing system groups the like images together.

Help 1
Help 2
Help 3
Exit 1
Exit 2
Exit 3

LINE 'EM UP

Nothing will embarrass you more than someone pointing out that your buttons are not lined up correctly. I'm not saying that you have to conform to a linear world where every image falls in line with the next. I'm talking about when you *are* trying to line up your graphics but, because you were in a rush and did not use guidelines, you accidentally offset the images. One way to prevent an object from being slightly askew from another is to use grids (Figure 5-14).

```
View>Grids>Snap to Grid
```

Grid marks can sometimes get in the way of developing when you are trying to implement graphics creatively, but there's no excuse for sloppy work when you are just being lazy.

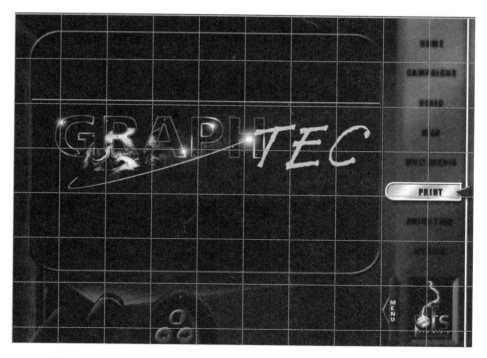

Figure 5-14   Grid lines.

A second option that allows you to be precise with the placement of sprites but not necessarily follow along the grid marks is a feature called align.

`Modify>Align`

With Align you have more control of how to line up your sprites. You can independently choose the alignments of vertical coordinates, horizontal coordinates, or both. Each pulldown menu contains a list of choices for which aspects of the selected sprites you wish to align (Figure 5-15). To use the align feature:

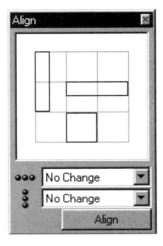

Figure 5-15   Align window.

1. Select the sprites on your stage that you wish to align.

2. Open the Align window.

3. Select between the different alignment options. A preview window shows you a sample of which portion of your sprites will line up.

4. Click the Align button to move your sprites into place.

Hold the Shift key to select more than one sprite at a time.

DESIGNING CUSTOM CURSORS

In the last chapter we told you how to change a cursor to improve the user's interaction with the interface.

As with anything you develop, you are going to want or need to create cursors that are better suited to the application you are creating. There are two rules to follow in order to have Director use a custom cursor:

1. Images must be 1-bit (black and white).
2. Images must be a maximum size of 16 x 16 pixels.

To create a custom cursor using Director Paint:

1. Open the Director Paint window.
2. To set a 16 x 16 pixel box, double-click on the Paintbrush tool and select the top square brush (default size is 16 x 16; Figure 5-16).

   Option: You can use the onion skinning feature (see below) to put the template in the background in order to help you see the image size without it becoming a part of the image you are creating.
3. Double-click on the Color Depth button at the bottom of the Paint window to open the Transform Bitmap window.
4. Select 1-bit from the color depth pulldown menu.
5. Hit the Transform button.

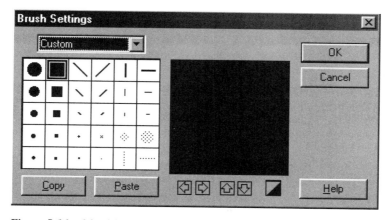

Figure 5-16   16 x 16 pixel square brush in Director Paint.

6. A warning will appear informing you that you cannot undo this function.

7. Select OK.

8. Design your icon to fit within the dimensions of the 16 x 16 template.

9. When you are finished, close the Paint window.

10. Enter the Lingo. There are two choices:

Changing the cursor for the entire movie:

1. Open the Movie script (Shift-Control-U for Windows; Shift-Command-U for Macintosh).

2. Enter the following Lingo command. The number inside the brackets indicates that it is looking for an object in that particular cast member number. Number values entered without brackets will interpret the number as one of the internal cursor codes.

```
on startMovie
   cursor [1]
end
```

3. Rewind and play your movie. The cursor should be in the design of the cast member that you have just created.

Changing the cursor for an interaction (i.e., rollovers):

1. Select the sprite that you wish to perform the event.

2. Open the Behavior Library.

3. Select New Behavior.

4. In the Event column, select `mouseEnter`.

5. Select Change Cursor in the Action column. Choose from any of the default cursors from the popup menu.

6. In the Event column, select `mouseLeave`.

7. Select Change Cursor in the Action column. Choose the arrow cursors from the popup menu to have Director return to its original cursor (Figure 5-17).

8. Open up the sprite script.

9. Find the `on mouseEnter` command and change the cursor line to read:

```
cursor [5]
```

10. Rewind and play your movie. The cursor should turn into the design of the cast member that you have indicated when you roll over that sprite.

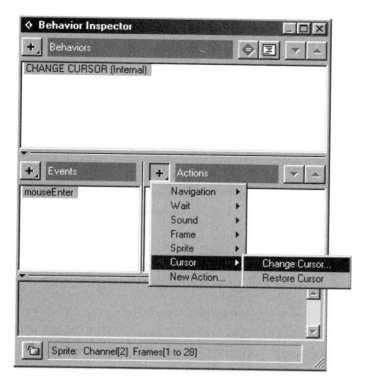

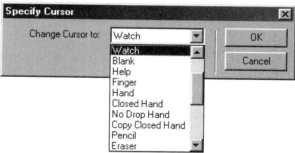

Figure 5-17   Changing cursors using the Behavior Inspector.

The number inside the brackets indicates that it is looking for an object in that particular cast member number. Number values entered without brackets will interpret the number as one of the internal cursor codes.

SETTING THE CURSOR'S REGISTRATION POINT

Setting the registration point may not seem very important at first, but may be more important depending on the type of cursor you are using or creating. The registration point, or hot point, is where the functionality of the cursor comes into play. This point reports, via Lingo, the `mouseH` (horizontal) and `mouseV` (vertical) position of your cursor on your screen. Therefore, if you are implementing an eyedropper cursor, you would want to set the registration point at the tip of the eyedropper (Figure 5-18).

To set the registration or hot point for an image:

1. Open an image into Director's Paint window.

2. Select the Registration Point (crosshairs) from the Tool panel.

3. Position the crosshairs over the desired location and click the mouse to set that position as the registration point.

4. Close the Paint window to save that point.

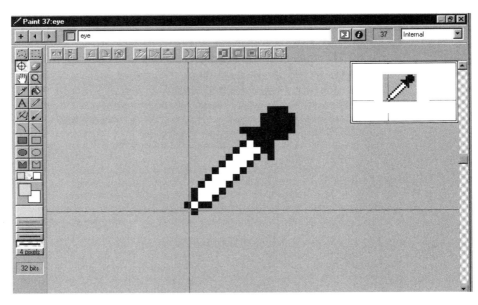

Figure 5-18   Setting the registration point on custom cursors.

ADDING A BORDER TO CUSTOM CURSORS

Designing custom cursors in Director is very limiting as to the creativity you can apply. To improve the look of your custom cursor (as much as you can jazz up a 1-bit image), add the opposite color border around the object you create.

To get a full 16 x 16 pixel cursor, design your image starting from the top left corner using a 17 x 17 pixel template. The "17th" or bottom and right rows of pixels will be used as placeholders when you shrink the marquee tool around your object.

1. Open the Director Paint window.
2. To set a 16 x 16 pixel box, double-click on the Paintbrush tool and select the top square brush (default size is 16 x 16).
3. Use the pencil tool to add in another row of pixels to one horizontal and one vertical side to create a 17 x 17 pixel image.

   Option: You can use the onion skinning feature (see following) to put the template in the background in order to help you see the image you are creating easier.
4. Double-click on the Color Depth window at the bottom of the Paint window to open the Transform Bitmap window.
5. Select 1-bit from the color depth pulldown menu.
6. Hit the Transform button.
7. A warning will appear informing you that you cannot undo this function (Figure 5-19).
8. Select OK.
9. Working from the top left corner, design your icon to fit within the dimensions of the 16 x 16 template. Keep it small using 1-pixel lines.
10. Copy the image (Control-C in Windows; Command-C in Macintosh).

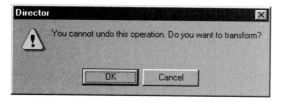

Figure 5-19 Warning indicating that you cannot undo certain procedures.

11. Click on Add New Cast Member on the top of the Paint window.

12. Using the Pencil tool, draw a 1-pixel border around your shape. This new object will act as our mask, or cutout shape for our cursor design.

13. When you are finished, close the Paint window.

14. Enter the following change to your existing cursor Lingo command:

```
cursor [1,2]
```

15. Rewind and play your movie.

The cursor command tells Director to change the standard cursor to the object in cast member number 1 and use cast member number 2 as the mask. Whichever shape is in cast member number 2 will allow the object in cast member number 1 to show through, adding the outlined shape to your cursor (Figure 5-20).

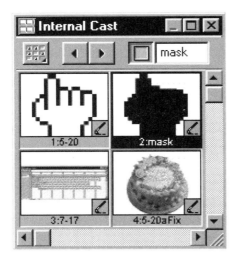

Figure 5-20   Cast member used as custom cursor and the mask defining the cursor's shape.

Unlike the mask ink effect, the cast members for cursor masks do not have to be in adjacent cast member panels.

DUPLICATING BEHAVIORS

To save yourself a great deal of time creating new behaviors for each sprite that will perform the same events and actions, you can duplicate a behavior in the cast and then make changes to the copy. To duplicate a behavior (also works for duplicating bit-mapped cast members):

1. Hold down the Alt key (Windows) or the Control key (Macintosh) and click on the behavior cast member, and drag it to any open frame in the Cast window. An exact copy of the cast member is created.

2. At the top of the Cast window, change the name of the new behavior right away to avoid confusion and errors with the settings of the original behavior.

3. Apply the new behavior to the next cast member that you want to have the same type of interactions.

4. Open the Behavior Inspector window for this cast member.

5. Change the name in the `Change Cast Member to` command under the Actions column to the name of the new cast member associated with this action.

ENHANCING THE LINKS

The next step to adding some visual enhancements to your multimedia project is to make the buttons look like they work when you click on them. You can choose to have them move slightly, invert colors, or give them the appearance of being pushed in. To create this effect:

1. Create and import all necessary images into Director.

2. Select a sprite to which you have already applied interactive rollover behaviors.

3. Open the Behavior Inspector window.

4. Choose `mouseDown` in the Event column.

5. Choose "Change Cast Members" to the Down button (alternate version of the initial sprite).

6. Rewind and play the movie.

The movie will start off and remain displaying the "normal" button, change to the "rollover" button when the cursor enters the area of the sprite, and then change to the "down" button when the left mouse button is clicked.

This is just one easy method for adding some life to each section of your multimedia program. You can apply rollovers and alternate the appearance of buttons and other links to give these objects the illusion of really being active. Experiment with these types of added features to come up with your own interesting variations.

ADDING VISIBLES THROUGH ROLLOVERS

Setting a rollover command is merely another type of interactive function that can perform just about any type of action, while adding so much more to the production value of your movie. Rollovers can be used to reveal hidden areas of a screen for games or display help-style balloons used in just about every piece of software written (Figure 5-21). Having these rollovers in random places encourages users to become more involved and interact with the program.

Figure 5-22 is an example that demonstrates that you do not always have to affect the actual object you are rolling over, but instead add other images to the screen. In this project, when the user rolls his mouse over the pressure gauge, steam begins to pour from the valves throughout the screen. To achieve this type of effect, keep the sprites invisible and only display them when the mouse enters a certain area of the screen:

Figure 5-21   Help-style balloons are displayed when an image is rolled over.

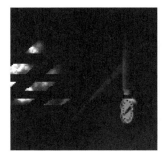 

Figure 5-22   Steam pours out of valve when cursor rolls over the image.

1. Drag the cast member you wish to reveal into position on the stage.

2. Create a score script on or directly before the first frame of the sprite you wish to hide. Enter the following Lingo script:

```
on enterFrame
    Set the visible of sprite (channel number) to false
End
```

When placing sprites that will be invisible in the score, do not place them in there for the full length of that section of your movie. In other words, if the duration of the section containing the invisible rollover is 15 frames long, do not put that invisible graphic into the score for all 15 frames. Start the invisible graphic on the second frame of that section. Place the score script that sets the variables for the invisible graphic on the first frame. This way the play head has time to interpret the script as it enters that first frame (Figure 5-23). If the graphic was present, you may see that sprite for a split second before disappearing once the script command takes full effect.

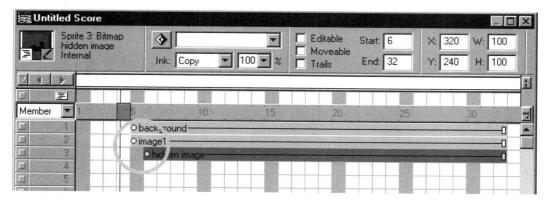

Figure 5-23   Placing the hidden image in the score starting one frame after the visible image.

Next, you will need to set a rollover spot on the stage. As the mouse rolls over this selected vicinity, the invisible sprite will appear. To create a designated rollover region:

1. Create an image (any shape) to set the boundary for the desired rollover area.

2. Place that object in the score on a channel where it can be concealed by the sprite above it.

3. Select the shape sprite.

4. Open the Script window and enter the following script:

```
On enterFrame
        if rollover (channel number) then
        Set the visible of sprite (channel number) to true
    Else
          Set the visible (channel number) to false
    End if
End
```

This Lingo command basically tells Director when the cursor rolls over the shape sprite in the channel selected, making the invisible graphic appear. If the cursor is not within the confines of that shape sprite in the channel selected, keep the graphic invisible.

 When implementing this type of rollover in your Director movie, place the invisible graphic on a channel all by itself and leave that channel empty throughout the rest of the score. Several programmers I know have occasionally experienced some trouble with sprites not appearing further down the line when placed in the same channel as the "invisible" sprite, even after using Lingo commands stating that the channel would be visible.

SUMMARY

With a little creativity, you can make design work very fast and easy when you know these techniques. As you know, the less time you spend wasting time doing cumbersome tasks, the more time you have to be creative. Many of the features and techniques described in this chapter will become useful in your programming skills with the topics covered in the next chapter, Adding Life through Animation and Layering.

chapter 6

ADDING LIFE THROUGH ANIMATION AND LAYERING

One of Director's main purposes is creating animations. Director offers you two general ways to create animated movies. Each one of these techniques offers various combinations that allow you to design your movie any way you want. Using the analogy of how cartoons were drawn (before the use of computers), single frames of illustrations, each slightly different from the next, when played back at a certain speed created the illusion of movement. This same principle is one way to utilize Director for creating animations. The playback head moves across the score, displaying images one frame at a time.

FRAME-BY-FRAME ANIMATION

As long and tedious as this process sounds, sometimes it is the only way to get the exact look of an effect you need for your project. Figure 6-1 shows a series of frames in storyboard format to show the separate images needed for this project. Use the following steps to create the effect using the frame-by-frame technique:

1. Model an object using any 3D modeling and animation software (Specular's Infini-D was used for this example).
2. Animate the object.
3. Export the animations as a serious of individual frames from the program showing the progress of movement over the course of time.

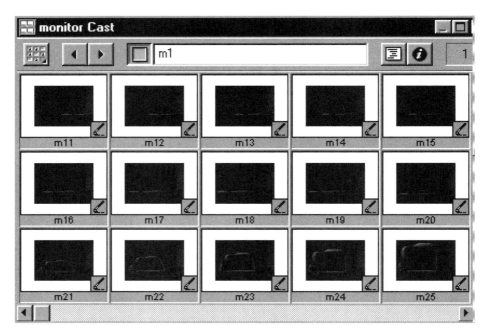

Figure 6-1   Storyboard display showing frame-by-frame animation.

4. Import each of these frames into Director.

5. Place them in the score, each for the duration of one frame (Figure 6-2).

6. Rewind and play back the animation. As the playback head travels progressively through each frame of the score, the object created appears to move around the screen into its final position.

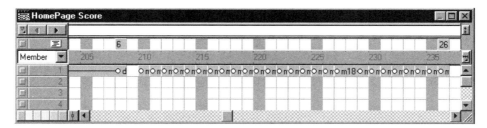

Figure 6-2   Frame-by-frame animation represented in score by individual sprites one frame each.

Check out the To Go Series website at www.phptr.com/togo to see samples of these and other examples in action.

ANIMATE MULTIPLE CAST MEMBERS IN A SINGLE SPRITE

Another technique for animating images in your movie is to combine multiple cast members into a single sprite in your score. There are numerous advantages to this technique, but keep in mind that they may not always be the best solution to meet the specific requirements of your movie. One very common reason for applying the multiple-cast-member-single-sprite technique is the ability to stretch or change the span of this single sprite.

Making changes to frame-by-frame animations can be quite messy if you don't know what you are doing and takes far too much time.

To create this type of animation takes a few minutes to set up but again offers you the flexibility of working with an animated sequence as a single sprite.

1. Place the first cast member in the score where you want your animation to start.

2. Adjust the span of the sprite to cover the duration that you want the animation to play.

3. Change the Sprite Labels to Changes Only in order to make changing cast members easier to see (View>Sprite Labels>Changes Only).

4. Choose Edit Sprite Frames under the Edit menu. This makes the score look more like working in Version 5, but makes it easier to select individual frames within the sprite for swapping cast members (Figure 6-3).

5. Select the frames where you want to play a different cast member. To select a continuous span of frame in the score, click on the first frame and then, while holding the shift key, click on the last frame. All of the inclusive frames should become highlighted (Figure 6-4).

6. Click on the cast member you wish to put in the place of the highlighted area of the score.

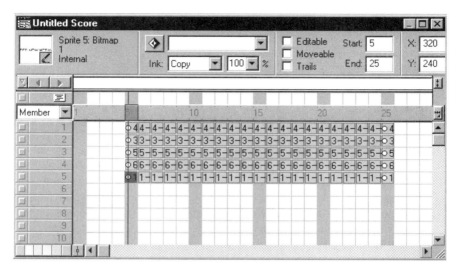

Figure 6-3   Sprites in score displayed as individual frames.

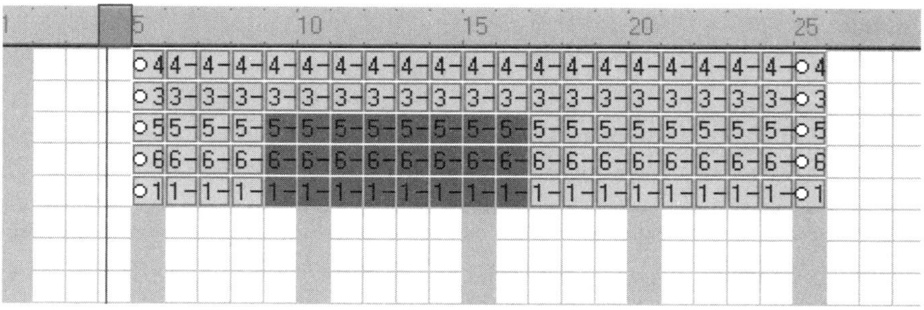

Figure 6-4   Highlighting portions of a single sprite to be replaced with another sprite.

7. Click on the Exchange Cast Member button along the top button bar. Notice how the new cast member fills in the selected area of the sprite.

8. Repeat Steps 5 through 7 to add the rest of the necessary cast members to complete the animation within the single sprite.

9. Once you have added in all the necessary cast members, select Edit Entire Sprite from the Edit menu.

Now you can begin manipulating the sprite (animating cast members) because it functions just like a single sprite made of a single cast member. You can now animate it by adding key frames and stretching the span of the sprite in your score.

CAST TO TIME

The best way to get a series of individual cast members to play back in your score and animated is by using a technique called "cast to time." The difference between frame-by-frame animation and cast to time is that cast to time is much faster to implement and provides you with a single sprite in the score instead of many individual frames. To create an animation using cast to time:

1. Import a series of images you would like to animate (Figure 6-5).
2. Rearrange the images in the order that you want them to appear. Start with the first image in the first available cast member position followed by the next successive image in the cast immediately following the previous one.
3. Click on the first cast member of this group.
4. Shift-click on the last cast member of this group.

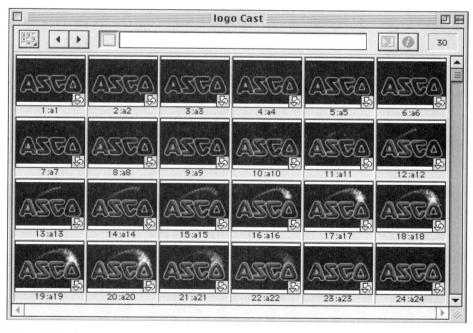

Figure 6-5   Cast of sequential images to be used for "Cast to Time" animation (see Color Figure 17).

5. Holding down the Alt key (Windows) or Option key (Macintosh), drag the series of frames onto the stage. A single sprite should appear in the score.

6. Rewind and play back the animation.

Change the length of the sprite to alter the speed of the animation. If you stretch it too far, your animation will appear to move with a stuttering motion.

CREATING FILM LOOPS

A film loop is very similar to the end result of cast to time, animating multiple cast members into a single sprite. Film loops are especially effective for animating repetitive motions over time. To create a film loop:

1. Select the sprites you want to create into a film loop. One advantage with creating a film loop is that you can select multiple channels, including sound channels, to create one cast member.

2. Choose Film Loop from the Insert menu.

3. Name the film loop. Notice in your cast window that Director has added a new cast member with the film loop icon in it (Figure 6-6).

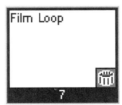

Figure 6-6   Film loop icon.

Another way to create a film loop is to highlight the frames and channels you would like to turn into a film loop. Drag them into an open cast member. Director automatically makes them into a film loop.

You can now add any film loop to your movie as a single sprite and manipulate it like you would any sprite. There are a few exceptions:

1. Film loops do not display the animation while stepping through the sprite frame-by-frame.

2. The animation will only occur during playback of your movie.

There is a significant difference when lengthening or shortening a film loop sprite compared to a regular sprite. Altering the span of a film loop does not affect the speed at which it plays back, but instead affects the number of times the film loop cycles. If the span of the film loop is shorter than the initial duration of the sprites creating the loop, the film loop will only play the same amount of frames that were in the original sprite sequence covering that same number of frames. For instance, if the initial sprites sequence contained four images each covering 10 frames and a film loop was created, the film loop would have to cover a total of 40 frames to play back the entire sequence. If the film loop sprite were shortened in the score to only 20 frames, then only the first two images would be displayed during playback. The opposite would occur if you doubled the length of the film loop sprite, resulting in the sequence playing twice.

TWEENING

Director's animation capabilities allow you to animate sprites across the stage with very little effort. Tweening (or in-betweening) basically means that the computer will figure out, calculate, and automatically draw in the frames of your animation that fall in between the start and end points that you have set. In its most primitive form, this will produce a linear animation, moving on a straight path between these two points. (Figure 6-7). In order to achieve any type of animation, whether linear or complex, you begin by separating the position of these points by adding keyframes to the sprite in your score.

To establish any type of animation, your sprite must span more than one frame long.

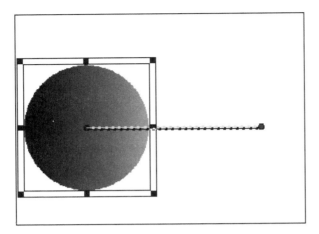

Figure 6-7   Tweening animation over a linear path.

KEYFRAMES

Keyframes can be defined as a set of instructions containing the sprite's characteristics and position information at a specific time (frame number) in your score. That means every time the playback head reaches a particular keyframe, that sprite will be in exactly the same position you set it in whenever your Director movie is playing. In the score, the first frame of your sprite contains a small circle indicating that it is a keyframe, always monitoring the precise location of that image (Figure 6-8).

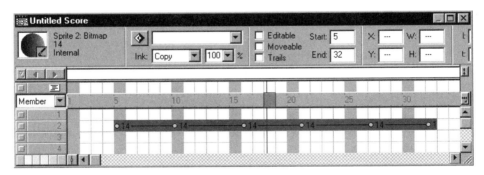

Figure 6-8   Keyframes displayed on sprites in the score.

To add keyframes:

1. Click on the frame of the sprite you are trying to alter.
2. Select Keyframe from the Insert menu. A new circle will appear on the sprite you had selected in the frame that you were parked on.

To delete a keyframe:

1. Click on the keyframe.
2. Hit the Delete key.

 TWEENING ANIMATIONS

Tweening has become one of the most powerful features in animation programs. Through the use of programs like Director, the computer is capable of creating all of the necessary frames to complete the movements between two keyframes. To use tweening:

1. Design any single image.
2. Import it into the cast.
3. Drag it onto the stage and set the sprite's starting position.
4. In the score, add a keyframe on the last frame (Modify>Add Keyframe).
5. Reposition the sprite to its ending position.
6. Rewind and play back the animation.

With the use of Director's tweening capabilities, all you have to do is create a single frame image and set the keyframes for the first and last frames of the sprite. Director will now animate your image across the screen by filling in the additional frames needed between these two keyframes.

SETTING TWEENING PROPERTIES

To adjust the way Director animates your sprites, you can select which properties you want to control for the animation (Figure 6-9).

1. Select Sprite from the Modify menu.
2. Select Tweening. The Sprite Tweening Properties dialog box appears. This is where you can set which parameters you want Director to control when it processes each frame of the animation all within one sprite.

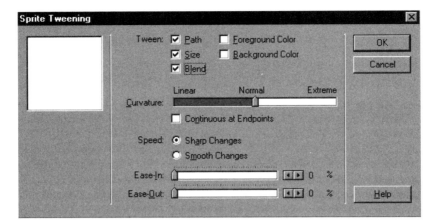

Figure 6-9   Sprite Tweening Properties dialog box.

 Turn off the tween size control and then change the size of the image on the first keyframe (Figure 6-10). When Director goes to play back the animation, the first frame will appear with the larger size image and the rest will play back with the normal size image. If you loop it, this flash frame will definitely catch your eye indicating that something is wrong with the animation.

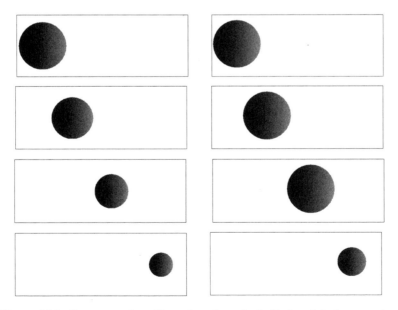

Figure 6-10   Demonstration of how size of a sprite is displayed during tweening animations.

ROTATING YOUR SPRITES

One of the tweening characteristics added in Director 7.0 is the ability to manipulate your sprites with more control and flexibility. With the addition of the rotation feature, all you have to do is import a single graphic and animate a rotation by setting its variables.

Prior to Version 7, you had to create a new graphic for each frame of the rotation.

To rotate sprites:

1. Select the sprite you want to animate.

2. Insert a keyframe (Ctrl-Alt-k for Windows; Alt-Command-k for Macintosh) on the last frame of the sprite (the first frame of every sprite is automatically created as a keyframe).

3. In the sprite toolbar at the top of the score, enter a variable in the Flip Horizontal—Rotation setting field for the number of degrees you want to rotate the sprite. For this example, try to make your sprite complete one full revolution.

   Or

4. Click the right mouse button (Control-click for Macintosh) to access the settings popup menu.

5. Select Transform.

6. In the submenu, select Rotate Left or Rotate Right. This will rotate your sprite in 90-degree increments.

Because only the last keyframe had a rotation value entered for it, Director will tween the playback of the sprite between its initial starting point and the final ending point.

When entering a variable to rotate an object that will loop, do not enter a full value of 360 degrees. Notice the image in the first frame (0 degrees) is at the 12 o'clock position and the image in the last frame (360 degrees) is also at the 12 o'clock position. (Figure 6-11). When you animate this for a complete revolution and loop it, the animation will actually be playing those two frames consecutively in that same position. This will appear as a slight pause or hesitation in your animation. It will not revolve smoothly. To avoid this problem, enter a degree value less than 360 for that last frame. Depending upon the tempo of your movie (number of frames needed to complete a rotation), an end frame value of 350 degrees seems to allow for a smooth and continuous rotation loop. This may be calculated out if the animation is 20 frames long; rotate each frame by 1/21st of 360 degrees. This will allow the animation to start and complete the looping rotation.

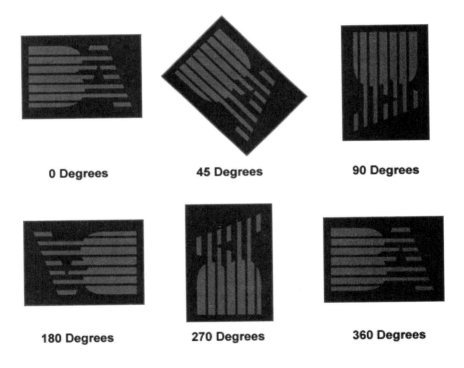

0 Degrees 45 Degrees 90 Degrees

180 Degrees 270 Degrees 360 Degrees

Figure 6-11   Logo rotating 360 degrees (Frame 0 degrees and 360 degrees are identical) (see Color Figure 18).

TUMBLING SPRITES IN AND OUT

Those of you who have been developing content on Director for years will probably appreciate the different rotation variables at some point. I have found that rotating the first keyframe slightly and scaling down the size of the image gives the illusion of rotating into position from infinity. The combination of changing the size and transparency level of the image gives it the illusion of flying in from a distant point. If you reverse the keyframes, you can basically move your sprite offscreen, flying it away into the distance. To create the zoom out effect:

1. Select the sprite you want to animate.
2. Insert a keyframe on the last frame of the sprite.
3. On the last keyframe, enter a variable in the Flip Horizontal—Rotation setting field in the sprite toolbar for the number of degrees you want to rotate the sprite (Figure 6-12).
4. Set the opacity level down to 0%.
5. Rewind and play back your animation.

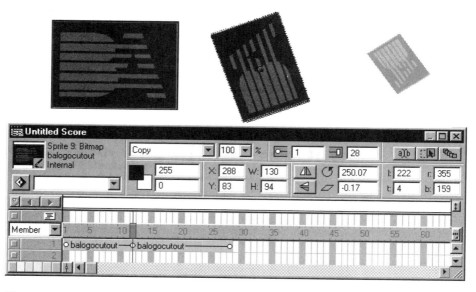

Figure 6-12   Score showing keyframes for rotating sprite.

GOING TOO FAR

It is very easy to start playing around with effects, warping and spinning sprites into oblivion. Sometimes experimenting like that is the best way to come up with new effects worth using in your next project. If you do not like the results, simply use the undo feature (Control-Z in Windows; Command-Z on Macintosh). The undo feature can only undo the last step that you have performed. In your quest to see how many ways you can distort your image from its original form, you can choose to reset different variables:

1. Select the deformed sprite.
2. Click the right mouse button (Control-click for Macintosh users) to bring up a Settings popup menu.
3. Click on Transform.
4. In the submenu, choose which variables you want to reset (i.e., width, height, or skew). Depending on which variables you changed, reset or revert all of the variables to return to the initial cast member settings.

Duplicating a cast member before making alterations is recommended if you want to experiment around with the attributes of that cast member. Some settings, such as converting bit depth, cannot return back to the original state once you proceed with the operation. By duplicating the cast member you always have a safety copy to use if you are not satisfied with the changes you have made.

ADVANCE TWEENING: USING MULTIPLE KEYFRAMES

With Director, you can use a combination of keyframes and tempo controls to create some intricate nonlinear animations. You can make images curve, speed up, or slow down. You can make images change size, change direction, and change transparency levels. Figure 6-13 uses a combination of keyframes and other properties to create more useful animations:

1. Insert keyframes on Frames 10, 20, 30, and 40.
2. Click on the first keyframe.
3. Reposition the sprite on the stage.

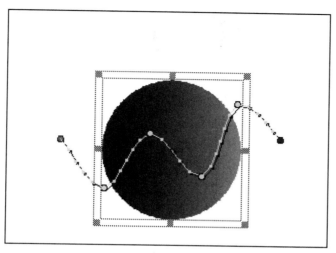

Figure 6-13   Multiple keyframes used for creating non-linear motion paths.

4. Repeat Steps 2 and 3 for the other keyframes.
5. Under the Modify menu, select Sprite.
6. Select Tweening from the submenu.
7. Use the various properties in the Sprite Tweening window to adjust the sprite's curvature and speed.

Director only animates on a 2D plane. You need to use combinations of different characteristics for your keyframes to give it the illusion of traveling on the third dimension.

LAYERING YOUR SPRITES

Just because Director comes with hundreds of channels does not mean you have to use them all. Every project you design will require that you use more than one. Layers allow you to stack multiple independent media files on top of each other, yet maintain control over each individual sprite. If you are interested in learning more about working with layers for graphics, take a look at the *Web Photoshop5 To Go* book by Jason Miletsky. It goes into much more detail than we can touch on in this book.

There are many ways to use different layering techniques to improve the appearance of your multimedia applications. Third-party graphics programs allow you to apply borders and shadows to images before you import them into Director. Digital video files do not have the same options available and tend to lack the same creative design as other graphic sprites. To add depth to digital video files using Director's Paint window:

1. Open up Director's Paint window.
2. Create a rectangle larger than the size of your digital video screen.
3. Name the cast member "border."
4. Add other rectangles, each slightly smaller than the previous to achieve a framing or border effect.
5. Add other design elements as you wish.
6. Copy the entire image.
7. Add a new cast member.
8. Paste the copy of your image in the empty Paint window.
9. Fill in the object to be completely black.
10. Name the cast member "shadow" and close the Paint window.
11. Place a background image into Channel 1 of the score.
12. Drag the "shadow" cast member into Channel 2.
13. Drag the "border" cast member into Channel 3.
14. Reposition the "shadow" sprite to be slightly offset from the "border" sprite (Figure 6-14).

Figure 6-14   Using layers to add a 3D look to your 2D images.

15. Lower the transparency of the "border" sprite to 30%.
16. Place the digital video cast member into Channel 4.
17. Rewind and play back your movie.

Using bright vivid colors in the border may distract the user from being able to watch the digital video clip. A combination of black, white, and grays seem to work the best.

CREATING BETTER TRANSITIONS

Director provides you with a set of standard single-frame transitions to be applied in the transition channel of the score. Normally, you place a transition in the end frame of the outgoing scene to transition into the next scene. The effects that come standard are rather blocky and generic. The dissolve transition is probably the most common transition used in any project, yet is quite possibly the most pixilated effect within Director (Figure 6-15). Instead, work with other tools inside of Director to create better looking transitional effects without actually applying a transition. Use the following procedure to create a smooth, non-pixilated one second cross-fade transition:

For this example, the movie frame rate is 30 frames per second.

Figure 6-15   Steps showing Director's standard pixilated dissolve.

1. Click on the sprite you want to animate using the tweening technique.
2. Select Sprite from the Modify menu.
3. Select Tweening from the Sprite submenu.
4. Make sure the Blending option in the Sprite Tweening window is selected and close the window.
5. Place the outgoing sprite in Channel 1.
6. Extend the sprite for 40 frames.
7. Place the incoming sprite in Channel 2.
8. Extend this sprite for 40 frames.
9. Position the sprite on Channel 2 to start 10 frames later than the sprite in Channel 1 (Figure 6-16).
10. On both channels, insert keyframes at Frame 10 and Frame 40.
11. At Frame 10, change the opacity value on Channel 2 to 0% (invisible).
12. At Frame 40, change the opacity value on Channel 1 to 0% (invisible).
13. Rewind and play back your movie. You should notice a smooth gradual cross-fade from one image into the other as opposed to the pixilated effect produced using the dissolve effect transition (Figure 6-17).

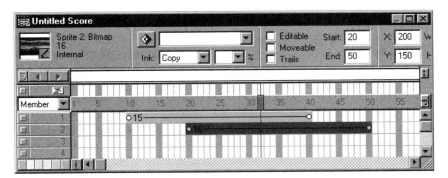

Figure 6-16   Sprites with offset starting positions.

Figure 6-17   Smooth transition showing even blend (not pixilated).

INKS

Apply one of the many different ink effects to change the appearance of your sprites on the stage. Each one holds a certain characteristic that affects different sprites in different ways. Director's Help section has a great interactive movie that demonstrates how all the different ink effects work. You can apply inks to various images over different style backgrounds to get a better understanding of how inks affect the related images (Figure 6-18). I highly recommend checking it out to broaden that "I already know how inks work" mentality that we all seem to have until we learn something totally new that blows us away.

In the score, select a sprite and hold the Control key when clicking the left mouse button (Windows) or hold the Option key when clicking the mouse (Macintosh) to see a complete list of inks.

Figure 6-18   *Effects of different inks applied to the same images (Lightest, Not Copy, Not Transparent, and Subtract) (see Color Figure 19).*

Certain Inks will look like they perform the same effect. Each one actually has its own unique characteristics. The results of the ink effect are dependent on both the foreground sprite that you apply the Ink effect to and the image below it. One of the most common uses for ink effects is to drop out a region of the image in order to isolate only the portion of that sprite you need to display (Figure 6-19). The Mask Ink works with a combination of two consecutive cast members to display only the portions of the sprite that you have masked (see Working with Masks for more detail). Another common ink effect is to animate images with different ink effects intersecting with each other to achieve a cycling color effect. To demonstrate the way certain ink effects interact with one another, set up this quick animation:

1. Create three geometric shapes using the Paint tool.
2. Make each one a separate color. For best results, use bright vivid colors.
3. Place each cast member at a different starting position of the stage. Leave Channel 1 open in the score at this point.
4. Using the Tweening technique, animate these objects across the stage so that each sprite comes in contact with one another at some point during the animation (Figure 6-20).

Figure 6-19   Comparing images with and without background transparent ink applied.

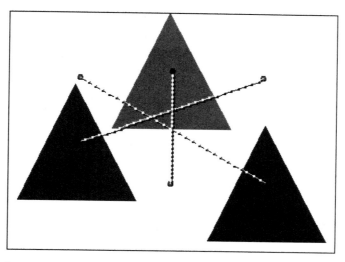

Figure 6-20   *Animating colorful geometric shapes to demonstrate effects of different inks and the interaction between the sprites as they intersect.*

5. Apply one ink effect at a time and play back your movie. Take notice of how each sprite interacts with the other sprites due to the ink effect applied to it.

Give each sprite the reverse ink and watch how the colors mix together as the sprites intersect one another. Enhancing this type of effect can make for a great splash opening on your next Director project.

Try applying different inks to different sprites and see what kinds of results these changes create. After you have tested a few different variations, add a bitmapped image to Channel 1. You should see that some of these ink effects change the hue and brightness level of the background image.

WHEN TO ANTI-ALIAS OBJECTS

Aliasing is a term usually referred to as the stair-stepping or jagged look of an object. Anti-aliasing is the computer's way of softening or blurring the edges of an object in order to make the image look like it has smoother edges (Figure 6-21). You will notice this effect in Director when you begin applying Ink effects to drop out the background color of an object. Generally, if you use an ink effect, such as background transparent, you may notice a ghosting or outline effect happening around the image when placed over a different color background. This occurs when an object is created with anti-aliasing turned on (Figure 6-22). For images created over a different color background than the color that they will be placed over, shut off anti-aliasing while creating these images. If you are placing an image over the same color background, you can choose to turn on anti-aliasing in order to create cleaner looking edges on your image.

Director's Paint utility does not default to anti-aliasing, thus giving you clean edges when applying inks. Photoshop users need to deselect the default anti-aliasing in Photoshop when creating objects, unless they will be placed over the same color background.

Figure 6-21   Comparison of aliased and anti-aliased text (magnified).

Figure 6-22   Ghosting effect with anti-aliased sprites.

MASKS

For those of you who have worked extensively with Photoshop or have a background in on-line video productions, you are probably familiar with the term alpha channel. For those of you who are not familiar with alpha channels, alpha channels are also referred to as masks in Director and are the best way to drop out unwanted portions of your image in order to display a clean cutout of an image when layering it on top of another image (Figure 6-23). If we apply the background transparent ink to the logo sprite, the white area inside the logo will be eliminated by the white area around the outside of the logo, which we want removed (Figure 6-24). There is only one way to get a complex image such as this logo to be displayed where only the areas that you want to be displayed are and all other areas are eliminated. The proper method is to create a Mask.

A mask is commonly referred to as a Hi-Con in the video world, meaning an image containing two colors of high contrast. You generally set up these images with the exact detail and shape of your object as black and the area you want transparent as white. In Photoshop, the channels for the mask show the reverse of this. Your object to keep is white and the area to be keyed out is black.

Figure 6-23   Example of mask used to remove the unwanted background.

*Figure 6-24   Background transparent ink does not always work if the image contains the
same color that you want to remove from the background.*

You can create a mask for any object, regardless of what software it was created in. This is where Director's Paint program really saves you time, allowing you to create the exact desired effect. Create a mask in order to make the logo appear correctly over the background image:

1. Set up your score with the background cast member on Channel 1 and the logo on Channel 2.

2. Double-click on the logo cast member to open it in Director Paint.

3. Choose Duplicate from the Edit menu so that you do not alter your original graphic. The Duplicate function automatically creates a new cast member and displays the cloned copy in the Paint window.

4. Click on the Transform Bitmap option under the Modify menu. The Transform Bitmap dialog box will appear.

5. To change this colorful graphic into a black and white image, use the Color Depth pulldown menu to select 1-bit.

6. Click the Transform button.

Create a mask or a Hi-Con image (see earlier note for explanation), turning everything either black or white. The best way to achieve this effect is to convert the image into a 1-bit image that only displays black and white. This will also help reduce the file size. If you plan to use several masked images throughout your Director movie, having two versions for each of these images will take up a tremendous amount of space, increasing the size of your movie, especially if you are working with 24-bit images.

7. In the Paint window, use the paintbrush or other tools to clean up the image. Fill in the parts of the image that you want to be opaque (visible) with black. The areas that you leave white will become transparent.

8. Close the paint window when you are finished.

9. Place the Hi-Con cast member immediately following the original cast member in order for the mask effect to work (Figure 6-25). There cannot be any other cast members or empty frames between the original image and the black and white image.

10. Select the Logo sprite in your score on Channel 2.

11. Click on the Ink Selector pulldown menu at the top of the score and choose Mask (Figure 6-26).

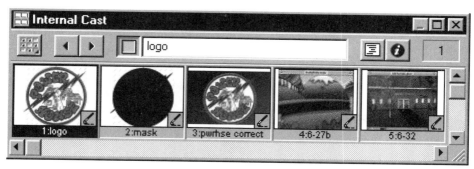

Figure 6-25   Cast with Hi-Con (mask) cast member directly following the regular cast member.

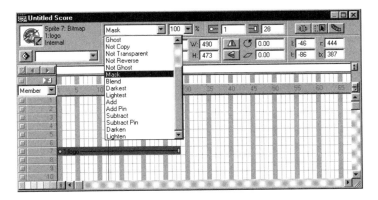

Figure 6-26   Ink selector pulldown menu.

12. Rewind and play back your movie.

Notice how the effect allows for a clean cutout of your logo on the stage. Use the mask ink and the technique described earlier when you need to separate a specific section of an image and layer that portion on top of another image.

 The more intricate the design of your object, the more careful you will have to be when filling in the areas to be masked. Any areas that you paint outside the borders of your object might produce a pixilated or ghosting effect when you apply the mask to the sprite.

SEPARATING IMAGES FROM THE BACKGROUND

In a perfect world, you would be supplied with every image designed over a clean, white background that you could quickly and easily separate when you need to layer it over another image. WAKE UP! Unless you are creating every single element from scratch, I highly doubt that you will be provided with all the images in a clean and ready-to-use format.

To separate an image from the background of an image:

1. Import an image into Director.

2. Open the new cast member in the Paint window.

3. Choose Duplicate from the Edit menu so that you do not alter your original graphic. The Duplicate function automatically creates a new cast member and displays the cloned copy in the paint window.

4. Paint out the shape of the object you want to separate from the background.

5. Rearrange the cast members so that the high contrast mask is in the cast window directly following the original image.

6. Place a new background image in the score on Channel 1.

7. Place the cast member of the original image into the score on Channel 2.

8. Apply the Mask Ink effect to your sprite in Channel 2.

This technique, even though masked perfectly, looks like the cutout image was just placed over the background image and was not really a part of the scene. To avoid this situation and create a more desirable effect, layer other portions of images above this sprite, concealing parts of the cutout image to give the illusion that it was a part of the scene (Figure 6-27).

Figure 6-27   Before and after image with the key element displayed over a new background (see Color Figure 20).

ADVANCED LAYERING

If you animate several sprites across the stage without ever rearranging the channel order of the sprites, the sprite in Channel 1 will always appear below the sprite in Channel 2, and so on. Many projects involve altering the layers of sprites over time to create the effect of objects moving in front of one another. When dealing with rearranging sprite channels, spend time sketching out drawings to figure out when and where to place each sprite. Create a movie with the race car sprites driving around a race track constantly changing layers (Figure 6-28):

1. Sketch out on paper when and where each sprit will be in relationship to the other sprites (this will determine which channel to place the sprite in).

2. Create the necessary graphics and import all of the images into Director.

Figure 6-28   Example of layering sprites using race car driving around track.

3. Following your notes taken during the planning stage, place each cast member into the sprite starting on Frame 1 leaving Channels 2 through 5 empty for now. This will allow you to keep the static layers on consistent channels throughout the movie (Figure 6-29).

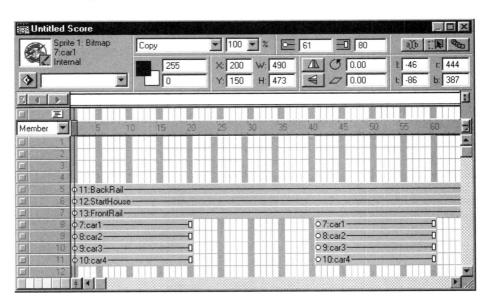

Figure 6-29   Score showing static images on higher channels with empty channels below to make layering easier.

4. Start with the back most layered object (Back Rail Cast Member) in Channel 1.

5. Place the Watchtower Cast Member in Channel 6.

6. Place the Front Rail Cast Member in Channel 11.

7. Place each of the four car cast members in Channels 7 through 10.

8. Color-code each of these sprites independently:

   A. Select a sprite.

   B. Click on one of the sprite color swatches in the lower left portion of the score window.

   C. Repeat Steps 2 and 3 for each additional sprite, selecting a different color for each one.

9. Select all of the sprites (Control-A for Windows; Command-A for Macintosh).

10. Using the End Frame field in the Score, enter 90. This will extend all of the cast members to span from Frame 1 to Frame 90.

11. Select Edit Sprite Frames from the Edit menu. This breaks up the long single-object sprite into individual frame elements, resembling how Director 5 displayed the Score.

Now your score is ready to begin setting the animation aspect of your sprites. Use a combination of animation techniques, including adding keyframes, tweening, and creating film loops.

12. Animate the car sprites to turn on the right side of the screen using tweening.

13. Create a film loop for viewing the cars going around the turn.

14. Select the portion of the sprites that will be animated on the far side of the track and move them to Channels 2 through 5 (Figure 6-30).

15. Because the cars looks like they are traveling in reverse, select these sprites and replace them with the appropriate cast members that show the cars facing the opposite direction. Click on the Exchange Cast Member button to replace the existing sprite with a different cast member. (For a more detailed explanation on using Exchange Cast Member, see Chapter 7.)

16. Create a film loop for viewing the cars coming around the turn toward the front of the track.

17. Loop the movie to show a continuous cycle around the track.

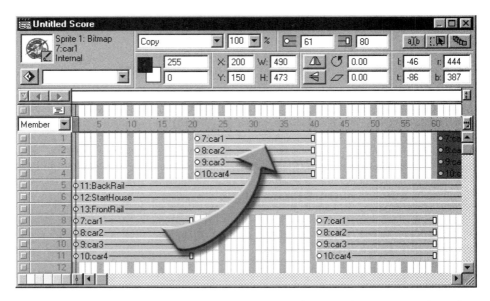

Figure 6-30   Moving portions of the sprites to the lower channels of the score to achieve the proper layering effect.

Swapping many layers of sprites around in the score can get confusing quickly. Two techniques become useful for being able to work swiftly and accurately in a score of constantly changing cast members across several layers. Name each sprite to keep track of which sprite is on which channel. The other tip that makes life much easier is color-coding the sprites. This project could have easily taken twice as long without color-coding each sprite. Visually, you will be able to see where and when a sprite moves vertically in the channels (layers) as time goes on.

COMPARING THE BACKGROUND TRANSPARENT AND THE MASK INKS

Sometimes certain Ink effects will work and other times they will not. Going back to the car racing example, let's suppose that when you created the graphics of the cars, the only white portion of the car was the glass windows. When you used the background transparent ink for each of these sprites, you were able to see the images layered below each car as it animated across the screen. Now, change the design of the car graphics. Suppose you want to give each vehicle a number on the side door and want these numbers to be white. Well, you already know that if you apply the background transparent ink to this sprite, the background images will show through the numbers just like it did for the windows on the car. How do you avoid this? This is a case where you would want to use the mask ink and create that black and white cloned copy of your image. To keep the white portions of your object that you want to be displayed and to key out all the other white areas, you will need to create a mask of your object (Figure 6-31).

Figure 6-31   Creating masks to display portions of the background images through the windows of the cars (see Color Figure 21).

DO YOU LIKE TO WORK IN PHOTOSHOP?

Because we are discussing how to work with layers, I figured this was the appropriate time to fill you in on a timesaving Xtra that you can use to make your design work much cleaner and more accurately, while allowing you time to be creative. How great would it be if you could build your interface once and not have to break it down to only piece it back together in Director? Wouldn't it be great if you never had to flatten another Photoshop graphic again? Well, would you believe me if I told you there is a way? There is an Xtra that I would recommend to anyone who uses Photoshop to design images for Director. There is a set of Xtras from Media Lab, Inc. called Photo-Caster and AlphaMania. Check out their website at www.medialab.com. These Xtras allow you to preserve all the layers of your Photoshop document and import them directly into Director. What is really a huge timesaver is that they create a new cast member for each layer of your Photoshop file (Figure 6-32). Best of all with Photo-Caster and AlphaMania, if your stage is set for the same dimensions as your Photoshop file, each cast member will retain the same transparency, position, and registration points to reproduce itself exactly as you had in Photoshop.

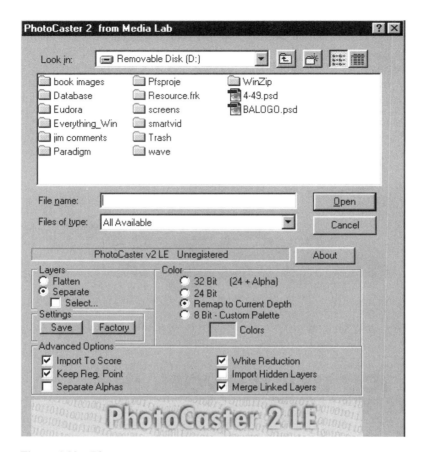

Figure 6-32   Photocaster screen.

Unregistered versions of this application will display blue lines through your image requiring you to register it to use it in your productions. Otherwise you can download the plug-in for demonstration and sample purposes from Media Lab's website.

Set the dimensions of your Photoshop file to be the same as the stage size of your Director movie.

1. Create a layered image in Photoshop and save it as a .psd file.
2. Open Director.
3. Under the Insert menu, select PhotoCaster.
4. In the application's main screen, select the file that you want to bring into Director.
5. Set any other options you wish. (Media Lab's Set Effect Xtras contains a set of filters that you can apply to the layer with an alpha channel.)
6. Click OK.

Once you have selected the file you want to import, PhotoCaster does all the work. These applications bring in every image layer and automatically align each one onto the stage in the exact layout that you created in Photoshop. What your image looks like in Photoshop is how it recreates itself in Director (Figure 6-33). Take a look in the color section of this book to see some of the filters applied to images using AlphaMania and Set Effects.

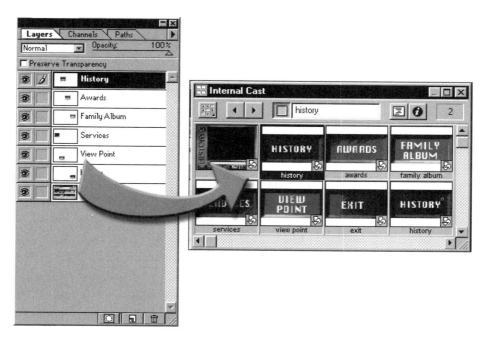

Figure 6-33   Comparison of layers in Photoshop and layers in Director using PhotoCaster.

APPLYING FILTERS TO SPRITES

Just like the high-end graphics programs such as Photoshop and After Effects, you can add third-party filters to Director that allow you to alter the appearance of your bit-mapped image. Even if you design your graphics in Photoshop, there might be situations that will require applying these filters in Director instead. If you make any changes to a sprite that has already been saved with the filter effect applied to it from Photoshop, any changes to this filtered image may adversely affect the appearance of the new image. By having these filters available in Director, you can add the effect to the sprite after the changes have been made. To add a filter to Director:

1. Copy the filter(s) from the filters folder of Photoshop, Kai Power Tools, or another program that contains bitmap image filters.

2. Paste the filter(s) into the Xtras folder in Director Root file.

3. Re-launch Director.

 You can apply filters to an entire cast member, portions of a cast member, or several cast members at once. However, not all filters work with Director. Check with each manufacturer for more information.

To apply a filter:

1. Double-click on a cast member to open it in the Paint Window.

2. Select the Xtras menu from the top of the screen and choose Filter Bitmap. A Filter Bitmap dialog box will appear, displaying all of the filters installed in the Xtras folder for Director.

3. Select a category in the left column.

4. Select a filter in the right column.

5. Click the "Filter" button to apply that filter or bring up the settings window for that filter.

ONION SKINNING

The best way to explain the onion skinning technique is to think back to your childhood when you used tracing paper to redraw the objects underneath. Cartoon artists still use this technique for animation to monitor the amount of change from one frame to the next. This is the same theory applied in Director's Paint window. Onion skinning allows you to see several adjacent cast members so that you can slightly alter each one in order to create the illusion of movement (Figure 6-34).

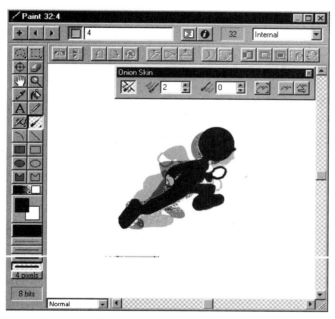

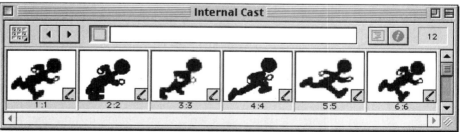

Figure 6-34   Viewing adjacent cast members using the onion skinning feature for proper placement.

Example: Create the illusion of a triangle morphing into a thin line as it animates across the screen. Having the ability to monitor each frame and control the variations needed between these frames will make the effect flow more fluidly (Figure 6-35).

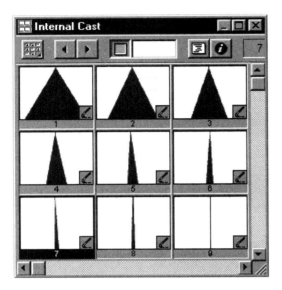

Figure 6-35   Triangular image transforming into a simple straight line over the course of several frames.

1. Open the Paint window.

2. Select Onion Skinning from the View menu.

3. Turn on the Onion Skinning feature (Figure 6-36).

4. Select the number of preceding cast members you wish to view underneath the one you are currently working on.

5. Using the line tool, draw a triangle.

6. Click the New Cast Member button to create the next image. The first image should now appear ghosted (Figure 6-37).

7. Repeat Steps 4 and 5, continuously manipulating the object from a triangle into a straight line.

8. When you are finished, close the Paint window.

9. In your cast, you should see a series of progressive cast members changing from a triangle into a straight line.

Figure 6-36   Turning on the onion skinning feature.

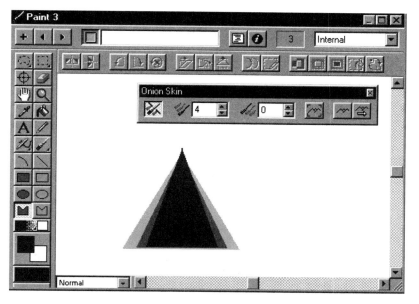

Figure 6-37   Current image is displayed clearly while adjacent images appear ghosted when using onion skinning.

10. Use cast to time to animate the series of frames:

    A. Click on the first triangle cast member.

    B. Hold the Shift key and select the last straight line cast member. All of the cast members between these should become highlighted.

    C. Hold down the Alt key (Windows) or Option key (Macintosh) and drag the series of cast members onto the stage. This will create one sprite in your score containing all of the various cast members.

11. Rewind and play back your movie. Depending on how many individual frames you drew, your triangle should animate smoothly across the screen changing into a thin line.

OPTIMIZING YOUR DESIGN TECHNIQUES

You have seen many different types of design techniques implemented to create some interesting effects in Director. There are additional steps that you can take to minimize the work Director has to do in order to play back your animations. The animated movie in Figure 6-38 utilizes the old style of cartoon animation—designing cels for only the portion of the screen that changes. This technique is especially useful in Director to help reduce both the file size of this project and the amount of memory required to play back the animations. It takes more memory to move a large object across the screen than it does a smaller object.

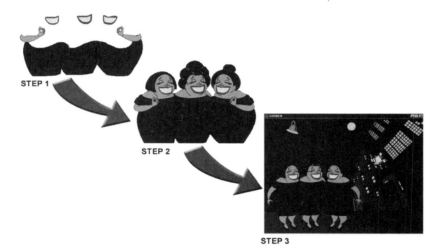

Figure 6-38   *Old-school animation technique of layered cels—designing only the aspects that will be changing frame by frame compared to the static background images.*

Figure out which parts of your image are going to be animated before you create the final image. This will save valuable time when you create the animation in Director. Create the animating images on a separate layer from the background.

1. Import all of the images you created for your project into Director (Figure 6-39).

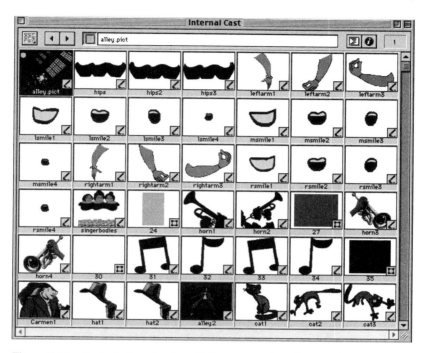

Figure 6-39   Cast window showing all the cast members for a project.

2. Place the background on Channel 1.
3. Add the different elements to be animated on higher channels.
4. Select all of the sprites in the score.
5. Choose Edit Sprite Frames from the Edit menu.
6. Highlight the portion of the lips sprites where you want to begin having the mouth move.
7. Click on the cast member (open mouth) that you want in place of the closed lips.
8. Click on the Exchange Cast Member button in the toolbar at the top of your screen or hit Control-E (Windows) or Command-E (Macintosh) on the keyboard.
9. Repeat Steps 6 through 8 for all the areas that you want to show animating.
10. Rewind and play back your movie.

Add a music track and try to time the animated sprites to match the beats of the music.

COMBINING ANIMATION TECHNIQUES

You can use a combination of all the techniques described in this chapter to achieve the exact effect you want.

For PFS New Media's demo CD-ROM, we wanted the digital video clips to have a bit more flare than just appearing in a rectangular box when the name of the movie was selected. We decided to create an animation of a space-age monitor coming out of the wall then rotating up 90 degrees into position to play back the video clips. Because Director does not fully work in a 3D world (not yet), the object had to be created in a third-party program that can operate on all three axes.

 You can use 3D objects within Director with the aid of the QuickDraw3D Xtra both for Windows and Macintosh systems. When you create your object in Extreme 3D and export it out in a 3DMF format, the Xtra allows Director to see it as a true rotatable 3D model.

To create the animation of the monitor sliding out from the wall and rotating upward 90 degrees, use a combination of layering, tweening, and film loops:

1. Create the desired monitor animation in any third-party animation program.
2. Export each frame as an individual file, such as a pict sequence.
3. Import each file into Director (Figure 6-40).
4. Place the background image in Channel 1.
5. Place the wall sprite in Channel 3. This will be used to cover the monitor as it comes out from behind the wall.
6. Add the first frame of the monitor sequence (in the flat position) to Channel 2.
7. Position the first key frame to be hidden completely behind the wall sprite in Channel 3.
8. Add a keyframe to the last frame and position it where you want the monitor to rotate up.
9. Add each cast member to the score for a duration of one frame each starting in the frame after the monitor slides into position.
10. Make these frames into a film loop and name it.
11. Open the Cast Member Properties window and deselect the loop option.
12. Drag the film loop from the cast, holding down the Control Key (Windows) or Command Key (Macintosh) to replace the individual frames in the score.
13. Add a script to the last frame of the film loop:

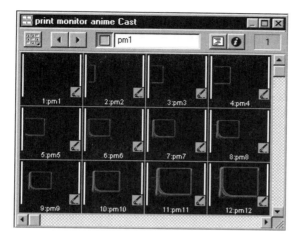

Figure 6-40   *Cast of images created in third-party programs that are being used for an animation.*

```
on exitFrame
  go to the frame
end
```

14. Add the digital video cast member to Channel 4.

15. Rewind and play back your animation.

If you experience the mouse flickering when you play back the movie, add the last frame of the monitor loop as a still frame directly after the film loop ends. The flickering is caused by the Lingo script that keeps playing the film loop and does not allow it to finish.

SUMMARY

You can see how much work goes into creating a simple animated scene for a Director movie. Do not be overwhelmed. Think creatively and break down your ideas into smaller elements. It is amazing what you can build by analyzing the designs and effects of your favorite multimedia pieces and by trying to emulate similar effects in your productions.

chapter 7

TECHNIQUES
EVERY
DEVELOPER
CAN USE

If there's one thing I have learned when working with programs as involved as Director, no matter how long you use them, there are always a few tips that you might not know that can wind up saving you invaluable time on your next project. Learning the basics of Director is not very hard. To become an expert takes a great deal of hard work and dedication. The more effort you apply and hours you spend trying to develop new ideas, the more you will improve the quality and level of your applications. This chapter covers a wide variety of topics, explaining many of the little techniques that will save you time and greatly improve the functionality of the programs you develop.

MOVING AND STRETCHING ONE- AND TWO-FRAME SPRITES

No matter how far you zoom in to a score, it is hard to stretch a sprite that spans only one frame (Figure 7-1). If you go and click on it and try to drag it, the single frame sprite will move from frame to frame instead of stretch to span over several frames. This can drive you crazy if you don't know what to do. To stretch a one-frame sprite:

1. Hold down the Alt key (Windows) or Option key (Macintosh).
2. Click and drag the sprite using your mouse. This will lengthen the span of your sprite more than one frame.

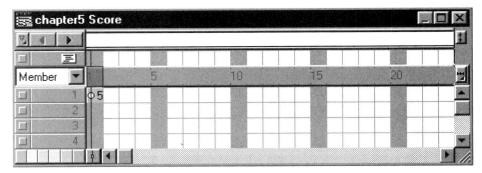

Figure 7-1   Sprite spanning one frame.

Conversely, trying to move a two-frame sprite without extending the span of the sprite is rather difficult itself. One of the features added to Version 6 was the ability to alter the span of sprites in the score simply by clicking on an end point and dragging it to its new length. The last frame (or second frame of this two-frame sprite) contains a handle that allows you to maneuver and manipulate the number of frames you want a sprite to span in your score (Figure 7-2). To move the position of a two-frame sprite around in the score without changing the length of it:

1. Single-click on that sprite.
2. Hold down the space bar.
3. Drag the two-framed sprite around in the score to its new location.

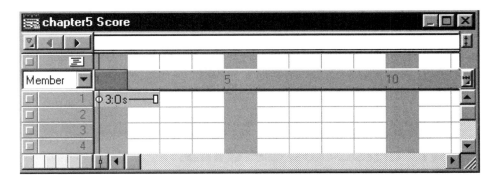

Figure 7-2   Sprite spanning two frames.

EXCHANGING CAST MEMBERS

The Exchange Cast Members feature will come in handy when you want to swap cast members in the score for part of an existing sprite or the entire thing (Figure 7-3). Where the exchange cast members function really adds benefit is when you have already set keyframes and other animation characteristics for the initial sprite. If you delete portions of the existing sprite to place in another, the new sprite will not have any of the animation characteristics or paths that were previously set for the original sprite.

Example: If you place a cast member of an image (i.e., person walking) on the stage and animate it around the screen using the tweening technique, you have set the keyframes for that sprite's position and motion path (Figure 7-4). Suppose you want to add other cast members into that animation to make the person actually move his legs (Figure 7-5). By replacing the new sprite over portions of the existing frames, you would have to try and manually set the new sprite's position and motion to match that of the rest of the animation you previously created. This would be nearly impossible to match up for a complex animation. Instead, use the exchange cast member feature to switch cast members and retain all of the keyframed positions and motion characteristics.

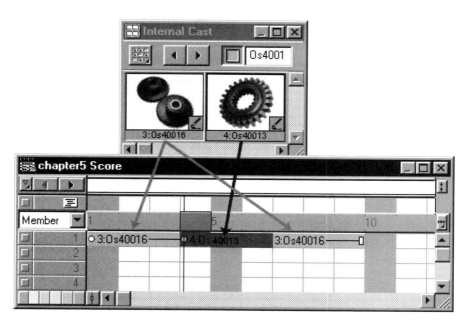

Figure 7-3   Use the exchange cast member feature to replace part of a single sprite with another cast member.

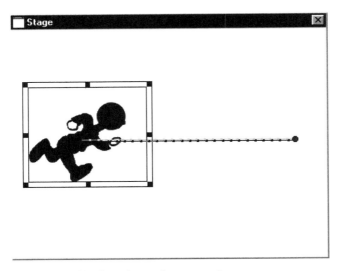

Figure 7-4   Single sprite moving across the stage.

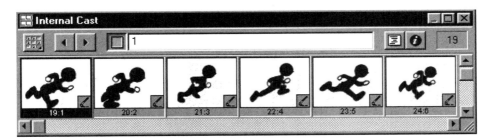

Figure 7-5   Cast of animated characters to make the character look like it's walking.

To implement this feature:

1. Add a cast member to the score.

2. Animate the sprite around on the stage using keyframes.

3. Select Edit Sprite Frames from the Edit menu.

4. Mark the region of the sprite that you want to change cast members. To select a range of frames:

   A. Single-click on the beginning frame of the area you want to select.

   B. Hold down the Shift key and click on the last frame of the area that you want to select. All of the frames in between the selected frame should also become highlighted (Figure 7-6).

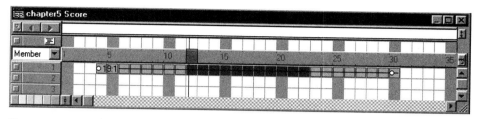

Figure 7-6　Highlight the frames in the score that you want to replace with a new cast member.

1. Single-click on the cast member you want to add in the place of the highlighted area.

2. Select Exchange Cast Members from the Edit menu or click on the Exchange Cast Members button in the toolbar at the top of the screen (Figure 7-7).

Figure 7-7　Exchange cast member button.

REGISTRATION POINTS FOR AN EVEN EXCHANGE

Director uses the registration points of sprites to align images when using the exchange cast members function. If similar images (altered versions of the same image) seem to shift during the animation or interactive action after using the exchange cast members feature, check that the registration points of the two images are lined up exactly (Figure 7-8). If they are not in the same position, you will need to reset their registration points. To change the registration point of a cast member:

1. Double-click on the cast member to open it into Director Paint.

2. Select the Registration Point tool.

3. Click the area of the image where you want to set a new registration point (Figure 7-9).

4. Close Director Paint to apply the changes to that cast member.

Figure 7-8   Registration points properly align the images used for the animation.

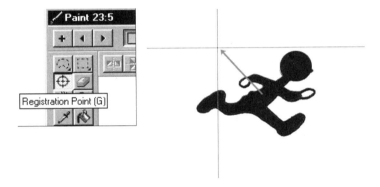

Figure 7-9   Setting new registration points.

Graphical cast members default to having their registration point in the center of the image. If you accidentally move the registration point and want to reset it, double-click on the Registration Point tool.

You can use the onion skinning feature to display other cast members to help visually line up registration points.

If you have changed the default editor for your cast member to something other than Director Paint (see Launch and Edit in Chapter 3):

1. Click the right mouse button (Windows) or Option-click (Macintosh) the sprite or cast member you wish to alter.
2. Select Edit Cast Member from the popup menu (Figure 7-10). The Director Paint window appears.
3. Use the previously listed steps to reset or reposition the registration point of your image.

Once you set an animation or interactive function (such as a rollover) to a sprite, the registration points are still used to evenly swap the cast members or sprites. If you move a sprite to another location of the stage, the registration points will move also and all adjustments will be made correctly when the animations or interactions take place.

Figure 7-10   Edit Cast Member
option from popup menu.

REVERSING AN ANIMATION

A portion of your program may require one or more sprites to animate on screen into a given position and then reverse themselves following the same path back to their initial starting point. Getting sprites to animate in the exact opposite direction by setting new keyframes to recreate the movements of how they came into position would be very difficult if not impossible. Fortunately, Director has taken all the guesswork out. To have Director reproduce the exact movement pattern in reverse:

1. Animate the sprite(s) around the stage as desired.

2. Highlight the sprite(s) in the score that you want to reverse.

3. Select Copy Sprites from the Edit menu or use the keyboard shortcut Control-C (Windows) or Command-C (Macintosh).

4. Single-click in the score on the first frame where you want to place the copied sprites.

5. Select Paste from the Edit menu or use the keyboard shortcut Control-V (Windows) or Command-V (Macintosh).

6. With the sprite(s) still selected, choose Reverse Sequence from the Modify menu.

7. Rewind and play back your movie. The sprite(s) should animate into place and then move along the same path in reverse back into the original starting position (Figure 7-11).

Figure 7-11   Reverse animation plays the sprite backward along the same path as it plays forward .

ADDING PRINT CAPABILITIES

Director allows you to print movie content in order to review and mark changes of screens, sign off sheets for client approval, show changes made to the rest of the design/ development team, or to make handouts for presentations. There are several print options during the authoring stages of your movie:

◆ Print an image of the stage, score, cast art, cast thumbnails, or contents of text cast members.

◆ All scripts or a range of scripts (movie, cast, score, and sprite scripts).

◆ The comments in the Markers window.

◆ The entire Cast window.

Depending on the nature of your finished program, most applications do not require the ability to print a page from a Director movie. However, there may be applications where having a print feature is beneficial. The print command is implemented using a simple Lingo command that will print a frame or series of frames of whatever is displayed on the stage during the specified frames. Use the following command:

```
printForm (fromFrame), (to frame)
```

All images are printed at 72 pixels per inch in the portrait (vertical) layout, regardless of the orientation of the Page Setup settings.

The command `printForm 1, 5` tells Director to print the images as they appear on the stage for Frames 1 through 5. You can also instruct it to change the percentage size of the image to one of three choices (100%, 50%, or 25%). To reduce the print size of the image, add the percentage value at the end of the Lingo command:

```
printForm (fromFrame), (to frame), (reduction value)
```

The command `printForm 1,5, 50` tells Director to print what is displayed for Frames 1 through 5 at half of the original size of the image.

There are a few third-party Xtras, including the PrintOMatic Xtra, which you can purchase to add more printing options when implementing print features in your Director movies. You can find the source for this and other Xtras at www.macromedia.com/software/xtras/director.

PLAYING SELECTED FRAMES

During the authoring stage of your project, Director allows you to play back only a specific range of frames that you select. This feature comes in handy when you want to keep testing a certain area without having to play back your entire movie every time you hit play. To select a region of the score to play back:

1. Open a Director movie.

2. Click on the first frame of the area you want to mark as the selected range of frames.

3. Hold the Shift key and select the last frame of the area you want to select. The marked region should become highlighted.

4. Open the Control Panel from the Window menu or press Control-2 (Windows) or Command-2 (Macintosh).

5. Click on the Selected Frames Only button in the lower right corner of the Control Panel (Figure 7-12).

Notice that a green line appears in the score indicating the marked area for playback. When you hit play, the playback head starts playing your movie from the first selected frame and continues to the last frame of the selected region (unless it comes across any Wait commands or Lingo scripts interrupting the playback of your movie). When the playback head reaches the last frame, it loops back to the first frame of the selected area, not the first frame of your movie (Figure 7-13).

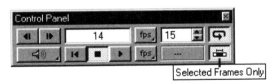

Figure 7-12   The Selected Frames Only button located in the control panel.

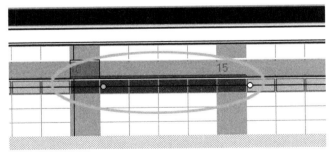

Figure 7-13   A green line indicates selected frames for playback.

WORKING WITH EXTERNAL EXECUTABLE FILES

There are many advantages to creating separate Director movies and linking to them from the current movie you working in. A common request is to develop a program that incorporates elements from existing programs. Usually, these programs have been authored in Director or Authorware. Instead of wasting the time trying to recreate these programs, use a Lingo command to open one of these movies and play it. You can also have it return back to your original Director movie when the external program is done playing. To set up this feature:

1. Open the main Director movie you are using that will launch other movies and programs.

2. Add a sprite script or frame script in the appropriate location where you want to launch an external program.

3. Type in the Lingo code:

```
play movie "name of movie"
```

4. Rewind and play back your movie.

Depending where in the file structure the new movie you are linking to is stored, you may have to add in the specific path for Director to locate the proper movies. The best solution is to keep all externally linked files in the same folder.

Director is able to open other executable files and applications, not just Director movies. Generally, any Windows application containing an .EXE file extension or Macintosh application program can be opened from a Director movie.

CUT, COPY, AND PASTE SHORTCUTS

Within the course of developing a project, you will be cutting and copying cast members and sprites all of the time. When working in just about any type of program, learning shortcut keys and alternate methods for doing certain functions quicker is a big timesaver. This is especially true for simple, yet repetitive functions that you perform constantly. The method that most everyone is familiar with is to:

1. Select the image you wish to cut or copy.
2. Click on the Edit menu.
3. Select Cut or Copy.
4. Go to a new frame or cast member window.
5. Click on the Edit menu.
6. Select Paste to add the cut or copied image into the new area.

Why do all those steps when you don't have to? Instead here are a few suggestions for saving you some time:

KEYBOARD QUICKIES

To cut, copy, or paste a sprite or cast member, select the image and hold:

♦ Control-X (Windows) or Command-X (Macintosh) to cut or remove a sprite or cast member.

♦ Control-C (Windows) or Command-C (Macintosh) to copy a sprite or cast member.

♦ Control-V (Windows) or Command-V (Macintosh) to paste or add a sprite or cast member.

KEYBOARD/MOUSE COMBOS

To duplicate a sprite or cast member:

♦ Select the image and hit Control-D (Windows) or Command-D (Macintosh). This will place the duplicate image into the next available cast window.

♦ Click and hold onto the sprite or cast member while holding the Alt key (Windows) or Control key (Macintosh) and drag it to a blank area or empty cast member window in your movie (Figure 7-14).

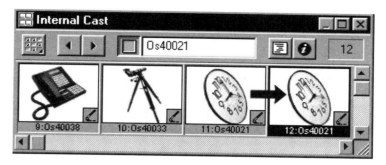

Figure 7-14 Using a modify key while dragging a cast member can create an exact duplicate cast member.

Duplicate is a function that is only available for cast members, not sprites.

WORKING IN THE SCORE

There are a number of things you can do as a programmer to make maneuvering around the score more efficient. The score is the main work area, or timeline, where you control the majority of elements used in your movie. These elements include all of your cast members (which become sprites in the score), scripts, layering hierarchy, ink effects, duration of sprites, and so on. The following points should provide a few methods for properly setting up and testing the sequence you constructed in the score.

TURNING SPRITE CHANNELS ON AND OFF

Because the score can contain upward of 1,000 channels, having the ability to turn some of these channels on and off could be a huge timesaver in troubleshooting multi-layered movies. The small gray buttons in the far-left side of each channel toggle the visibility and functionality of sprites located in that particular channel (Figure 7-15). This allows you to isolate whether a particular channel is causing a conflict with the playback of your movie (a sprite with a lingering script that is adversely affecting other sprites in the same channel). You may also want to hide certain channels for aesthetic purposes. Turning off a particular channel allows Director to play your movie without displaying the sprites in that channel. You can compare playback with and without the channel displaying the images, scripts, or effects contained in that channel. This technique is the easiest method for hiding channels without having to delete any of the sprites contained in those selected channels.

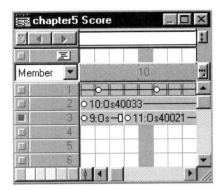

Figure 7-15   Toggle any channel in the score on and off.

Hiding channels is a good technique while still in the development stages of your program. However, the sprites in these hidden channels are still factored into the file size of your movie. Eliminate any unnecessary channels when you have finished building your movie and are ready to package the final project, either as a Projector or a Shockwave movie. This will reduce the overall size of your movie.

TURNING EFFECT CHANNELS ON AND OFF

Turning channels on and off in the effects channels is essentially the same as turning channels on and off for the regular sprite channels. To toggle any channel on or off, click the button to the far-left side of the channel. The advantage for turning these channels on and off can help you troubleshoot your movie, especially when trying to find out whether a tempo setting or script is causing your movie to play incorrectly if at all. By turning a channel off using this technique, you can test to see if your movie plays back correctly when not activating the options selected in those particular channels of the score.

Example: If a playback or display error occurs between two screens, check the transition channel. Play back your movie with and without that channel selected. If the movie plays the same in both cases, the problem lies somewhere else in your movie. If hiding the transition channel fixes the problem, then you may need to go back and recheck the settings for that troublesome transition or remove the transition altogether.

ALTERING THE DISPLAY OF YOUR SCORE

For those of you who remember (or still work with) Director 5, you remember what a tough time it was working in the score. Sprites were represented by their cast member numbers, which were displayed for each frame that the sprite spanned in the score (Figure 7-16). In Chapter 1 we covered the new way sprites are displayed since Version 6 and higher. More important than just looks, you can now see and utilize more information pertaining to each sprite. The one obvious factor is that sprites are now displayed as single objects (Figure 7-17). This allows:

◆ Sprites to be stretched in either direction just by simply dragging either endpoint to cover more or less frames.

◆ Sprites to be moved to a new channel or set of frames by clicking on any part of the sprite and dragging it as a unit to the new location.

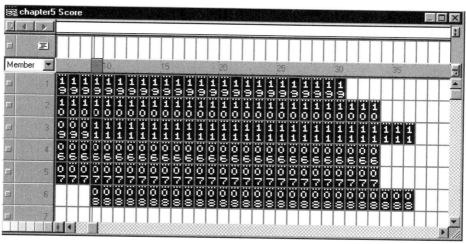

Figure 7-16   Reverting your score to look like Version 5 display.

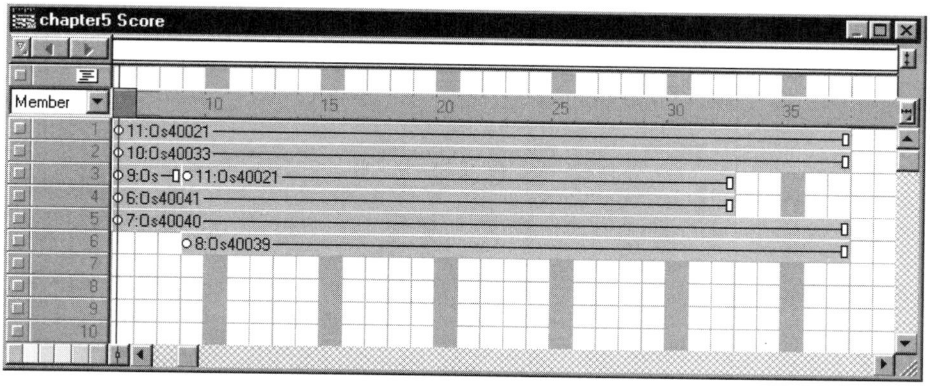

Figure 7-17   Sprites are displayed as single objects since Version 6.

◆ Sprites to display additional information directly inside the sprite in your score. Click on the Sprite Content pulldown menu (Figure 7-18). These various displays make reading and editing a complex score easier. You can select between:

Figure 7-18   Sprite content pulldown menu.

1. Member—displays the name and/or number of the associated cast member (Figure 7-19).

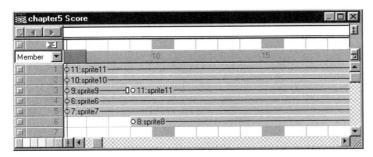

Figure 7-19   Sprite display: Member.

2. Behavior—displays the associated cast member's name and/or number of any behaviors applied to any sprites in the score. The sprite remains blank if no behavior was used (Figure 7-20).

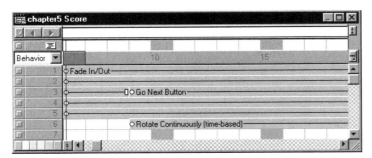

Figure 7-20   Sprite display: Behavior.

3. Location—displays the location of the sprite (top left corner of bounding box) on the stage (Figure 7-21).

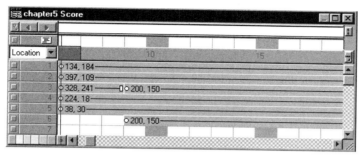

Figure 7-21   Sprite display: Location.

4. Ink—displays the type of ink effect applied to each sprite (Figure 7-22).

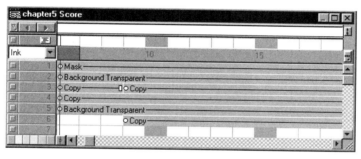

Figure 7-22   Sprite display: Ink.

5. Blend—displays the transparency level for each sprite; 100% is opaque, 0% is completely invisible (Figure 7-23).

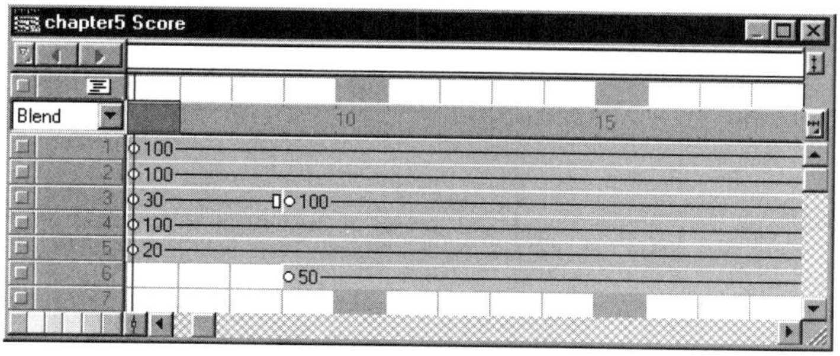

Figure 7-23   Sprite display: Blend.

6. Extended—a unique combination of all of the sprite content choices (Figure 7-24).

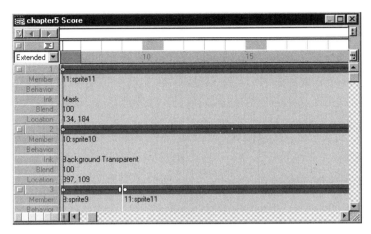

Figure 7-24   *Sprite display: Extended.*

You can also change the information that is displayed for sprites in your score by choosing how and when sprite information is displayed within the sprite itself. This is referred to as sprite labels. To select how and when the information selected in the Sprite Content menu is displayed:

1. Choose Sprite Labels from the View menu.

2. Choose from one of the following sprite label displays:

◆ Keyframes—displays the information (selected in the Sprite Content menu) at every keyframe marked in the score for every channel (Figure 7-25).

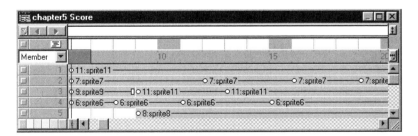

Figure 7-25   *Sprite label: Keyframes.*

◆ Changes Only—displays the information in a sprite only where a new sprite is added to the score (Figure 7-26).

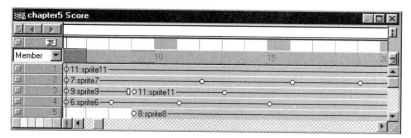

Figure 7-26 Sprite label: Changes Only.

◆ Every Frame—displays information for every frame of every sprite. Unless zoomed all the way in to your score, it becomes very difficult to work with this setting and distinguish which sprite you want to work with (Figure 7-27).

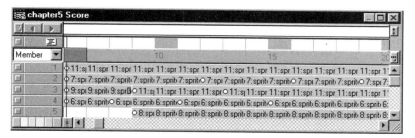

Figure 7-27 Sprite label: Every Frame.

◆ First Frame—displays the information for each sprite only at the beginning of each sprite (Figure 7-28).

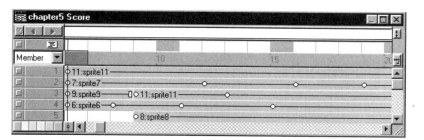

Figure 7-28 Sprite label: First Frame.

◆   None—does not display any information for any sprites in the score (Figure 7-29).

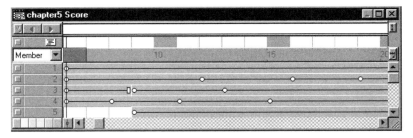

Figure 7-29   Sprite label: None.

CHANGING THE FOCUS OF YOUR TIMELINE

Depending on the size of your movie and the number of frames a sprite spans in your score, you may need to change the zoom factor of your timeline. To do this:

1. Click on the Zoom menu on the right side of the score window.
2. Choose from one of the preselected zoom percentages listed in the popup menu (Figure 7-30).

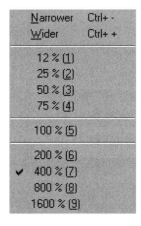

Figure 7-30   Zoom menu for the score.

OR

Use the shortcut keys Control-(+) (Windows) or Command-(+) (Macintosh) to zoom in closer to the timeline to see more detail and less number of frames displayed. Use Control-(-) (Windows) or Command-(-) (Macintosh) to zoom back to a wider view of the timeline.

Being able to see more detail will come in handy when you need to add or change things to a single frame or small group of sprites (such as adding a keyframe). Displaying a wider view of the timeline will come in handy when trying to move a sprite or group of sprites to a section of the score much further down in time (Figure 7-31).

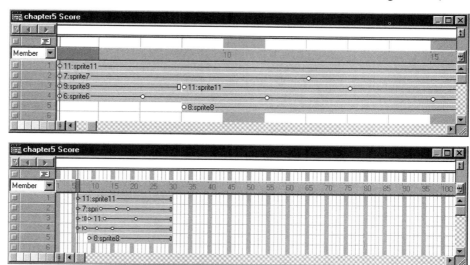

Figure 7-31   Comparing different views of the score (800% vs. 75%).

To assist in adding keyframes (single frames) or other subsets (portions) of a larger sprite, change the display under the Edit menu from Edit Entire Sprite to Edit Sprite Frames (Figure 7-32). This gives the score the look of Version 5, allowing you the access to break up and change any sprite frame by frame.

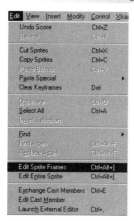

Figure 7-32   Changing the view of the score from edit entire sprite to edit sprite frames.

LOCATING THE PLAYBACK HEAD

When developing a program in Director, many times it is easy to lose sight of the playback head in the score. You might have clicked on a navigational link that has taken you to a frame much further down in your timeline than what is currently displayed in the score. Or you might be trying to troubleshoot a movie and want to stop the playback head at the precise moment of the problematic frame. You must be careful not to click anywhere in the score or you will move the playback head to the new location that you accidentally clicked on. The other alternative is to scroll through your score to try and locate the position of the playback head. This can waste time and be quite cumbersome.

Instead, Director provides a quick-find locator that automatically finds the frame that your playback head is in and changes the view of your score so that the playback head and adjacent frames are now displayed in the center of the screen. To perform this function, click on the Center Current Frame button located in the lower left corner of the score (Figure 7-33).

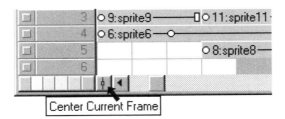

Figure 7-33   Center Current Frame button.

TROUBLESHOOTING TECHNIQUES

DEBUGGING YOUR APPLICATION

No matter how simple you may think your program is or how sure you are that every element you added to your movie will work correctly, there is always room for error when the gods of multimedia want to step in and have some fun. There is always the possibility that a typo occurred while typing in a Lingo script, sprites and cast members were rearranged while trying to test something and were not put back into their proper positions, or linked files were not able to be found or recognized by your Director movie. Therefore, it is very important to go through and debug your program thoroughly before considering it ready for distribution. Debugging basically means trying to maneuver through your program from start to finish, accessing every possible navigational combination, and trying to see if clicking something at the wrong time doesn't screw up the program or cause it to perform incorrectly. Many times developers will go through their program and click on all the right buttons. As expected, the program usually performs the way it was designed to play.

Sure enough, however, there are going to be times when items that were not supposed to be clicked caused the program to malfunction in unexpected ways. There is no way to prevent users from clicking around on the screens. Therefore, you must take the time to check all possible areas that may lead to an error in your program (as if you are trying to get it to fail). If you can get through the entire program several times without encountering a single error, then I would say your program is ready for distribution.

 Have someone else, who has not had any involvement in the development of the program, go in and try to maneuver through the program. You should be observing carefully to make sure that all of the buttons and links are navigating to the right sections.

FIND A PROBLEM, FIGURE IT OUT, AND FIX IT

While in the process of debugging your Director movie (or even just in the development stages), it is important to analyze a problem before rushing in to fix it. The first thing to do (after panicking that your movie doesn't work) is to write down exactly what went wrong. Be specific and document the details of what caused the error. If an error message appears, write it down. This message may be helpful in determining what needs to be fixed. This error message will also be helpful if you wind up calling Macromedia's Technical Support.

 Create a developer's journal that you can use to keep track of notes on all of your multimedia projects. This can be useful to find out relevant information about project requirements, dates and version numbers of phases presented to clients for approval, special or unique developing techniques used, and troubleshooting hold-ups and their appropriate fixes.

Once you have come across the error and have logged it in your developer's journal, begin to focus on the problem. Try to track down the cause of the problem. Can you easily identify what is causing the error to occur or is it more involved than that? Work your way backward through the steps that you performed to see if you can figure out precisely what caused the error. Use Director features, such as the Debugger window, Watcher window, and Message window with Trace, to check through your scripts to display the line that is causing the problem.

The last step is to eliminate all other potential factors or external variables that may be causing the problem. If you can isolate the error to a specific incidence every time it occurs, even under different circumstances (i.e., running your program on another system), then you should be able to go in and correct the problem or eliminate it altogether.

To double-check that the problem you have diagnosed is truly the correct reason causing the error, try and recreate the error in a test movie. Make a simplified version of the real application and see whether or not the problem occurs. If you know the steps it takes to successfully reproduce the error, then you will know the steps to take to correct the problem.

STEP-BY-STEP COMMANDS WITH TRACE

Turn on the trace feature while playing your movie to see exactly how Director is functioning. The Message window will display all the commands and scripts as the playback head encounters them. Scroll back through the trace list to find out where any errors in your application are originating from. To activate the trace feature:

1. Select Message from the Window menu. The Message window appears.
2. Click on the Trace button in the top of the Message window (Figure 7-34).
3. Run your movie with the Message window visible. All Lingo scripts and Behavior commands will be displayed every time the playback head encounters a command. You can stop the movie after experiencing an error in your application to check the code that is causing the problem.

Playing your Director movie with the Message window open and running Trace can slow down the playback performance of your application.

Figure 7-34   Trace button located in Message window.

USING THE WATCHER

The Watcher window is another type of troubleshooting feature available in Director. It is used to check variables and other simple expressions while your movie is playing, similar to the Message window's Trace option. To use the Watcher to check a specific variable:

1. Create a Field Text List and name the cast member (Figure 7-35).
2. Create a new script and set the values for the given variable.
3. Select Watcher from the Window menu.
4. Open up the Script window that contains the variable code that you want to test.
5. Copy the text from your script and paste it into the top field of the Watcher window.
6. Click the Add button. Because the variable has no value assigned to it yet, the equation should return a <VOID> statement.
7. Close the Script window.

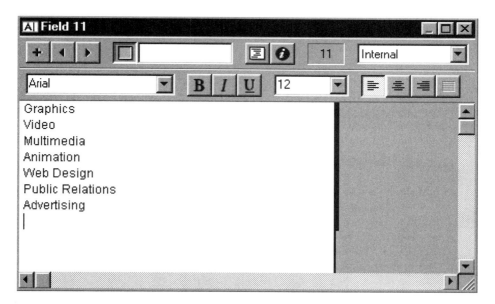

Figure 7-35   Field text list.

8. Play your movie. The values set in Step 2 should appear next to the variable command in the Watcher window (Figure 7-36). If this happens, then you know that your movie is recognizing the values set for the variable(s) in your movie.

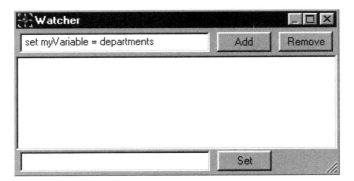

Figure 7-36   Watcher window recognizing script values.

Always copy and paste the text from your scripts. Do not try and retype them. This is to make sure that you are testing the same scripts in the Watcher as you have them set (and spelled) in your movie. Any alterations will not allow the Watcher to perform correctly.

STEPPING THROUGH SCRIPTS WITH THE DEBUGGER WINDOW

The Debugger window is a great troubleshooting feature to utilize if you are having trouble with a script and cannot figure out what is wrong. The Debugger window is also a good tool for developers just getting their feet wet with Lingo scripts because it allows you to walk through your script step by step when you play your movie. When activated, the Debugger window will display the script handler that is currently running and a list of variables used in the current handler (Figure 7-37). To use the Debugger window to check that your scripts are performing the correct procedures line by line:

1. Open a Director movie that contains a movie script variable.
2. Open the Movie Script window. (Select Script from the Window menu).
3. Click in the left margin of the script window to add a breakpoint. A red dot should appear next to the handler you select.
4. Close the script window.

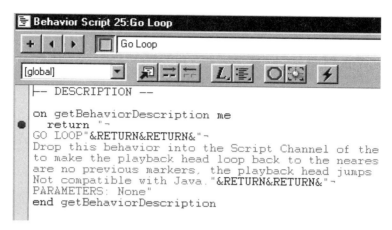

Figure 7-37   Debugger window.

5. Play the movie. As the movie plays, it will automatically open the Debugger window. The green arrow indicates the statement that is about to be executed (Figure 7-38).

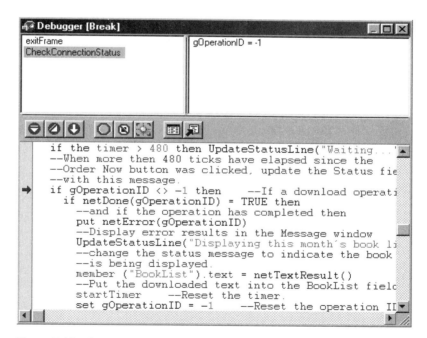

Figure 7-38   Green arrow indicates the command next in line.

6. Click the Step Into Script button to move through the script line by line. This should allow you to monitor the procedure of your scripts to make sure they are being executed in the correct manner as you had intended them to work.

A breakpoint is used to tell Director that once it comes across this particular handler when running your movie it should access the Debugger window. Before Director executes that handler, the Debugger window will open (if closed) and allow you to step through the script one statement at a time.

To remove a breakpoint from the Script window, click on the red dot in the margin and close the window.

ADDING JUST THE RIGHT COLOR

When working with any type of image in Director, setting the right color palettes is information that is critical. What actually determines the way an image is displayed is the types of colors available in its associated color palette (Figure 7-39). This is especially true when working with images created as 8-bit color depth or less. Working in Director involves two types of color depth settings:

◆ Setting a general palette for the entire movie.

◆ Setting color palettes for individual sprites or cast members.

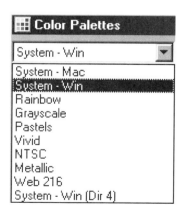

Figure 7-39   List of standard color palettes.

Director offers the unique ability to change color palettes along the way (via the color palette channel) or import custom palettes associated with individual graphics (Figure 7-40). Director has the ability to create customized palettes by selecting the most commonly used colors and then saving that for the most optimal playback display of all your images. (Check out the color section in this book to see some examples of how custom color palettes can work for you.)

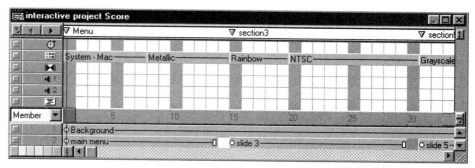

Figure 7-40   Various color palettes can be applied directly in the score.

OPTIMIZING YOUR GRAPHICS

Every bitmapped image imported into Director has its own color depth setting. When you import a graphic into Director, if the color depth is not the same as the color depth set for your Director movie, an Image Option window appears prompting you to choose which color depth setting you want to apply to the graphic being imported. (Figure 7-41). If the image has a higher color depth than that set for your movie, Director will automatically strip out the extra colors not found in the movie's color palette. The downside is that the graphic will still sustain the same characteristics of the larger file, meaning that the image will use up more RAM as if it still contained all the discarded colors causing it to animate more slowly across the screen. If you want to display an image at its natural color depth, you must change the color depth setting of the movie.

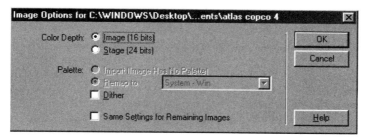

Figure 7-41   Image options (color depth settings) during import.

◆   1 bit = 2 colors (black and white only)

◆   2 bit = 4 colors

◆   4 bit = 16 colors

◆   8 bit = 256 colors

◆   16 bit = thousands of colors (32,768)

◆   24 bit = millions of colors (16.7 million)

The color depth of your movie is set outside of Director. How you set the color depth for your monitor determines the color depth available for your movies. Therefore, if you only set it for 256 colors, you will only be able to display 8-bit images. For Windows systems, use the Display Properties Settings in the Control Panel to set the color depth of your monitor. For Macintosh systems, use the Monitor and Sound Settings found in the Control Panels folder.

Inside Director, graphics with a 2-, 4-, or 8-bit color depth identify with colors set to a particular position of a color palette, referred to as index colors. Higher bit depths do not rely on color palettes to display accurate colors and use the adjustable luminance, hue, and saturation levels of the color wheel (Figure 7-42).

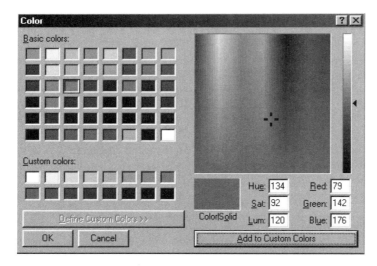

Figure 7-42   Color wheel with adjustable luminance, hue, and saturation controls.

Map your images to as few color palettes as possible. This will increase the quality and performance of how Director displays your images.

CHANGING IMAGE COLOR DEPTH

To get your images to look their best, create a custom palette optimal for most of the graphics you have imported now as cast members. This may be the best solution for working at lower bit depths with reduced file size, and still having images look as close to normal as possible. This new optimized palette will allow you to remap all of your cast members and have them utilize one color palette instead of trying to load a new one for each individual cast member displayed. To set up an optimized custom palette:

Your stage must be set for 8-bit (Windows and Macintosh) or 4-bit (Macintosh only) color depth in order to create a custom palette in Director.

1. Select a cast member to utilize its color palette as the basis for the optimized palette.
2. Choose Color Palettes from the Window menu. The image's color palette appears.
3. Choose Duplicate from the Edit menu. This way you will not destroy the original color palette of the selected cast member.
4. Enter a name for the new palette in the Create Palette window that appears.

In Director or any other program, get into the habit of naming files in a manner that makes them easily recognizable. Name the new palette you created in Step 3 something descriptive and easily identifiable, such as "custom palette" or "optimal palette."

5. Click on the Select Used Colors button at the top of the color palette window. (Figure 7-43).
6. Click on the Select button in the Select Colors Used In Bitmap window. Director will put a black outline around the colors of the palette present in the cast member.
7. Use the Hand tool and drag one of the selected colors to the second color panel in the top row (next to the white color chip). Director automatically rearranges the selected colors in a continuous row next to the one you just repositioned (Figure 7-44).
8. Click the Invert Selection button to highlight the unused colors of the palette.
9. Click the In-Betweening button to convert the unused colors into an even-toned color blend to make it easier to identify and separate the actual colors used in the original cast member (Figure 7-45).

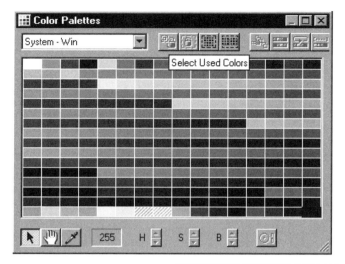

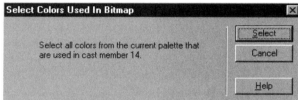

Figure 7-43   Select Colors Used In Bitmap window and Select Used Colors button.

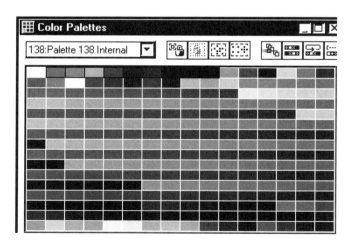

Figure 7-44   Rearrange used colors in color palette.

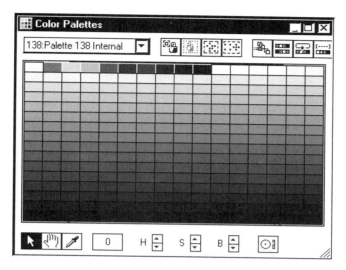

Figure 7-45   The In-Betweening button separates unused colors into an even color blend.

10. Click the Palette popup menu in the Color Palettes window. Choose a color palette used by other cast members.

11. Select another cast member and click on the Select Used Colors button again.

12. With the new selection highlighted, choose Copy Colors from the Edit menu.

13. Select the Optimized Palette from the Palette popup menu.

14. Select the first chip after the colors used in the original cast member.

15. Choose Paste Into Palette in the Edit menu to add these newly selected colors from the second chosen cast member to your optimal palette.

16. Repeat Steps 10 through 15 for each cast member or until the optimized color palette is full.

Now, you must remap all of your images (graphical cast members) to this new optimized color palette you just created:

1. Select the cast member you want to remap.

2. Select Transform Bitmap from the Modify menu. The Transform Bitmap window appears.

3. Select the Remap Colors radio button.

4. Select the optimized palette you created from the Palette popup menu (Figure 7-46).

5. Click transform to apply the new color palette.

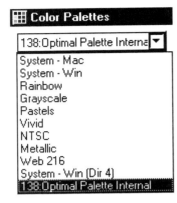

Figure 7-46   Palette popup menu containing new custom-made optimized palette.

It is important to plan this procedure from the beginning of your project in order to get the best quality images while creating the most optimal Director movie.

There are only two color depths that have customizable palettes. Both Window and Macintosh systems allow you to modify an 8-bit color palette. Only Macintosh systems allow you to modify a 4-bit palette.

CREATING A LIMITED TIME DEMO

There are many reasons why you should consider adding a feature to prevent your application from running after a certain date:

◆ You do not want incomplete versions (alpha and beta phases for evaluation only) of your software floating around forever. Clients and end users are likely to think it's the final version, when in essence, there may be several changes that need to be implemented.

◆ You want to get approval from your client, but want to make sure you get paid before releasing the final version.

◆ You are sending out a trial version for people to examine your program before they purchase it.

Whatever the reason may be, all you need to do is program Director to compare the current date of the system that is running your program versus the date you set for it to cease running. To add this feature to your movie, type in the following Lingo script:

```
on startMovie
   expirationDate = date("20000101")
   -- where January 1, 2000 is the desired Expiration Date
   if the systemDate > expirationDate
   alert "The trial period for this application has expired!"
   -- add in your own message
   halt
   end if
end
```

This script will be executed when you play the original Director movie or a projector created from it. An alert window will appear displaying the message you input in the alert line of the script. (Figure 7-47). Once the user clicks on the OK button, the program will automatically quit. The projector file will quit and no longer be accessible. The Director movie will just stop playing, not allowing the application to run any further. However, you still have full control of the program and can go back in to alter the script for further development.

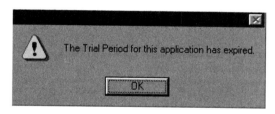

Figure 7-47   Alert window indicating trial period for application has expired.

TOP SECRET: ADDING A PASSWORD

Director's ability to interact with the user via Lingo scripts and Behavior commands allows developers to include features that can be used for applications that you do not want to make accessible to the general public. The user would be required to type in a predetermined password that is created during the development of the program. This does not give the user the ability to enter his own password or change the existing password. Director 7 has added a password Behavior to make adding a password into your program easy. To implement a password into your Director movie:

1. Open the Tool Palette from the Window menu or press Control-7 (Windows) or Command-7 (Macintosh) on the keyboard.
2. Create a Field Text window on the stage using the Field button.

3. Open the Library Palette from the Window menu.

4. Select Text from the Library List pulldown menu (Figure 7-48).

5. Click and drag the Password Entry Behavior onto the Field Text box. The Parameters for "Password Entry" window appears.

6. Enter the desired password in the Password field (Figure 7-49).

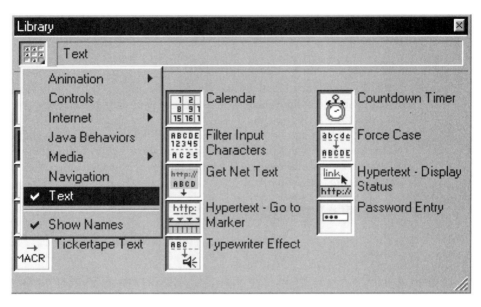

Figure 7-48   Display the text behaviors accessed from the Library List.

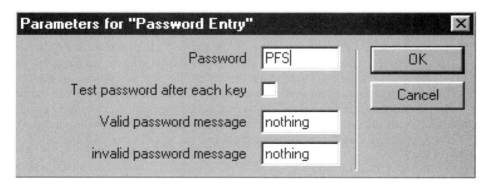

Figure 7-49   Enter the desired password in the parameters for "Password Entry" window.

7. Enter a command or handler in the Valid password message field.

   Example: `myHandler`

8. Enter a command or handler in the Invalid password message field.

   Example: `quit`

9. Click OK.

10. Create a new movie script and set the following global variables:

```
global gFlag


on exitFrame
   if gFlag = 1 then
      go to frame (frameNumber or markerName)
   else
      go the frame
   end if
end
```

11. Create a new movie script. This can be done by clicking the Plus sign to add a new script:

```
global gFlag


on startMovie
   set gFlag = 0
end



on myHandler
   set gFlag = 1
end
```

12. Rewind and play your movie.

13. Click on the stage to make it the active window. Use the keyboard to type in a password.

For the aforementioned example, if the password is entered correctly, the playback head will navigate to the frame number or marker name set in the script, allowing the user to begin the program (Figure 7-50). If the user enters an incorrect password, you can set the program to either stay in the frame or quit on the user.

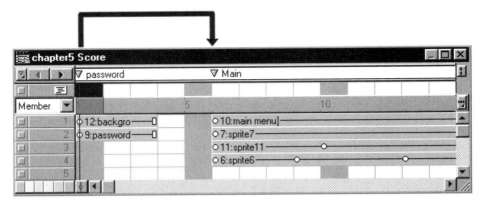

*Figure 7-50   Playback head navigates to main section of movie upon entering the correct
           password.*

**Do not use Editable text for the Password Field text. This will
cause the password feature to not function properly.**

**You cannot enter a GO TO command for the Valid or Invalid
password message field. (Thanks to Dave at Macromedia Tech
Support for figuring this one out.)**

**Make sure to add a Loop On Frame command (or similar) in the
score so that the playback head does not continue playing past the
password section of your movie until the user enters the correct
password.**

Password-protected applications can be used for programs intended to be distributed
over the internet via Shockwave that you want to make available only to selected individuals. This can be useful for posting projects to key clients around the world before
releasing to the public. This application now functions more like an intranet site accessible over the pipelines of the World Wide Web.

Password Entry requires a system-specific font in order to function properly. Set up your Field text to use the Arial font for Windows and Helvetica for Macintosh systems. Bullet points appear in the Field window to hide the actual password being entered.

HELPING USERS WITH TOOLTIPS

Just like the majority of programs on the market, Director allows you to add popup labels identifying the name of the button or link when the cursor is left sitting over one of these functions for a short period of time (Figure 7-51). This type of feature is very helpful to the user when trying to learn where each link is located on an unfamiliar interface. To add this feature to your application:

1. Build a Director movie as you would normally or open an existing movie.
2. Open the Tool Palette window from the Window menu or press Control-7 (Windows) or Command-7 (Macintosh) on the keyboard.
3. Select the Field text box and drag a new Field window on the stage.
4. Open the Library Palette from the Window menu.
5. Select Controls from the Library List pulldown menu (Figure 7-52).

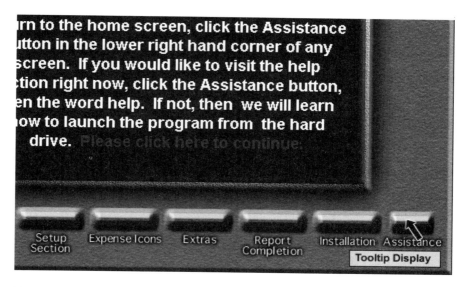

Figure 7-51   Standard popup message window called "Tooltips."

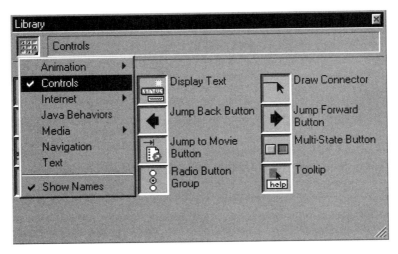

Figure 7-52   Display the controls behaviors accessed from the Library list.

6. Click on the Display Text Behavior and apply it to the Field sprite. The Parameters for "Display Text" window appears.

7. Select Tooltip from the pulldown menu (Figure 7-53).

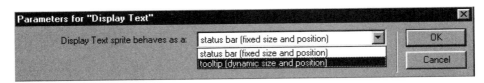

Figure 7-53   Select tooltip in the parameters for "Display Text" window.

8. Click OK.

9. Select Tooltip from the Library and apply it to the sprite that you want to have the Tooltip feature. The Parameters for "Tooltip" window appears.

10. Type in the text you want displayed as the "tip" in the "Text of Tool Tip" field (Figure 7-54).

11. Set the timing and position options as desired.

12. Important: Select the cast member number of the Field Text box that you added in Step 3 by dragging the slide bar located on the bottom of the parameters window.

13. Click OK.

14. Rewind and play your movie. The Tooltip is displayed when you park your cursor over the sprite.

Parameters for "Tooltip"			✕

Text of tool tip: `Insert your single-line tool tip here`   OK

Pause before showing tool tip (ticks): ⟨slider⟩ ◄ ► 30   Cancel

Hide tool tip if user clicks on sprite? ☑

Tool tip position relative to sprite (see notes): `centered` ▼

Use which sprite to display tooltip? ⟨slider⟩ ◄ ► 1

Figure 7-54   Parameters for "Tooltip" window.

Leave the Field window empty when you add it to your stage (see Step 3). This window will not be displayed when you play the movie.

MAKING MOVIES SPECIAL WITH XTRAS

Xtras are software plug-ins or extension modules that increase the functionality and capabilities of Director in a variety of ways. These modules come in all shapes and sizes. Some appear in a separate cast window and others are accessed through their own user interface to allow for customized settings (Figure 7-55). Director comes bundled with certain Xtras and allows you to install third-party Xtras. Depending on which Xtras are used in your program, make sure that the user has the required Xtras installed on his system or is provided with a copy of these Xtras with the final version of your movie. Director 6 and 7 have the ability to embed most of the commonly used Xtras into a projector file. Therefore, you may not be required to distribute a separate Xtras folder with your movie (see Chapter 9 for more information regarding packaging and distributing your movies).

To install Xtras, place them in the Xtras folder found in the Director application folder located on your hard drive.

Figure 7-55   Interface from (Beatnik) third-party Xtra.

There are five general types of Xtras:

◆   Image Filters—consist of third-party filters, such as Adobe Photoshop and Premiere filters, that alter the way your images appear on stage.

◆   Transition Xtras—consist of third-party plug-ins that add new transitions to the standard ones that come with Director.

◆   Xtra Cast Members—consist of a variety of items, including images, digital media, databases, and utility applications, which add different functionality to your movie. All Xtra Cast Members are accessed from the Insert menu and place a copy of the Xtra into the Cast. (Figure 7-56).

◆   Lingo Xtras—consist of added scripts and commands to add more control and flexibility to your interactive movies.

◆   Tools Xtras—consist of small applications that assist you in developing certain aspects of your movie, including simple animations and effects.

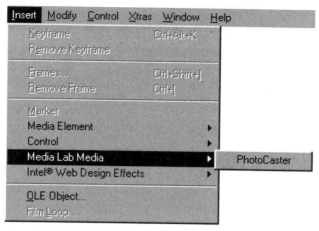

Figure 7-56   Xtra cast members are accessed from the insert menu rather than the Xtras menu.

Director 7.0 projectors and Shockwave movies can be designed to automatically download the required Xtras if available from a specific URL address. To select this option:

1. Select Movie from the Modify menu.

2. Select Xtras from the submenu.

3. Click on Xtras in the list to be downloaded from the Movie Xtras window (Figure 7-57).

4. Click the "Download if Needed" check box in the lower left corner.

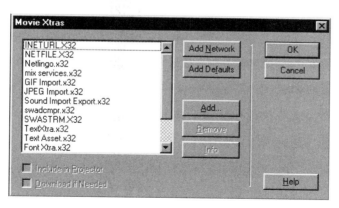

Figure 7-57   Movie Xtras window.

FINDING THE MOVIE XTRAS

Director can display a list of all the Xtras used in a movie to assist you in making sure that you have either bundled all the right Xtras internally with the movie or provided a separate folder containing the required Xtras. Enter the following command in the Message window:

```
put movieXtraList
```

This command will return a linear list of all the Xtras used in the current movie (Figure 7-58). Each of these Xtras will contain one of two possible properties displayed in the list:

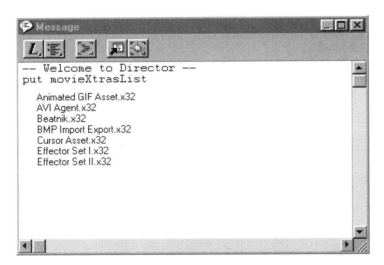

Figure 7-58   List of Xtras necessary for current movie.

◆   #name

◆   #packagefiles

The #name property describes the name of the Xtra used on the current platform. If a #name description does not appear, it means that the Xtra listed is only available on the current platform. The #packagefiles property describes an Xtra marked for downloading. This property contains a sublist of the #name and #version. Having this information is useful when gathering and making sure all of the required Xtras are available for packaging and distribution.

SUMMARY

This chapter included a mixture of "features to improve the capabilities of your programs" as a Director user. Obviously, there are millions of tips, tricks, and other techniques that I would love to put into this book, but I needed to focus on just a select few in order to keep this book down to a short, quick reference guide. The features listed here were features and techniques that I seem to find myself using on a wider base of projects. I hope they save you time and come in handy.

AVOIDING AUDIO AND VIDEO NIGHTMARES

I think one of the first experiences with video in multimedia came from a trade show where a company was demonstrating video on a computer. I saw a 10-second long video clip that was not much larger than a postage stamp with a frame rate (if you want to call it that) barely fast enough to be considered a video file and not a slide show.

Fortunately, things have come a long way. Today's technologies allow for full-screen, full-motion video and stereo-quality audio to be played off of a computer. As much as you would like to have these features in every multimedia project you create, it is not always feasible. The real challenge with developing for multimedia is presenting the best quality product within the limitations set by the guidelines of the project, especially within the system requirements that the client will be using. The challenge lies in knowing what guidelines you have to follow and how to then provide the best types of files for the project.

OPTIMIZING DIGITAL MEDIA FILES

Working with digital video and audio files takes time to set up the different attributes and compare the results. You will quickly learn what are the best settings for certain aspects and be able to make your adjustments accordingly. Unless your client tells you specifically how they want their audio and video files, you need to be the expert on knowing what will work best for their particular situation. Clients rarely understand that there *are* limitations when it comes to putting video and audio in their projects.

Rule #1

Always start with the best quality source material. The better the quality, the cleaner the end result.

Rule #2

Always start with the best quality source material. I'm sure you have heard this rule before, but it's true. Obviously, ideal situations don't always exist. But now that we are going to be compressing files, we need to understand that putting garbage in only gets you garbage out.

TEMPO CONTROLS

Initially, you might think the logical place to adjust the playback of sound and video files is with the Tempo slider found using the Tempo channel of the score. Actually, digital audio and video files are brought in to Director with the duration set when you compress the clips. Director does not have the ability to play back your files any faster or slower than the overall duration at which you created them, prior to import. Director looks at these files, calculates the total duration time, and plays back that file as best it can, to finish within that given duration. Director will not slow down the speed of digital audio or video files to make sure it plays every single frame of that file. Instead, Director is more concerned with the total duration time of the clip and achieving that time on playback. If the system cannot handle the frame rate that has been set for that file, Director will begin to randomly drop frames when it cannot keep pace with the set frame rate.

If your audio or video files are getting cut off:

◆   Your Director movie's tempo might be set too fast.

◆   You did not stretch the sprites far enough to span the necessary frames in the score.

◆   Implement a wait command using the properties in the tempo channel (Figure 8-1).

◆   Use the Wait for Cue Point setting.

Figure 8-1   Frame properties: Tempo window.

WAIT FOR CUE POINT

The Wait for Cue Point setting is designed to deal with the aggravation of digital audio and video files being chopped off or cut short. Using this feature instructs Director's playback head to wait at the frame where you have placed this command in the tempo channel for the media file you have selected to finish playing. This works regardless of how long or short you set the span of the sprite. Generally, the best place to set this command is on the last frame of the sprite. Otherwise, there will still be portions of that sprite that the playback head will still read after the audio or video file has completely played. Putting a wait for cue point command in an early part of a sprite can have some unpredictable behaviors. To add a wait for cue point command:

1. Place your media clip in the score.
2. Double-click on the tempo channel in the same frame where your sprite ends.
3. In the Frame Properties: Tempo window, click on the Wait for Cue Point button.
4. In the Channel pulldown menu, select the channel and sprite that is utilizing this command.
5. In the Cue Point pulldown menu, select End (this will command Director to wait for it to reach the end of the media file before continuing on).

WORKING WITH DIGITAL MEDIA FILES

Before you can consider using digital video or audio in your next project, you must first understand some basics about where to get these files and how to work with them. You may experience situations where, due to one factor or another, you need to sacrifice one facet of the file in order to meet the requirements of another technical specification. These types of trade-offs are frequent when you are developing for systems without the ideal performance levels. The more you begin to work with digital media files, the more you will be able to know which factors will be acceptable to reduce in order to execute the project successfully.

AUDIO

SOURCE MATERIAL AND DIGITIZING SOUND

With most of the projects you work on, your audio elements will not be ready for use in Director. It is very likely that you will be provided with the original raw elements that were used to record the sound initially. You will usually be working with some sort of audio media:

◆   Audio cassette

◆   DAT

◆   Compact disc

◆   MiniDisc

If this is the case, you will need to get access to some additional hardware and software for capturing the sound elements and converting them into digital media files on your computer system. You may also want to look into some type of audio editing program. I suggest adding a standard sound card (SoundBlaster or equivalent) that has audio capturing capabilities. Most consumer sound cards come with a stereo mini-connection input jack, output jack, and ports for your audio speakers. You can then use a basic audio editing program to record and manipulate your sound files, like Macromedia's Sound Edit 16 (Mac) or Sonic Foundry's Sound Forge XP that comes bundled with the Director Multimedia Studio package.

There are many books on the market that describe the best procedures for capturing and editing these sounds that go beyond the scope of this book.

Even if you are not the person responsible for capturing and editing the sound files, you will need to have an audio card installed into your system and a set of multimedia speakers (any brand is usually adequate) in order to play back the files.

FILE TYPES

Once you have the digital sound file in your system, you must make sure it is in the proper format for Director. Just as there are many different types of file formats for graphics and each have their own unique qualities, the same holds true for audio files.

Depending on the criteria of your projects (this goes back to the preplanning stages discussed in Chapter 2) you must be aware of the different characteristics and applications that each type of file holds unique to itself. Issues such as file types and cross-platform compatibility seem to pop up with projects that will use multiple operating systems. The good news is that Director supports most of the basic sound files for both the Macintosh and PC environments.

Director supports the following digital sound files:

♦ AIFF (most often used for cross-platform use)

♦ WAV (Windows)

♦ System 7 Sound (Macintosh)

♦ QuickTime (sound-only movies)

♦ Video for Windows (sound-only movies)

♦ MIDI

♦ SWA (ShockWave Audio)

If you are not sure what platforms you are going to be developing for, then go with a file format that can be used on more than one operating system or is supported by the computers that will be playing your movies, such as AIFF.

The decision for which file type to use depends on:

♦ Cross-platform compatability

♦ Xtra or plug-in required

♦ Type of capture card

♦ Type of editing software

♦ File conversion capability

Remember to flatten your Quicktime movies. This is what makes them applicable for cross-platform use.

CONVERTING FILES

As a multimedia developer you should have several different programs available for converting files, audio, and video. If you do not, I strongly recommend getting them. Many of these types of programs are not very expensive. There are some you can download from the Internet. Some of them are even free. One great program well worth purchasing from Terran Interactive is Media Cleaner Pro. This program is designed for converting and compressing most digital media files (Figure 8-2). Check out their web site at www.terran.com. Another audio program that is great to have in your arsenal is AudioToolbox, used to convert files to and from many different formats (Figure 8-3). Their web site can be reached at www.voiceinfo.com/products/toolbox/audtbx.asp.

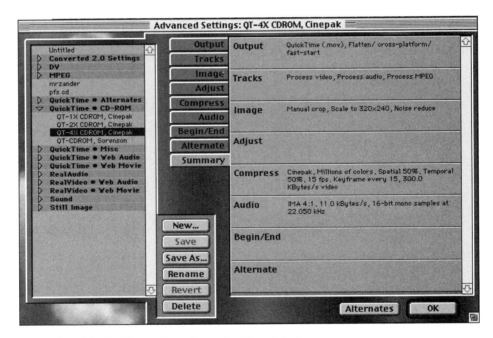

Figure 8-2   Media Cleaner Pro advanced settings interface.

Because video clips usually have audio with them, don't overlook your video editing programs (Avid and Premiere) as a means for editing, compressing, and converting your audio files. Some video editing packages come with outstanding audio formatting capabilities.

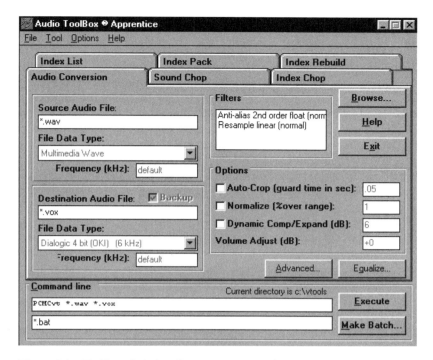

Figure 8-3   ToolBox digital audio conversion interface.

DOWNSAMPLING YOUR AUDIO FILES

The problem with audio when developing for multimedia is that it is not always necessary to have the highest quality audio. Limitations abound when working in the multimedia world, including:

◆   Limited storage space

◆   Delivery platforms

◆   Client's computer system

Because there are still many limitations in technology when developing for multimedia with Director, compress your files into the smallest possible size without reducing the quality beyond the acceptability level. Fortunately, compression for sound and downsampling rates hold up the quality of the original files remarkably well.

So What Is Sample Rate?

The quality, or clarity, of an audio file is a result of the sampling rate and bit depth. The higher the sample rate, the better the sound quality of the file. The better quality sound file is generated with the higher sampling rates because the sampling rate determines the highest frequencies that can be reproduced. Therefore, by lowering the sampling rate, the more high-end frequencies you will loose. That is why you can sample good quality voices at a lower sample rate than the New York Philhamonic. A more detailed explanation of sample rates and bit depth qualities goes beyond the scope of this book.

CD quality audio takes 44,100 samples or "snapshots" of the sound file for each and every second the sound is being captured. You will generally see this represented as 44.1 kHz. Rarely will you use audio files of this quality. In most cases you will want to sample down your file to 22.05 kHz or even 11.025 kHz. I generally try to use 22.05 kHz when possible. It is about half the size of the original file, yet retains enough of the quality to be acceptable for multimedia productions. A huge drop in quality occurs if you sample music at 11.025kHz. It sounds like you are listening to an AM radio station over a telephone. However, due to the more consistent dynamic range and minimal variation in tonal range, sampling voiceover narrations at this rate, especially female voices, seems to be acceptable for many applications. You can usually set the sample rate for your audio files when actually digitizing and creating them. Otherwise there are a number of third-party applications, including Media Cleaner Pro, that can downsample your files for you. Another variable that affects the clarity of your audio file is the bit depth. The best way to understand the difference is to take several different files, make two copies of each, convert one to 16-bit and the other to 8-bit, and then play and compare the same exact file at the different bit rates to hear the difference.

 16-bit files are of much higher quality than 8-bit sound files.

Mono or Stereo

Another factor that will determine the size of the file more than the quality of a file is whether it is saved as a mono or stereo file. The difference lies with the number of audio tracks and the placement (panning) of the sounds on those tracks. Keep in mind the application that you are creating this Director piece for. Most of the time you will opt for using a single-track mono sound file. This does not mean that your sound will only be played out of one speaker. It means that all of your sounds in your audio source will be played back out of both your left and right speaker equally. The advantage is that when storage space and delivery platforms are an issue, reducing the file size to a mono signal can help your Director movie play back with more efficiency.

IMPORTING

There are basically two ways Director looks at importing audio files:

1. Import the sound file into the Director movie internally. Importing sound files internally stores all of the sound information inside of the Director movie, within the cast file.

2. Link a cast member to a file that remains external from the Director movie. With this method, Director does not store any of the actual sound information inside the movie, only the link to the external file.

When you go to import a sound file into Director is when you will need to choose whether you prefer to have this sound file as an internal or externally linked cast member. Because internal sound files are stored inside the Director movie, they do increase the size of your movie. External files reside outside of your movie having very little effect on the size of the Director movie. Internal and external cast members are represented differently in the cast (Figure 8-4). To import a sound file:

Figure 8-4 Comparison of internally and externally linked file cast icons.

1. Use the Standard Import option located at the bottom of the Import Dialog Window.

2. Use the Link to External File option when importing external sound files (Figure 8-5).

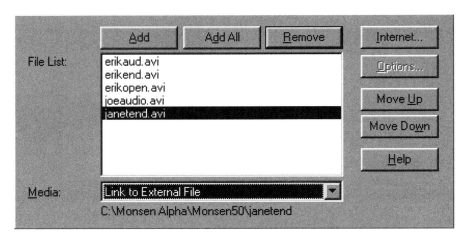

Figure 8-5   *Import digital media files using the Link To External option.*

 See Chapter 9 about packaging your Director movie with externally linked files.

GLITCHED SOUND FILES

You may have experienced a project where the sound files did not play back smoothly. This can be due to both the size and type of file you are using. Depending on the hardware configurations of your system and the size of your audio file, you may have some trouble with the sound file playing through completely without any pauses or hesitations. Internal sound files tend to play back better if they are kept short. Long internal audio files have a hard time playing back smoothly because the entire file is loaded into RAM before it begins to play. Director handles the playback of larger files better externally, but there may be a slight delay with initial playback. Director uses a feature known as file headers, which tells Director how large the external audio file is to assist with a quicker response for playback.

QUICK RESPONSE SOUNDS VS. LONG TRACKS

As a developer, you will quickly realize whether your sound files are responding to their commands and playing properly. If you are uncertain about which way to import your audio files, test them out both ways and see which works better for your application. Experiment with different size files (both in quality and duration). Director works with short quick sound files internally very well. A good example is any type of file that requires precise playback timing. It can load into memory quickly and play the instant you activate the command. Small file sizes, such as sound effects for rollovers and mouse clicks, are the types of files you need to keep internally. If you are planning on looping any audio files, these must be stored as internal cast members. Director will not be able to loop a file store externally.

Longer sound files such as voiceover narration and full music cuts will be too large to play from RAM smoothly (if at all on some older systems) and will have better playback capabilities coming from a hard drive or CD-ROM. For a recent project, the client wanted several testimonials to play under images of the products they use. Some of these audio files were several minutes long, too long to be used as internal cast members. You can see in Figure 8-6 how we set up the cast and the score accessing the external files.

Figure 8-6   Cast showing rollovers as internal sound files and long narrations as external files.

If you need to import long sound files instead of using external links to the files, consider breaking up the file into smaller sections. Find clean break points and edit your long clip into several subclips. This works especially well for voiceover, by cutting files at the end of a sentence or paragraph. Your system will perform much faster by working with smaller files. Cutting out the pauses in between sentences will help eliminate any noise or hiss that might occur during these silent periods.

REDUCING ACCESS TIME TO LINKED FILES

This technique works for both audio and video files. One way to decrease file access time comes from the naming structure of your files. Because the computer generally copies files in alphabetical order, naming associated files with a similar beginning structure can help reduce the amount of work and search time that your computer or CD-ROM's playback head needs to take to find the files. To demonstrate:

1. Name your Director movie "Test.dir."

2. When possible, name the audio files externally associated with this movie "Testaud1.aif" and "Testaud2.aif" (Figure 8-7).

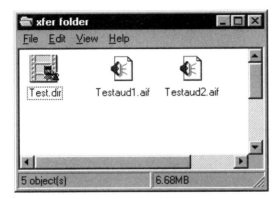

Figure 8-7   Using similar names to group files from the same project together.

These file names will be copied from a CD-ROM or other media and saved on the hard drive closer together, avoiding the drive's playback head from bouncing all over searching for files to play. This may not always be the most convenient or even preferred way of naming files; however, it can be used as a means of troubleshooting if the playback system is getting hung up trying to access files with random file names. For older systems, it can make enough of a difference on whether or not your movie will be able to play without any glitches.

Contiguous drive space on the end user's computer may not be available and results will vary, especially if their drive is full or has not been defragged recently.

LOOPING AUDIO

The shorter the duration and size of the actual file, and whether it is stored internally or externally, Director will be able to access and play the sound much quicker, no matter what type of system you are on. What can you do then if you need a music bed to span the duration of your entire presentation? The best way to handle this type of situation is to incorporate a shorter piece of music that can be smoothly looped without any abrupt connection points. Finding a piece of music that can be looped easily can be difficult. There are stock music libraries out there that contain short sound bites geared toward being looped in multimedia applications. Making it loop in Director is easy. To make an audio file loop:

1. Double-click on the sound file Cast Member or the sprite in the score.
2. The Sound Cast Members Properties window appears.
3. Click on the Options: Loop check box in the middle of the window (See Figure 8-8).

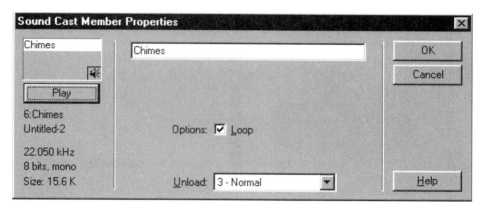

Figure 8-8   Loop check box located in the Cast Members Properties window.

VOLUME CONTROLS

The volume of sound files in the score of your Director movie are actually determined by the volume set in the computer sound level control. You can use Lingo controls to readjust the levels of your sound files. Why would you use Lingo commands? Lowering the speaker volume will not work if you need to adjust the levels for one of two sound files playing at the same time. Assume you were given two audio tracks to work with, a narration and a music bed. Suppose the music was too loud in comparison to the narrator's voice. The easiest way to fix this in Director is to alter the level of one of the audio channels. To set the volume for a particular channel use the following Lingo Script:

```
set the volume of sound whichChannel
```

You can enter a value of the volume between a range of 0 (mute) to a maximum volume of 255.

Example: If you wanted to change the volume of the sound in the score on Channel 1 to a medium level, use the following command:

```
set the volume of sound 1 to 140.
```

The lower you set the value of the volume of sound, the more likely you will hear noise or the hum of your speakers. Setting a value of the volume of sound too high, especially on a Windows system, may distort the sound.

CREATING ADJUSTABLE VOLUME CONTROLS

Every end user has his own comfort level for sound. Instead of you trying to program your movie to please everyone, why not give them the control to adjust the volume of the sound tracks? Figure 8-9 shows a screen from my company's demo CD-ROM of the volume remote control. This interactive feature uses a combination of some creative graphics and technical Lingo to adjust the volume of the movie in small increments. To design a functional volume control application in your Director movie:

Figure 8-9   Audio volume control.

1. In the graphics program of your choice, design at least two buttons (one for raising the volume, the other for lowering it).
2. Import your graphics and position them on the stage.
3. Select the sprite that will raise the volume.
4. Open a sprite script and type the following "if-then" Lingo command:

```
on mouseUp
   if soundLevel = 0 then
   set the soundLevel = 1
else
   if soundLevel = 1 then
   set the soundLevel = 2
else...
```

(and so on for as many increments as you would like to set).

The same script in reverse would then be applied to the down button sprite:

```
on mouseUp
    if soundLevel = 6 then
    set the soundLevel = 5
else
    if soundLevel = 5 then
    set the soundLevel = 4
else…
```

(and so on for as many increments as you set high, continue the pattern to return to 0).

Make sure to add the end command as the last line of your script.

In essence, this `if-then` statement tells Director to look at the value set for the volume of the movie. For each click of the mouse, update the variable to the next value. If raising the volume, add to the value to make the volume louder. If lowering the volume, decrease the value to soften the volume. A value of zero will mute the sound and play nothing but silence.

DIGITAL VIDEO VOLUME CONTROLS

The previous example affected the volume level for an audio channel of your movie. What happens if you need to adjust the volume levels for a digital video file in a sprite channel? You can use a Lingo command to adjust the volume of a particular sprite similar to the way you adjusted the volume of the entire audio channel. Use the following command to control the volume of a digital video movie cast member:

```
set the volume of sprite (channel number) to (value)
```

This command will tell Director which channel of your score the digital video sprite is in and adjust the volume accordingly. You can enter values for the volume range from 0 to 256. Zero and any value below will mute the sound completely.

Example: If we want to set a different volume for the Quicktime movie that is in Channel 4, we might use the following script:

```
set the volume of sprite 4 to 200
```

FADING SOUNDS IN AND OUT

Having a sound file start or end suddenly may seem too abrupt for your viewer. If you know the specific beginning or ending points of your sound file, you might choose to add the fade ins or fade outs back in your audio editing software, such as Sound Edit 16 or Sound Forge.

If you create your sound file in your audio editing program and choose to loop it inside of Director, it will always play with that fade-in effect. That is why it is better to create the fade-in and fade-out effects in Director using a simple Lingo Command.

Most of the time with an interactive movie, you will not know when you need a sound file to fade out. The timing is determined by the user's interaction with the program. For instance, you want a sound to fade out when the user clicks on a button to jump to another section of the movie. Without a Lingo script to tell the sound file to gradually fade out, the sound file will stop playing abruptly when the playback head jumps into a new section of the score. To add a Lingo script for fading in or fading out sprites in sound channels.

To fade a sound channel in, use the Lingo command:

```
sound fadeIn which channel
sound fadeIn which channel, ticks
```

Ticks are used as a timing element in Director. Each tick is equivalent to 1/60 of a second. Lingo can accept mathematical functions for certain commands (2*60 tells director to multiply 2 times the 60 tick counts to produce a 2 second effect).

Example: If you want to fade in a sound sprite in Channel 1 over the course of 3 seconds, you must write it in one of two ways:

```
sound fadeIn 1, 180 or sound fadeIn 1, 3*60
```

Some commands do not always work correctly on the first frame of your score. This is because certain Lingo commands call for an action to take place upon entering the frame. Director may not execute that command due to the fact that it may not be able to read that script ahead of Frame 1 and actually start playing your movie from the perspective of already being in Frame 1.

Workaround: To fade a sound file in, move everything else over one frame and begin on Frame 2. This way you can place your Fadein script into Frame 1 (Figure 8-10).

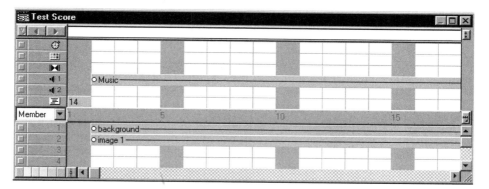

Figure 8-10   Placing the "Fade In" script before the other sprites allows Director to perform the task correctly.

The script command would read:

```
on exit frame
    sound fadeIn 1, 180
end
```

USING LINGO TO PLAY EXTERNAL SOUNDS

Director uses a Lingo command to play external audio files that are not in the cast. The command sound `playFile` tells Director which audio file to play and in which channel. These external sound files must be in either AIFF or WAVE file format. For example, to play a sound file named Jazz.aif in the music folder on the main hard drive on Channel 2, enter the following script:

```
sound playFile 2, "C:\music\jazz.aif"
```

Playing external sound files helps minimize the size of your Director movie. The advantage is that the external sound file minimizes the amount of RAM that is used to play the file, because external sound files do not get completely loaded into RAM in order to play. The disadvantage is that the computer can physically only read one file at a time from your disk. Director may experience a delay because it cannot load up or play any other cast members.

TURNING SOUND ON AND OFF

Some applications will require the ability to turn the sound on and off for a specific channel or for the entire movie. Most computer-based training projects that my company develops incorporate at least a button to toggle sound on and off. Example: A training application may be developed and installed on a large company's intranet site (Figure 8-11). The application may be used in a classroom-type environment where employees work on exercises at their own pace. Imagine 20 people in a room working on different sections of the program. Any audio playing would be a major distraction to the rest of the group. You will need to include audio capabilities for those employees who choose to work alone at their own workstation. Listening to the narrator's audio while maneuvering through the program would be very beneficial in this type of situation.

Figure 8-11   Button allows user to toggle the sound on and off.

To turn off all sound in a movie, use the `soundEnable` command:

```
set the soundEnabled to False
```

TOGGLE CHANNEL SOUND ON AND OFF

Use the following command to have Director play the opposite of the current setting. Therefore, if the current sound is set to off, this script will turn it on. If the current setting is on, it will turn the sound off.

```
set the soundEnabled to not (the soundEnabled)
```

Sometime you are going to need to shut off sounds in a particular channel as opposed to turning the sound off for the entire movie. Here is an example of when you may want to turn off the narration set on Channel 1 but do not want to turn off the sound effects and button clicks on Channel 2. For this type of situation, use the sound stop command:

```
on enterFrame
    sound stop 1
end
```

CONTROLLING SOUND FILES

Sound Edit and QuickTime files support cue points that are used to track the time and position of a sound file. This means Director can continue to play a file from the point at which it was stopped. If you hit play again, the sound file should continue from where it left off when it was stopped initially. AIFF and WAVE sound files do not support any control of time. If one of these files is stopped before it plays through completely, Director has no way to determine where and when a sound file was stopped, leaving you very little control of the file.

A good workaround for this problem is to associate WAVE and AIFF sound files as if they were audio-only digital video files. You can use Lingo commands to gain better control over these files. Use the `movieTime of Sprite` command to track where and when a file stopped playing so it can begin playing the rest of the sound file from that point.

```
set the movieTime of sprite (which sprite).
```

To gain even more control over your sound file by associating it as an audio-only digital movie file, you can control the rate at which the sound plays forward, backward, or just stops. Use the `movieRate` command to determine the playback property of a particular sprite in a designated channel. A value of 1 means the file will play at normal speed forward. A value of –1 means the file will play in reverse. A value of zero stops the movie. You can use other variables, such at 0.5 or 2.0, but the results will vary from system to system as to the playback capabilities of your file.

PuppetSounds

The more advanced your programming becomes the more you will need to rely on Lingo scripts to execute playing complex situations successfully. Puppet files are usually referred to as channels under Lingo's control. As with the rest of Director, Lingo continues with the metaphor of the theatre. Lingo acts as the puppeteer controlling the actions of the sprite in that channel.

The `puppetSound` command can be used either to play sounds or turn them off, overriding whatever is set in the sound channels of the score. The correct syntax for setting up a puppetSound is the command `puppetSound`, followed by a channel number, a comma, the name or number of the sound file cast member, and finally the cast in which it is associated with if there are multiple casts.

Example: `puppetSound 2, member "Music" of castLib "Audio Cast"`

This command is telling Director to play the sound file called Music from the cast called Audio Cast and play it in Channel 2 of the score. PuppetSounds are useful when you need to play a sound while a new movie is loading. This Lingo command enables Director to continue with one sound file while another is being activated. You need to keep these puppetSounds as internal cast members so they can be played directly from the RAM buffer. A typical puppetSound command (Figure 8-12) for having a sound file play while jumping to another section of the score is:

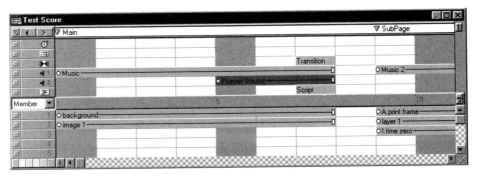

Figure 8-12   Puppet sound in audio Channel 2 allows for sound to continue playing during jumps to other sections of the movie.

```
On mouseUp
    puppetSound "Sound Effect"
        go to "Scene 3"
end
```

This script will tell Director when the user clicks and releases the mouse button to play a sound file called "Sound Effect" while the playback head jumps to the frame indicated by a marker called Scene 3. This type of command is very common and allows the movie to play more naturally. Otherwise, the playback of your movie might seem a bit jarring if no sound or visual is playing while Director navigates to the next section.

Once you put a puppetSound command in your script, no sound sprites play in that sound channel until the puppetSound finishes playing.

ADDING SOUND EFFECTS TO ROLLOVERS

You can enhance any interactive movie by adding sound effects in the right places. Warning: Do not go crazy adding them to everything that moves, shakes, or rattles. Too many sound effects can destroy a movie and make it "cheezy." Simple sound beeps and tones are pleasant to hear and do not detract from the content of the movie. Adding sound effects to buttons and other interactive links is very easy since the addition of Behavior with Version 6.

For best results, the sound file should be small in file size and be imported as an internal cast member.

Example: In Figure 8-13, add a thunder sound effect as a rollover feature to the logo sprite. If you are unsure of how to set up graphic rollovers, see Chapter 3.

To add a sound file as a rollover:

1. Import the sound effect file into your internal cast.
2. Open up the Behavior Inspector window for the sprite.
3. Choose New Behavior and name it.
4. In the Event column, select mouseEnter.
5. In the Action column, select Sound.
6. Choose Play Cast Member from the popup menu (Figure 8-14).
7. In the dialog window, select a sound cast member you want to activate when the mouse enters the area of the selected sprite.

    OR

    Use the actual Lingo scripts instead of behaviors.

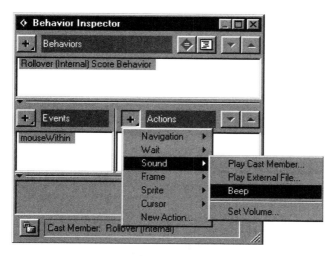

Figure 8-13   Adding sound effects to rollovers.

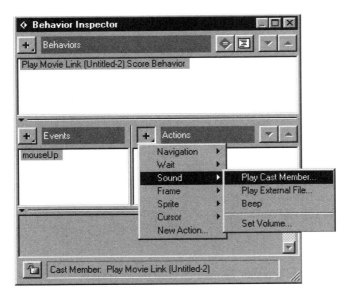

Figure 8-14   Applying the sound: Play Cast Member using the Behavior Inspector.

8. Enter the cast member script or sprite script for the small square image:

```
on mouseEnter
    puppetSound (name of cast member)
end
on mouseLeave
    puppetSound 0
end
```

Either way you choose to set up your commands, Director will play back the sound cast member (thunder sound effect) when the mouse rolls over the area of the logo. The way these behavior and Lingo commands work for rollovers, adding sound effects to mouse clicks and other interactions works the same. Simply substitute the `mouseEnter` commands with `mouseUp` commands. This way, when you click the left mouse button and release it, the selected sound effect will play.

 Due to the internal architecture of the machines, Macintosh systems handle the playback of multiple audio files better than Windows systems. To play back more than one sound file in a Windows system, you must have the Macromix.dll file installed on your system (Figure 8-15). This file mixes multiple audio files and plays them back as one file.

Figure 8-15   *The Macromix.dll file must be installed on your Windows system to play multiple sound files at once.*

If you have background music playing or other sounds and you want to add sound effects to rollovers, make sure to put the background sound file in audio Channel 2. This way both sound files will play, with only a slight pause on the puppeted rollover sound. Puppet sounds are automatically placed in audio Channel 1. Therefore, if you leave the background music in Channel 1, Director will cut off that sound in order to play the rollover puppet sound.

TWO-CHANNEL AUDIO

There are a few things that you should know about how Director works with audio files that can potentially save you hours of aggravation and frustration. Macintosh and Windows systems are made up of a different architectural structure for handling sound. The Windows architecture only has one channel of audio. Whichever program you are working in, Windows has to convert it down to one single track. Windows requires the use of a Director Dynamic Link Library file (commonly referred to as DLL files) called MacroMix.dll. This .dll file basically acts as a mixer to combine multiple layers of sound files from Director down into one audio track that windows can handle. Depending on the speed of the playback system, this usually causes some sort of noticeable delay.

MacroMix can combine Aiff and Wave digital audio files. It cannot mix digital audio files and the audio from digital video files at the same time. Director will play whichever sound file reaches the sound channel first. The other file will not begin until the first file has completely played through.

The Score in Director contains two sound channels. You can place your audio cast members into these channels to incorporate sound into your movie. As the playback head enters the frame of the sound sprite, Director begins to play that audio file as quickly as the system allows. More often on Windows platforms, when you start using both sound channels at the same time is when you might begin to experience some problems. Director for Windows has to mix the sound files for Channel 1 and Channel 2. The sounds will be able to play together as long as they are not both linked audio files (external files). The system is not capable of reading two large external files residing on the hard drive in two different locations at the same time. To hear both audio channels at the same time, at least one if not both of the files needs to be imported internally into Director. This way the internal files are loaded completely into RAM and play from there.

The two audio channels in the score do not function as right-channel/left-channel. Stereo audio files (if created that way) will play as one sprite occupying only one audio channel in the score.

To avoid running into the problem of having two externally linked audio files attempt to play at the same time while developing your movie, you may choose to set up your score by putting only internal sound files on Channel 1 and external sound files on Channel 2.

VIDEO

One thing about interactive applications that people still seem to be interested in is video. Although it has been a part of multimedia for years, the fact that video has been on such a slow pace evolving into the multimedia world with its ever increasing sized clips, it still has the ability to captivate people. Due to this tremendous size of each digital video file, movies need to be compressed in order to play back on a computer.

CAPTURING VIDEO CONTENT

Just like with audio, you need to capture, edit, and compress your digital movie files outside of Director. These digital video workstations can range in price from a few hundred dollars to hundreds of thousands of dollars. Depending on the applications you are developing and the requirements of the programs, you may only need access to one of the basic packages. If you have the privelege of working on a high-powered editing system, you will be able to work with better quality source footage and have more editing features available. Your source footage can come from almost any type of video tape, depending on the type of equipment you have available. To capture video clips into your computer, you will need:

◆ A video capture card

◆ Capture and editing software (i.e., Avid or Premiere)

◆ Multimedia capable high-speed hard drive

◆ Sound Card (to record audio)

The most common formats that you may experience:

◆ VHS

◆ S-VHS

◆ 8mm

◆ Hi-8

◆ ¾" U-Matic

◆ Beta SP

◆ DVC Pro

◆ DV

DIGITAL VIDEO APPLICATIONS

As a developer of multimedia products, you must be aware of the ever-changing formats that people are using to display and distribute the movies you design using Director. It is your responsibility to learn about the different requirements for your digital video files and which are the optimal formats to use. This type of information goes beyond the scope of this book, but nevertheless, will greatly impact your development capabilities using Director. Some common platforms today include:

◆ CD-ROM

◆ DVD-ROM

◆ Kiosks

◆ Websites

◆ Intranet training sites

SIZE AND FRAME RATES

Video frame rates are very similar to the frame rate of your Director movies with one exception. Where a certain frame rate may work fine for a Director movie, a digital video file may not be able to play back at that same rate. The cumbersome file size of digital video clips can cause some less powerful computer systems to hang up or skip frames. When you are capturing your video clips, the original source material (the video tape) is playing at approximately 30 frames per second (fps; 29.97 to be exact). Unless you have a extremely high-end computer with lots of RAM and high-speed hard drives, you will not be able to play back your video clips at 30 fps. Keep in mind, even if you are capable, the average end user's system will not be able to handle such a high frame rate. Most multimedia projects use somewhere around 15 fps. If you are processing these files to be played over the Internet, slow modem connection speeds may even require fewer fps. The standard frame rates are:

◆   30 fps—Output to any video tape format

◆   15 fps—CD-ROM quality

◆   10 fps—CD-ROM quality

◆   7.5 fps—Internet quality

◆   5 fps—Internet quality

The physical size of your video files will also affect the allowable frame rate. The larger the physical size of your video, the harder the computer will have to work to meet the demands of playing back the digital video file. You generally set the physical size of the video (how many pixels wide by how many pixels high) when you export your video out of your capture or editing program. Figure 8-16 shows you the setting controls that allow you to customize the exact configurations to optimize the performance of your video file. Programs like Movie Cleaner Pro allow you to recompress and reshape the properties of your digital video files.

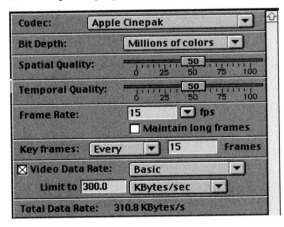

Figure 8-16   QuickTime export options.

MOVIE RATE

Use the `movieRate` command to determine the playback property for a digital video file in a particular channel. Using this Lingo command, you can control which way the video plays. A value of 1 means the file will play at normal speed forward. A value of −1 means the file will play in reverse. A value of zero stops the movie. Altering the speed and direction of your digital video files can be very memory-intensive on your system. The configuration of each system will determine the quality and smoothness at which the video clips play back. You can use other variables, such as 0.5 or 2.0, but the results will vary from system to system as to the playback capabilities of your file.

```
the movieRate of sprite (which sprite) to (value)
```

If you attempt to apply these settings and the digital video sprite is not currently on the stage, you will get an error message:

```
Not a digital video sprite"
```

TYPES OF FILES

When developing your Director movies, keep in mind the platform that it will be running on. This is especially important when using digital video files. Currently, QuickTime (.MOV) is the digital video standard for cross-platform multimedia development. When you create and compress your video to be a QuickTime file, there is generally an option to "flatten" your movie and make it cross-platform (Figure 8-17). Macintosh systems usually have the QuickTime extension loaded when you install the operating system, thus having the capability to play back QuickTime movies. QuickTime on Windows platforms, however, requires the QuickTime plug-in to be installed on the system.

You can download any of the QuickTime plug-ins and extensions for free at www.apple.com/quicktime.

Format:	QuickTime Movie ▼
☒ File Suffix:	.mov
☒ Flatten, Cross-platform, Fast-start	
☐ Compress Movie Header	
☐ Movie Information:	
☐ Create HTML:	

Figure 8-17   Using the Flatten Movie option allows digital video clips to be saved as cross-platform files.

If you are developing your Director movie for PC-compatible systems only, you may opt for using the Video for Windows format (AVI). This file format will play on any Windows system without the need for a plug-in. Whichever file format you choose, you will still need to compress your digital video file to make it playable on most computer systems.

 If you need to convert a QuickTime movie into an .AVI file or vice versa, there are some free and shareware conversion programs available for download off the Web. SmartVid is extremely easy to use and will convert your files in either direction. You can download this application from www.intel.com/sg/support/ technologies/multimedia/indeo/smartv.htm.

CODECS

As technologies change and the requirements to produce larger, cleaner video files increase, many different companies have entered the world of digital video compression for playback on your computer. The object: Get the best quality video playback while taking up the least amount of storage space. How is this possible? With the use of codecs.

A major innovation in the development of multimedia has been the development of codecs. Codecs have the ability to compress large files into the smallest possible components while conversely trying to preserve the best possible quality. Codec stands for **Co**mpression **Dec**ompression. Basically, you use one of these compression applications to compress your original digital video file to reduce its files size and optimize it for playback on a computer. Then, using that same type of technology, you play that file back on your computer with the assistance of the decompression portion of that application. There are several different formats available for you to choose from when creating your digital video files depending on the specifications of your project (Figure 8-18):

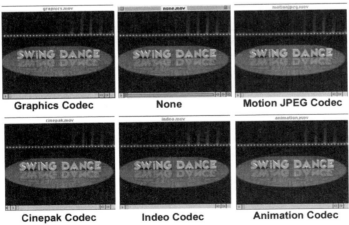

Figure 8-18   Comparison of different video codecs and quality settings.

- Cinepak
- Animation
- MPEG
- Indeo
- None
- Video
- Sorenson

Some of these formats require the codec to be installed on the system in order to view the movies.

A program like Terran Interactive's Media Cleaner Pro is one of the best compression applications available. You can choose to repurpose just about any type of digital media file into any format and custom set the quality that is required for your project. Generally, the settings used during the compression determine the quality of the entire digital video file. The decompression portion of the codec is usually a very small file, in the form of some type of plug-in or system extension, used as a key to unlock and play back the video file.

If you are distributing Director movies that require a codec to play back the movie compressed with a specific codec, either distribute a copy of the codec with the application or let your user know where they can obtain a copy. To find out more detailed information about codecs, check out www.CodecCentral.com.

Check with each vendor for information concerning distribution of their codecs and licensing issues. Most companies allow you to distribute it for free.

WORKING WITH MPEG

One of the file formats growing in popularity is MPEG. Although MPEG is not one of Director's standard type of cast members, it can be played with the assistance of MPEG drivers. These drivers come in the form of hardware acceleration boards or software-only controllers. Note: The hardware boards offer better quality and playback performance.

There are now some companies providing Xtras that contain an MPEG decoder so that you can distribute your Director movies with MPEG quality video and only need to make sure the Xtras folder is provided with the projector and individual MPEG files. Companies like Visible Light have created easy-to-use Drag-N-Drop Xtras or customizable parameter windows to optimize the performance of your digital video files (Figure 8-19). Check out Visible Light's OnStage MPEG Xtras at www.visible_light.com for more information.

MPEG movies are not internal or linked to Director, but instead use a type of control referred to as MCI calls. You can set up these calls via Lingo commands:

```
mci "play" && the pathname & "videofile.mpg"
```

QuickTime 3.0 for Windows does not support playing MPEG digital video files, unlike QuickTime 3.0 for Macintosh, which does support MPEG playback.

Although MPEG is a standardized file format, the different brands of hardware and software decoders handle the playback of your digital video files differently. This can lead to problems in the implementation and testing phases of your project. Be sure to test your movie on a system that uses the same type of MPEG decoder software or hardware that will be used by the end client.

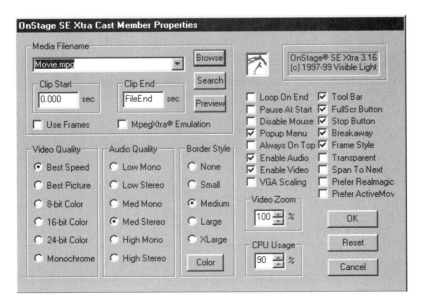

Figure 8-19   Settings Properties screen from Visible Light.

IMPORTING DIGITAL VIDEO FILES

Importing digital video files into Director is the same process as any other media element.

1. Choose Import from the File menu or click the Import icon on the tool bar (Figure 8-20).

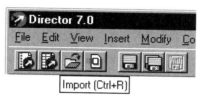

Figure 8-20   Import icon located in the toolbar.

2. Using the standard file hierarchy to locate the correct location, select the file you want to import (Figure 8-21).

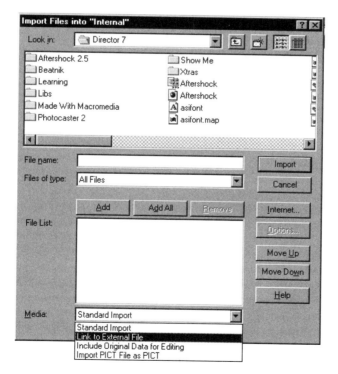

Figure 8-21   Select file to import.

3. Click the Add button to bring the selected file into the bottom window. Or, click the Add All button to move all of the files within that folder.

4. Click Import.

The only difference between importing still graphics and digital video files is that these digital video files are imported as linked files and remain outside of the regular Director movie. Director indicates these cast members are linked files by displaying an ellipses in the cast member icon (Figure 8-22).

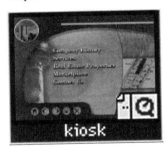

Figure 8-22   *Linked External Cast Member icon.*

Because Director references a digital video clip as an external file and is not stored inside of the Director movie, any changes made to that file will be reflected inside your Director movie as it plays back that file, even after it has been imported.

DIGITAL VIDEO CAST MEMBER PROPERTIES

It is important not to overlook the cast member properties for digital video files for information, playback characteristics, and setting options that affect the display and performance of your videos. To open the Digital Video Cast Member Properties window:

1. Select a digital video file in the cast.

2. Select Cast Member from the Modify menu.

3. Choose Properties. The Digital Video Cast Member Properties window appears.

   OR

4. Use the keyboard shortcut keys: Control-I for Windows; Command-I for Macintosh.

VITAL STATISTICS

The Digital Video Cast Member Properties window (Figure 8-23) is very helpful for finding out information about your video file and using this information for troubleshooting problems with any video playback errors. The top and left-hand side of the window displays all the basic information about your clip:

1. Cast member name
2. Path (where external file is residing)
3. Cast nember number
4. Total duration of the clip (time)
5. Physical dimensions (size) in pixels
6. Total file size (storage space)

Using a combination of these factors along with a general understanding of what variables affect the playback of digital video clips in Director, you will be able to troubleshoot common problems associated with the improper playback of your digital video files.

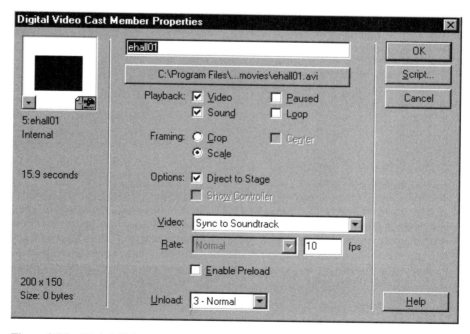

Figure 8-23   Digital Video Cast Member Properties window.

SEPARATING SOUND AND VIDEO FROM DIGITAL VIDEO FILES

The playback properties include the option to independently choose whether or not you want to display the video or hear only the audio portion of the file. Deselecting video is a great way to use the audio portion from a video clip without having to create a separate audio file. With the video file being external, it will not increase the size of your Director movie.

LOOPING VIDEO CLIPS

The only way to have a digital video file loop is to select the loop option in the Digital Video Cast Member Properties. Even if you place a digital video sprite in a frame that is set to loop with a Lingo script, the video file will only play once (Figure 8-24):

```
on enterFrame
    go to the frame
end
```

This script will keep the playback head in that particular frame, giving the user an infinite amount of time to interact with any navigational elements. However, the digital video file will only play through once and then stop.

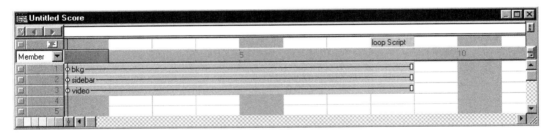

Figure 8-24   Digital video sprite only plays once even with script set to loop.

PAUSING VIDEO

Director begins to play a digital video file once as the playback head enters into the frame containing the video sprite. Some situations may require having control over when the digital video file begins to play. To have the video start in pause mode and not play until otherwise instructed, select the Pause option in the Digital Video Cast Member Properties. With this option selected, the video display area will hold on the first frame until a play command is activated (see Video Controllers).

SHOW CONTROLLER

The controller option determines whether you want to have a video control slider under the video display area in your movie. Some applications will find having this feature available onscreen very useful (Figure 8-25). Training programs and instructional design applications that have the video controller directly onscreen allow the user to pause the video at any point, rewind to review a section, or skip ahead to any point and play again.

Only QuickTime movies have the option to select and deselect the control slider in the properties window. If you want to have a control slider available on video for Windows (.AVI) files, you need to design and implement custom Lingo scripts. You can also use the Widget Wizard Button Library located in the Xtras menu to put together some graphical navigation controls to combine them with video control behaviors to control your digital video clips.

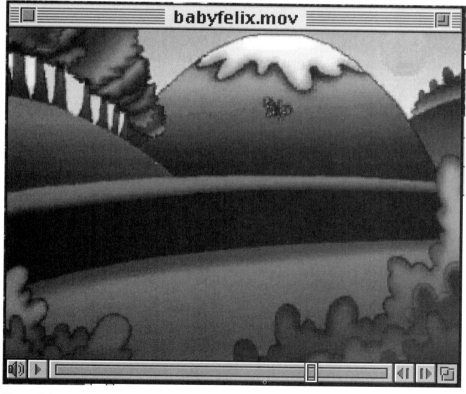

Figure 8-25   Digital video clip with control slider (see Color Figure 22).

TROUBLESHOOTING WITH THE PROPERTIES WINDOW

Use this window to determine errors or inconsistencies between the playback of your digital video files (Figure 8-26). Some basic problems include:

1. Verify that the file is in the proper external folder (check the file path).
2. If you do not see video, check to see if Playback: Video is selected.
3. If you do not hear audio, check to see if Playback: Sound is selected.
4. If video displays appear to be different sizes, check the dimensions of each file. See if either file has been cropped or resized.
5. If the video appears to be dropping frames on playback, check the files size, frame rate, and sync to sound.

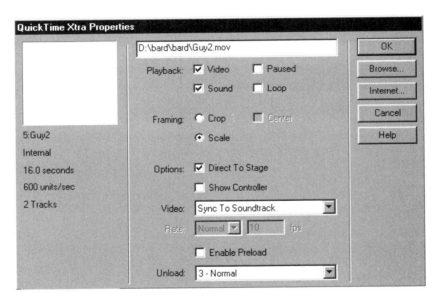

Figure 8-26   *Digital Video Cast Member Properties window.*

TRANSITIONS AND DIGITAL VIDEO FILES

Digital Video files are probably the most memory-intensive portion of any multimedia project. Adding transitions to the score greatly increases the strain on the system's playback capabilities. Depending on the throughput speed on your system and the amount of RAM installed, less powerful systems may experience some flickering with the video clip if you try to play a transition and a digital video file at the same time.

WAITING FOR DIGITAL VIDEO FILES TO FINISH

Playing back digital video files in Director can be as easy as dragging the imported cast member onto the stage or into the score and playing your movie. Make sure that the sprite spans enough frames to play back the entire duration of the digital video file. To check the total length of the file, open the cast member properties window. You may need to stretch the sprite to cover more frames in that channel. Using more score frames does not increase the file size or memory requirements of your Director movie. There are several ways to control the playback of your digital video files to ensure that the entire duration will be played:

1. Extend the length of the sprite to span more frames (Figure 8-27).
2. Slow down the tempo of your Director movie (a frame rate of 1 fps will require less frames).
3. Use a tempo control such as "Wait for Cue Point...[End]" (see the section "Wait for Cue Point" in the beginning of this chapter).
4. Use frame script Lingo commands.

Using the Wait for Cue Point option will not allow any interactive controls to be active while the digital video is playing. Director will record these events and perform them once the movie is completed. Instead, try using a Lingo command to allow the digital video to completely play while interactive controls still function.

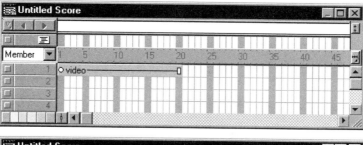

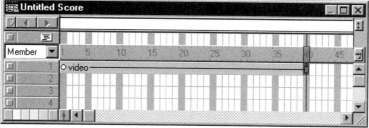

Figure 8-27   Extending the digital video sprite to span more frames.

LINGO COMMANDS FOR DIGITAL VIDEO FILES TO FINISH

To this point we have discussed several reasons why your Digital video clip may not completely play for its full duration or even play at all. Advanced developers usually choose to control the flow of their movies using Lingo. To set your digital video sprites to play through completion:

Figure out the total duration of the digital video file.

Enter the following frame script command:

```
on exitFrame
  if the movieTime of sprite (sprite number) < (number of ticks) then
    go to the frame
end
```

This Lingo script is instructing Director's playback head to determine whether the exact time (in increments of ticks, with one tick equalling 1/60th of a second) is less than the total duration of the sprite specified. If that value is less than the total duration entered (number of ticks) then go back and loop in that frame until the movieTime value equals or exceeds the total number of ticks set in the equation. When it reaches that number, the digital video file should be done playing and the playback head can continue on into the next frame.

SIMULTANEOUS INTERACTIVE CONTROLS AND DIGITAL VIDEO PLAYBACK

If you need to have access to the interactive buttons and navigational links on your screen while a digital video clip is currently playing, you will need to use a frame script that will allow these events to occur. Enter the frame script:

```
on exitFrame
    if the movieRate of sprite (sprite number) = 1 then
      go to the frame
end
```

This command allows the user to maintain control of the interactive buttons and links on the current screen, while continuing to play the video until it is complete. When the video finishes playing (movieRate is reached or True in this case), the script instructs the playback head to "go to the frame" or continuously loop in the current frame until the user selects one of the navigational choices available on the screen.

INTERACTIVE SCROLLING THROUGH DIGITAL VIDEO FILES

This command offers the user control to scroll through the video clip either ahead or in reverse a few frames or a few seconds at a time (Figure 8-28).

1. Set the digital video playback to pause. You can do this either for the entire movie upon entering the frame by selecting Paused in the Digital Video Cast Member Properties window or use a Lingo script to pause the movie (movieRate of sprite [channel number] to 0).

2. Apply either sprite or cast scripts for the navigational buttons (i.e., forward and backward arrows).

3. Enter the following script to scroll forward through the digital movie by 2-second intervals:

```
on mouseUp
    set the movieTime of sprite to 1 to (the movieTime of sprite 1) + (60*2)
    updateStage
end
```

This script is telling Director to advance through the digital video sprite in Channel 1 to the current time/position of the video plus 2 seconds (60 ticks per second times 2 = 2 seconds). UpdateStage instructs Director to refresh the image on the screen and show the new frame of the digital video clip. To create the script for a back button, simply change the plus sign to a minus sign. You can set the variable for how many seconds or frames you want the video to change from with the click of these buttons by entering a different value in the last part of the math equation.

Figure 8-28　Digital video clip with virtual fast forward and rewind controls.

◆   60*2 = 2 seconds

◆   60*1 = 1 second

◆   60*5 = 5 seconds

EDITING VIDEO IN DIRECTOR

A glitch at the end of a file or a white frame flash of video unexpectedly occurs from time to time. Don't panic. Director has the ability to do some simple editing by cutting and pasting video frames without having to go back to your raw materials and compress new files.

To edit a movie:

1. Select the cast member you want to edit.
2. Select Video from the Window menu (Control-9 for Windows; Command-9 for Macintosh). This automatically opens a video preview window.
3. Select the frame(s) you wish to copy or cut out.

   To select a continuous range of frames:

1. Go to the first or last frame that you want to select.
2. Hold the Shift key down.
3. Use the Step Forward or Step Backward buttons located at the bottom of the window or drag the slider to select the other end. The highlighted region turns black indicating that this is the section you have selected (Figure 8-29).

Figure 8-29   Highlight area in control strip to mark area to be edited (see Color Figure 23).

4. Choose Cut Video, Copy Video, or Clear Video from the video editing commands in the Edit menu (Figure 8-30).

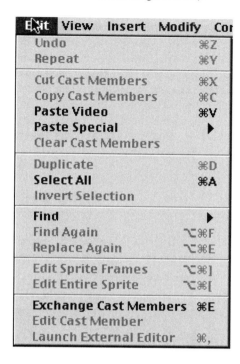

Figure 8-30   Cut Video, Copy Video, and Clear Video selections found in the Edit menu.

To paste frames into a video file:

1. While still in the Video window, use the Previous and Next Cast Member buttons to select a different video cast member that you want to insert or paste in video frames from a video clip you previously cut or copied.

2. Using the Slider or Step keys, select the frame prior to where you want to paste in the new video portion.

3. Choose Paste Video from the Edit menu.

If you are inserting frames into a video file, Director will create a new cast member and prompt you to enter a new file name.

RESIZING AND RESHAPING VIDEO FILES

The cut and paste video features are a way of altering the duration of your video clip. Director also allows you to alter the viewing size of your video display area. The scale feature will take the entire size of the original video file and stretch it horizontally and vertically in any rectangular form while always showing the entire content area. Figure 8-31 shows three different clip sizes: original, 50%, and 150%. The crop feature works in a different way. The actual size of the content inside the visible area never changes size, just the borders around the video clip. Cropping your video will actually alter the aspect ratio of the clip's visible area. You can crop out part of the image on the side of the screen or make a letterbox movie effect (Figure 8-32). You can crop the size of the original video file to make it smaller, eliminating portions of the visible area; however, you cannot crop a file to be larger than the full size of the original video file.

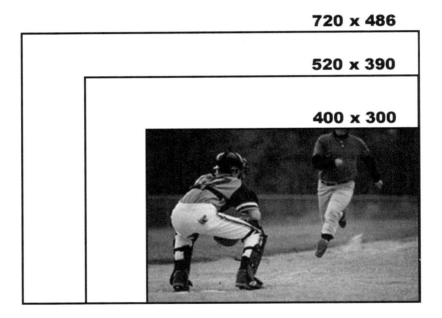

Figure 8-31   Comparison of resized video clips.

Figure 8-32 Use the crop feature to remove unwanted portions of the video clip.

TO SCALE A DIGITAL VIDEO FILE

1. Select the video cast member you wish to resize.
2. Click on the Cast Members Properties button in the score or right click (Windows) or Option-click (Macintosh) the cast member. Select Cast Member Properties from the popup menu (Figure 8-33).

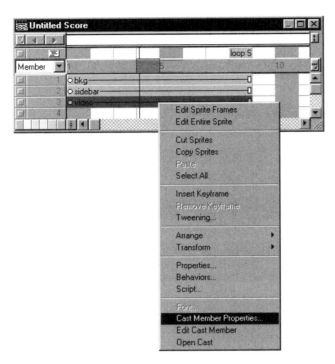

Figure 8-33   Cast Member Properties button located in the score.

3. Select the Scale option in the Digital Video Cast Members Properties window.

4. Click OK.

5. Select the sprite in the Score window.

6. Use the handle surrounding the video sprite on your stage to manipulate the size of the viewing area.

TO CROP A DIGITAL VIDEO FILE

1. Select the video cast member you wish to crop.

2. Click on the Cast Members Properties button in the score or right click (Windows) or Option-click (Macintosh) the cast member. Select Cast Member Properties from the popup menu.

3. Select the Crop option in the Digital Video Cast Members Properties window. Click Center if you want the center point of your video to be the registration point from which you crop the movie (Figure 8-34).

Figure 8-34   Registration points determine the center point when cropping screen sizes.

4. Click OK.

5. Select the sprite in the score window.

6. Use the handle surrounding the video sprite on your stage to manipulate the amount of cropping you wish to alter the viewing area.

Director requires a lot of RAM to adjust digital video files. For best results, size and set the video properties during the editing, exporting, or compression stage before you import them into Director.

RESHAPING VIDEO FILES

As an AVID Certified Instructor, trying out new video editing tricks and techniques is a passion of mine. In a high-end video editing system, designing these interesting video special effects is easy. Most multimedia programs present their video clips in the standard rectangular shape that they come in when the digital video files are made. Director's unique layering capabilities and support of digital video files allow you to create some new ways to present your video clips. Figure 8-35 shows video clips not in the standard rectangular form. Some are circular while others actually have portions of other graphics covering an area of the video screen. These types of effects are relatively easy to create, and yet catch the attention of every viewer.

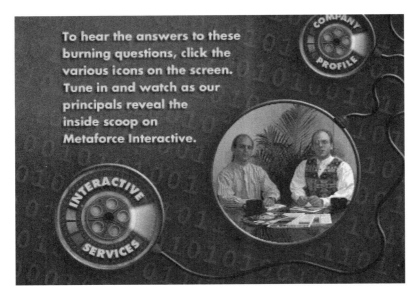

Figure 8-35   No more rectangular video displays; video clips can be displayed in just about any shape (see Color Figure 24).

MASKING YOUR VIDEOS

The trick to getting odd-shaped video files is achieved not by affecting the actual shape of the video, but instead manipulating the images layered over the video file. If you experience the video display always on top of the other images, regardless of which channel you put your sprites in, deselect the Direct to Screen option in the Cast Member Properties window. This will give the digital video files the same layering capabilities as any other sprite (Figure 8-36). To mask your video files:

1. Select the video cast member in your cast that you wish to manipulate.

2. Choose Cast Member from the Modify menu at the top of the screen and select Properties from the popup menu.

3. Deselect the Direct to Screen option.

4. Click OK.

5. Drag the video cast member to the proper position on the stage.

6. Create or import a new cast member to be used as a mask or overlay graphic. Make sure it is large enough to cover the entire video image. The shape of this image you create will determine which portions of the video clip are visible and which parts are covered.

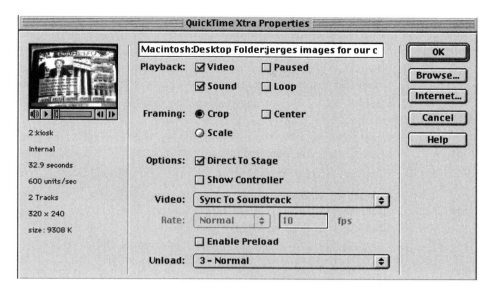

Figure 8-36   Direct to Screen option displays the digital video clip on top of all other images, regardless of its layer in the score.

Deselecting the Direct to Screen option allows you to layer digital video files as you would other sprites in the score. Where the video is placed in the score in relation to sprites in the other channels will determine what is displayed above and below the video.

If the overlay graphic contains no white in it other than the area that will ultimately shape the video, move on to Step 6. If you are planning to create a custom mask (as discussed in Chapter 5), move on to Step 11.

7. If you have not done so, create the area on the overlay graphic in white for which portion you want to cut out in order to display the video clip.

8. Place the overlay graphic cast member in the channel directly below the video sprite in your score (remember how layers work in the score; a sprite in Channel 3 will be displayed on the stage over a sprite in Channel 2).

9. Move the overlay graphic into the correct position on the stage completely covering the rectangular video display area.

10. Apply a background transparent ink to the sprite. This will make the white portion of the overlay graphic transparent and the video play in the shape of the cutout area.

11. Rewind and play back your movie. Only the portion of the video clip that was positioned underneath the transparent (white) area of the graphic should be visible.

12. Double-click on the overlay graphic cast member to open it into Director's Paint window.

13. Choose Duplicate from the Edit menu. The Duplicate function automatically creates a new cast member and displays the cloned copy in the Paint window.

14. Click on the Transform Bitmap option under the Modify menu.

15. Change the color depth to be 1-bit. This will change the graphic into a black and white image.

16. Click the Transform button.

17. Use the paintbrush and other tools to clean up the image. Use black to paint the portion of the image you wish to leave opaque (visible). The areas that you leave white will become transparent.

 The more intricate the design of your object, the more careful you will have to be when filling in the areas to be masked in order to get a clean cut out shape.

18. Close the Paint window when you are finished.

19. For the mask effect to work, you must place the new black and white cast member immediately following the original in the cast (Figure 8-37). There cannot be any other cast members or empty frames between the original image and the black and white image.

20. Drag the original overlay graphic cast member and place it in the channel directly below the video sprite in your score.

21. Move the overlay graphic into the correct position on the stage completely covering the rectangular video display area located directly below.

22. Apply the Mask Ink effect to the sprite. This will make all of the white portion in the cloned overlay graphic transparent to see the video play in the shape of this custom cutout area.

23. Rewind and play back your movie. Only the portion of the video clip that was positioned underneath the transparent (white) area of the graphic should be visible.

Figure 8-37   Mask cast member placed directly after original cast member.

DIRECT TO STAGE

Direct to Stage is a feature that Director uses to allow QuickTime and Video for Windows controls to drive the playback performance of your digital video files. Use Direct to Stage to get the best possible frame rate from your digital video files in Director. But with all good things come the bad.

Disadvantages for using Direct to Stage:

1. Digital video files always appear on top of all other images, no matter on which channel of the score they exist.
2. Ink effects are not applicable.

Turn off Direct to Stage in the Cast Member Properties to layer your digital video behind other sprites or apply ink effects (except matte ink) to the video file itself.

The Direct to Stage option needs to be turned on in order to use QuickTime digital video files in Director on the Windows platform. Video for Windows (AVI) files on a PC-platform and QuickTime on a Macintosh system do not require Direct to Cast to be active.

EXPORTING DIGITAL VIDEOS

Director is a great program to design and build your animations and interactive movies. When you are finished, you can export your entire Director movie out as a single digital video file. There are a few pitfalls to keep in mind. Chapter 9 covers in detail all the exporting options and limitations that Director has when outputting your movie as a digital video file.

PACKAGING EXTERNAL FILES FOR DISTRIBUTION

Because Director only imports a link to external audio and video files, you must remember to include these files when you distribute your Director project. See Chapter 9, It's All Finished … Now Deliver It, for more details on packaging your external digital video and audio files.

TEST, TEST, TEST

Time is generally everyone's biggest enemy. I have yet to meet a multimedia developer who works 9 to 5.

However, 2:00 a.m. last-minute changes for the client are no excuse for not taking the proper time to go through and test your work, especially on other systems. If you have access to the actual system(s) that you are going to be running your movies on, then that is the ideal true testing situation. You will know right off the bat whether the hard work you have just killed yourself to complete has paid off. Testing is especially true when you are working with digital audio and video files. These files tend to be the most notorious for causing headaches. They require more detail when creating them and even more detail trying to play them back. Every system out there seems to be able to play basic Director animations of bitmapped images. Generally, color palettes or monitor display settings are to blame for more of the problems with graphics not playing correctly. But when it comes to audio and video media, the files are much larger, require more RAM and fast access hard drives, and usually need some type of media player installed in the system. Depending on which codecs you choose to compress your files, you may require the use of additional hardware or software applications in order to even open the media files.

SUMMARY

As computer and television technology merge closer together, people want to see and hear the full-screen, full-motion video clips and the thunderous quality of surround sound audio on their laptops. (I'm not talking about little postage stamp sized files.) What is more scary than these people's request is that the manufacturers are developing the technology so that soon you will be able to interactively see and hear any video or audio file available. This Video-On Demand concept is partially here today and will soon be the way everyone watches programming. There are millions of clients who want to use the features and capabilities of multiple audio and high-quality video. Now, through the use of Director, you can design your best applications using one of the numerous audio and video files in your next production.

chapter 9

IT'S ALL
FINISHED ...
NOW DELIVER IT

Once you have finished importing files and animating sprites, it's time to show the world ... well, almost. There are a few things that you should be aware of on how best to get your Director movie to the end user. Right now your raw Director movie (.DIR file) is inherently cross-platform compatible. This means you can take any Director movie you have created and open it on any system that has Director installed on it. Whether you built your movie on a Windows-based platform or a Macintosh-based system, Director movies can open on either platform. Be aware, however, movies that link to files that are platform specific (such as .avi digital video files) will not be able to play on the opposite system.

You can open movies created on the same version automatically. Movies created in a lower version need to be converted and saved when bringing them into a higher version of Director. A confirmation dialog box will appear prompting you to convert the file (Figure 9-1).

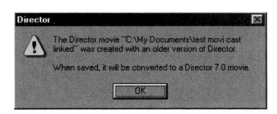

Figure 9-1   Confirmation dialog box when upgrading Director movie to new version.

295

PREPARING YOUR MOVIE FOR DISTRIBUTION

Distributing your Director movie "as is" requires the end user to have a compatible version of Director installed on his system. Obviously, the majority of your viewing audience will not have a copy of Director on their systems. Distributing your original Director movie in this format is not recommended. People who do not have Director will not be able to play your movie. People who do have Director will be able to open your files and make changes to it. This can lead to many serious problems down the road. This chapter describes the best solutions for finalizing and distributing your movie to the end user.

Most of the concepts covered in this chapter discuss what options you have with your finished movie. These concepts should be considered during the developmental phase of your project, not just when your movie is complete. Preplanning some of these steps will ensure the best results with the fewest headaches in the end.

TESTING YOUR MOVIE

Do not wait until your movie is complete before deciding to test your application to make sure everything is functioning properly. One of the worst feelings you can experience while authoring a program is to have it not work when you think you are done. Testing is immensely important if you are designing applications to run on both Windows and Macintosh platforms. Throughout the process of your development, continually check that the files and functions work properly on both systems. As you import files, make sure graphic images appear correctly and digital media files play the same way inside of Director as they do outside of Director (Figure 9-2). If not, bring your files back into their respective editing applications and see if they look or play correctly there. It's possible to have files corrupted while being compressed, converted, or transferred between locations. Another reason to test your movie often is to make sure external files do not lose their links with their associated cast member. Many times externally linked files are moved to a different location on your system and Director is unable to match up the proper link. If you move these external files, you must relink or reimport these files back into your Director movie. If you do not recreate the links before you play the movie, a window will appear prompting you to manually select the location of the unlinked file (Figure 9-3).

Figure 9-2 *Cast member image will show whether or not a graphic file has been successfully imported properly.*

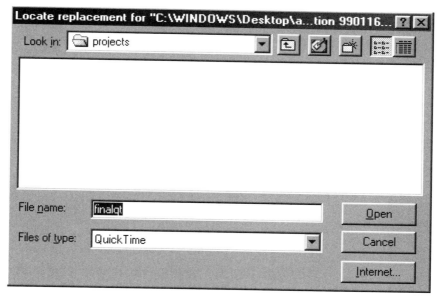

Figure 9-3 *A "Where Is..." file prompt appears if director has lost its link with external files.*

Testing your movie regularly can be very crucial when you begin to develop applications that will be delivered via the Internet. Here you do not have the same control of knowing which platform the end user will be viewing your program on, let alone the performance level of that system. That is why it is so important to test frequently on multiple types of machines and keep track of how your movie performs on each system. For more information about creating your movies for the Internet, check out Chapter 10, Shock It for the Web.

SYSTEM REQUIREMENTS FOR PLAYBACK

Every movie you create and distribute should contain a list (either on the packaging or as a read_me file) for the end user to review before trying to launch your application. This list will probably vary for each project you create based on the size of the program and the type of media it contains. If you are using simple graphics and text created inside of Director, you will be able to run this application on a low-end computer containing at least the following minimum requirements:

For Windows:

1. 386/33 MHz processor
2. 8 MB RAM
3. Windows 3.1, 95, 98, or NT 3.5.1 operating system
4. Enough hard drive space required to fit your project

For Macintosh:

1. 68020 processor
2. OS 7.0
3. 8 MB RAM
4. Enough hard drive space required to fit your project

These system requirements will hardly do any movie justice. I highly recommend increasing the specifications in all areas to the highest degree possible while still maintaining the system's lowest common denominator required by the end user. Director is a memory-intensive program and functions much better with more RAM, faster processors, and better supporting peripherals. Advanced applications will probably require:

1. Pentium (Windows) or PowerPC (Macintosh) Processors
2. 16 MB RAM or more
3. CD-ROM drive
4. High-resolution monitors
5. Graphics accelerator cards with extra video RAM
6. Sound card and multimedia speakers
7. Any required software, plug-ins, or extensions (i.e., QuickTime)

The faster the system, the better performance you will experience when playing back movies that contain multiple animations of large-sized sprites and digital video movie clips.

DIFFERENT WAYS TO SAVE YOUR WORK

Saving your work is something that I do not believe I have to explain. I do however want to explain the different ways Director allows you to save your movies.

1. Save
2. Save As
3. Save and Compact
4. Save All
5. Save as a Shockwave Movie

Each method provides a slightly different purpose when saving your Director movie. The Save feature works by adding new information to the end of the existing file, never actually deleting the place holders of the unwanted information, as new changes are made to your movie. This process takes very little time but can actually increase the file size of your movie. This method is fine to use during the developmental stages of your movie (and I highly recommend doing this often), but use the Save As or Save and Compact command when saving the final version. Both of these methods rewrite a completely new file. The Save As command optimizes your file while allowing you to save the movie under a different name, replace the existing file, or move it to a new location. The Save and Compact command allows you to only replace the existing file, but goes inside to clean out any unwanted information. To optimize your movie:

1. Open any Director movie.
2. Click on Save and Compact from the File menu. A progress bar will appear on your screen, indicating the clean-up process of your file. The smaller the file, the quicker this process takes.

The Save All command allows you to save a copy of all of your files at once. This is a time-saving feature so that you do not have to select each window and save each cast one at a time. With the release of Director 6, the Save as a Shockwave Movie command has been added to the File menu. This function allows you to save and compress your movie for use on the internet. Shockwave movies are indicated with a .DCR file extension after the name. These compressed files can be used over the Internet or played on a stand-alone media platform as long as the Shockwave plug-in has been installed on the user's system.

 Because Director only has limited undo capabilities, use the Save As function to make back-up copies of your movie before trying out a new feature. If you change your movie beyond a quick repair, delete the current file that got messed up and open one of the backup copies you saved to pick up where you left off before making any alterations (Figure 9-4).

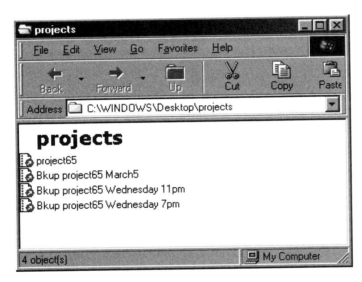

Figure 9-4   Use the date, time, or version number when naming files to help identify the correct version.

CLEANING UP DIRECTOR MOVIES

Updating your Director movie is one way to optimize it in order to be used in the correct format and have the most up-to-date files. The Update Movies option allows you to convert older versions of Director movies (from Version 5 to 6 and 6 to 7) and casts to the latest version you have on your system. It also cleans up your files to keep only the necessary files used in your movie, removing all of the unwanted information. Consolidating your movies using the Update Movies function also reduces the overall file size of your movie by eliminating any garbage information still lingering around in your fragmented movie file. To update a movie:

1. Select Update Movies from the Xtras menu.
2. Select Actions: Update from the Update Movies Option window.
3. Choose either to Backup Original File or Delete.
4. Click OK.
5. Select the Director movie you want to update.
6. If you chose to back up original files, select a folder where you want to save the original files.
7. Click Continue to Update and Compact your Director movie.

You cannot save the original movie files in the same folder as where you are saving the updated file. Director puts the updated file in the folder where the original movie was in order to keep all links to other files functioning properly.

CREATING A PROJECTOR

A projector is a very small stand-alone application that you create from the original Director movie. The projector contains enough of the run-time codes to play your Director movie in a play-only environment without the need for Director to be installed on the end user's system. Depending on the complexity of your movie, the projector file may be the only file required for distributing your application to the end users. To create a projector:

1. Select Create Projector from the File menu. The Create Projector window appears.
2. Select the Director movie(s) and external cast(s) (if applicable) that you want to add to this projector (Figure 9-5).
3. Click the Add button to transfer the file name to the File List window below.
4. If selecting multiple movies, use the Move Up and Move Down buttons to rearrange the order of the movies.
5. Optional: Click the Options button to further customize your movie. (See projector options later.)
6. Click the Create button to make the projector.

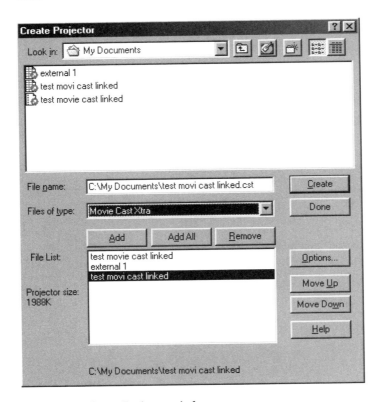

Figure 9-5   Create Projector window.

7. Name the projector and save it to the location on your system where you would like.

When you open that folder, notice that a new projector icon has been created with the name that you saved it as in Step 7 (Figure 9-6). Double-click on this file to view the play-only version of your movie. This is the packaged file of your application that you will distribute to the end user.

Although Director movies are platform independent, projectors are not. To create a Macintosh projector, you will need to perform the previous steps using the Macintosh version of Director. To create a projector capable of playing on a Windows system, you need to perform the same steps using a version of Director for Windows.

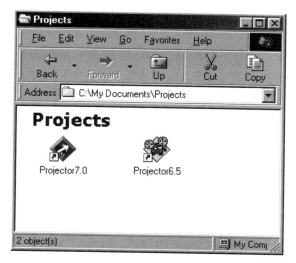

Figure 9-6   Projector icon.

CUSTOMIZING PROJECTOR OPTIONS

The Projector Options window contains the basic settings for determining how your movie will play back on the end user's system (Figure 9-7). In this window, you have several different choices for optimizing your movie and determining how it will be displayed when the user launches the projector application.

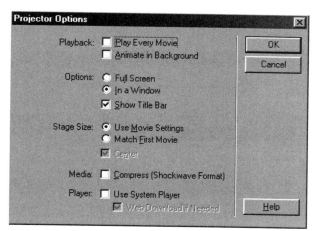

Figure 9-7   The Projector Options window.

Director keeps these option settings from the previous project when you create a new Director movie. Therefore, if you distribute your movies under the same general guidelines, you will only need to set these settings once.

PLAYBACK

Playback Every Movie is an option that tells the projector to play every movie that was added to the play list (Figure 9-8). If you did not select this option when adding multiple Director movies to the list while creating a projector, only the first movie in the list will play. The only way to get the other movies to run is to have them launch from within the first Director movie via the `playMovie` Lingo command, which can navigate to each individual movie.

 Rearrange your movies in the Playback List window to select the proper playback order. Place the movie you want to play first at the top of the list. The order that is listed from top to bottom indicates the order that the movies will play back.

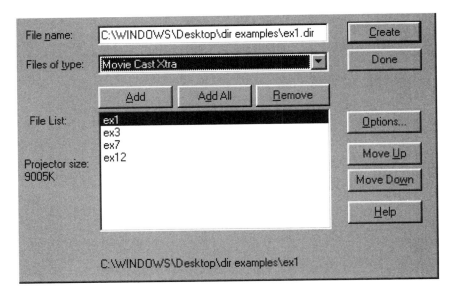

Figure 9-8   Add multiple movies to play back in the play list.

Animate in Background is a feature that allows your movie to continue running even if the user switches to another application. If the option was deselected at the time of creating the projector, your movie will go into a pause mode when you select another application as the active window. The movie will continue to play when it is selected as the active window (Figure 9-9).

The Reset Monitor to Match Movie's Color Depth is a Macintosh only feature that allows your computer display to automatically adjust to match the color depth settings of the current movie. This function will adjust the color depth for each movie independently if you have added several Director movies to the play list. This ensures that the playback of all your movies and its images are displayed correctly.

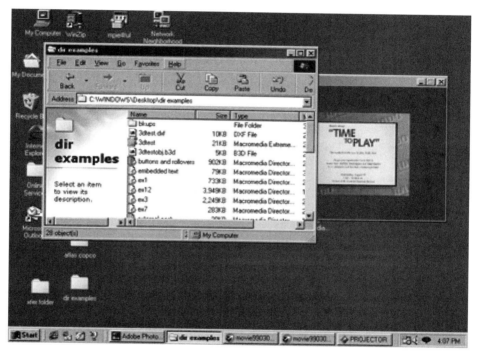

Figure 9-9   Director movie pauses if it is not the active window on the desktop.

OPTIONS

Full Screen Display is a very important feature to have selected. Most applications run covering the entire screen. If you set your monitor's resolution to be higher than the stage size of your movie, the user would wind up seeing parts of his desktop around the outside of the movie display (Figure 9-10). By selecting the Full Screen Display option, the projector file fills the remaining visible portions of the screen outside the area used to display your movie with the color selected for the stage color. This will mask out and cover up any signs of the desktop display around the outskirts of your movie (Figure 9-11). If this option is not selected, your movie will play in a box with the desktop visible on all sides. This feature is referred to as In A Window.

Displaying movies set to play In A Window will only play at the size of the original movie settings. These windows cannot be sized.

Figure 9-10   *The desktop is usually visible around projectors saved with the "In A Window" feature selected (see Color Figure 25).*

Figure 9-11   Full screen display projectors cover the entire screen, regardless of resolution (see Color Figure 26).

The Show Title Bar option is only available if In A Window is the current display setting for the movie. With this option selected, your movie will play back in a window that has a title bar attached to the top of the window (Figure 9-12). Use this title bar to reposition the playback window to a new location anywhere on your screen.

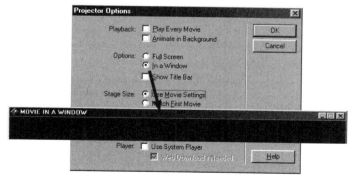

Figure 9-12   Adding a title bar to projectors saved with the "In A Window" feature selected.

STAGE SIZE

The next group of settings in the Projector Options window determines how to best display the size and position of your movies when you add multiple files to the playback list. Use Movie Settings adjusts how the stage size of the movie will be displayed. This will allow you to set whether the movie will take on the size of the current movie or whether it will use the size from the new movie.

The Match First Movie option affects the appearance of movies used in a multiple movie play list. This function resizes and repositions the way all of the other movies listed in accordance with the settings from the first movie.

If you have problems with the appearance of all of the movies in your play list, double-check this setting. This can cause the rest of your movies to all conform to the dimensions of your first movie's settings.

If the user of your application has his screen set to a higher resolution than the size of your movie, the Center option will automatically position your movie in the center of the screen (Figure 9-13). Otherwise, your movie may default to an undesirable position on the screen that cannot be changed once the projector has been created.

MEDIA

The next section in the Options window deals with compressing your movie and how best to play the compressed movie back. Select Compress (Shockwave Format) to compress the file size and movie data into a Shockwave format. For anyone to view this movie, the user would need to have the Shockwave plug-in installed on his system. You can choose to include a player within the projector file or reduce the file size by selecting Use System Player to use the Shockwave player. Turn on the Web Download If Needed feature to prompt the user to download the free Shockwave player from the Macromedia website (Figure 9-14).

Compressing your movie with Shockwave will reduce the size of the projector, but may increase the time required to open your movie as it decompresses.

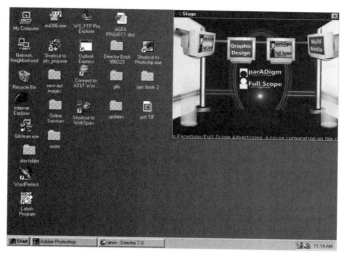

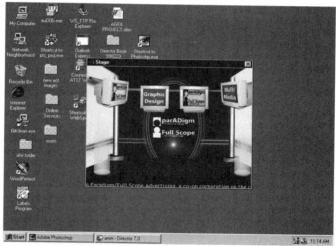

Figure 9-13   Comparison of movies playback position onscreen.

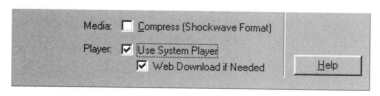

Figure 9-14   Selecting the Web Download if Needed feature .

Once you have selected all of the options for the movie:

1. Click Create in the Create Projector window.
2. Enter a new name for the projector.
3. Select the location where you want to save the projector.
4. Click Save.

Director will now package the movie(s) that you had added to the play list, the associated casts, and required Xtras and will create one projector file.

Moving projectors to a new folder different from where they were originally created can cause linked files not to be recognized. When the user goes to play the movie, they will be prompted to select the location of these external files.

CREATING SMALL MOVIES

A good technique to incorporate into your development skills is to design several small movies instead of working with one large file. For example, create the main interface of your application as one movie. Have each button or link on that interface open a new Director movie via a Lingo command (see Branching in Chapter 3 for more details). Therefore each subtopic would be reliant on its own independent movie (Figure 9-15). There are several advantages to packaging your movie in this fashion:

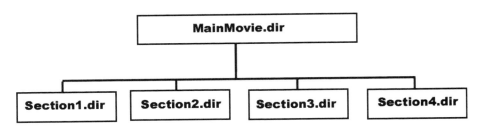

Figure 9-15   Schematic layout for individual subtopic movies.

1. Smaller files are easier to work with. The score for each smaller movie will be less cluttered than trying to work with all of your sprites in one giant score.

2. Smaller files are easier to troubleshoot. You can make changes in your score more accurately without having to worry about altering another section of the movie. If something is not functioning properly, you can quickly narrow down the location of your errors.

3. Smaller files will perform better, especially on low-end systems. The system's RAM will not be bogged down with unnecessary files. It will only need to load up the required information for the current movie.

4. Creating smaller movies allows you to build your own library of Director movies. You can use these movies as templates if you ever need to reproduce the same functionality for another application without having to recreate it from scratch or dissect through a lot of unwanted information contained in a single larger movie.

Director movies do not have a maximum file size. However, the larger you make the movie, the more potential you face for running into playback problems.

THE BENEFITS OF CREATING TEST PROJECTORS

One technique that will save you time testing your movie during the entire development process is to create a stub or test projector to be used over and over again. This process will allow one projector to activate each movie you create, saving you the hassle of constantly creating new projectors every time you want to test your movie. To create a test projector:

1. Name the movie you are currently developing "Movie1.dir."

2. Create a new Director movie.

3. Add the following Lingo command to Frame 1 of the script channel (Figure 9-16):

```
on exitFrame
    go to movie "Movie1.dir"
end
```

4. Choose Save from the File menu.

5. Name the movie "Test.dir."

6. Save it in the same folder as Movie1.dir (Figure 9-17).

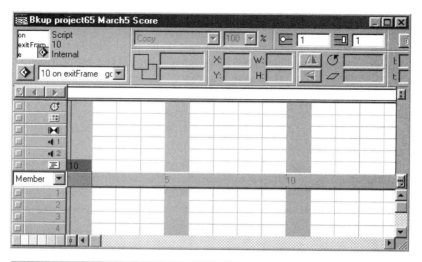

Figure 9-16   Creating a test projector.

Figure 9-17   Place Test.dir and Movie1.dir in the same folder.

7. Choose Create Projector from the File menu.

8. Add the Test.dir movie to the playback list window (Figure 9-18).

9. Click Create.

10. Save the projector as "TestProj."

Now you have a projector that can be used for each movie you create that you initially name Movie1.dir. As you keep saving your movie, this useful tip allows you to continually use this test projector (TestProj) to launch your application at any stage of the authoring process. Testing this process will ensure that your movie functions properly every step of the way. When you finish your movie, save your final Director movie under a new name using the Save As command and create a final projector for this movie.

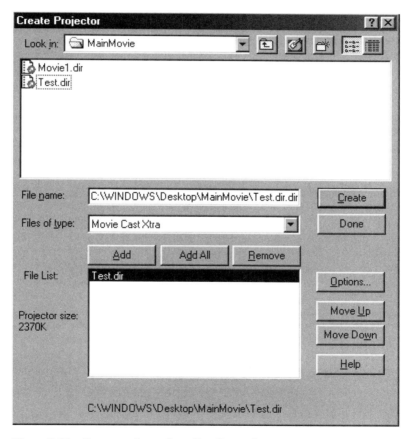

Figure 9-18   Create projector from Test.dir movie.

PROTECTING EXTERNAL MOVIES FOR DISTRIBUTION

If you are sending out movies that are external to the main movie contained in the projector file, you probably do not want the end users to have the ability to open up your existing .DIR files and make changes to your movie, steal your images, or copy your custom Lingo codes. Protected Director movies play back exactly the same as the original movie but do not allow you to open them back up in Director to edit the file. Once you create a protected movie, it is displayed with a new extension (.dxr). To protect a movie:

1. Open Director.
2. Select Update Movie from the Xtras menu.
3. Select Protect from the Update Movies Options window (Figure 9-19).
4. Select the Director movie you want to protect (original .dir files only).
5. Click the Proceed button.
6. Select the folder where you want to save and back up the original raw file. You must select a different folder than the one containing the protected file. An error message will prompt you if you try to save the backup and the protected file to the same location (Figure 9-20).

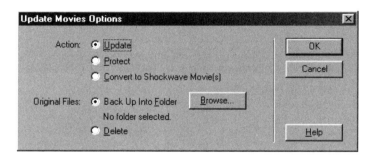

Figure 9-19   Update Movies Options window.

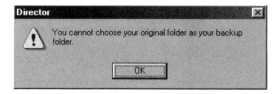

Figure 9-20   Error message warning that you cannot save the original file in the same place as the protected file.

You can choose to delete the original file and save only the protected file by selecting Delete from the Movies Options window. I strongly recommend saving a backup copy of your original file just in case you need to add anything to it or make any changes. Otherwise, you will need to start over from scratch.

Open up the folder to verify the location of the protected file. Launch the file to make sure it was saved correctly. The .dxr icon is displayed differently in the folder than regular .dir files. These files cannot be opened by Director and can only be played by a projector. All of the information required to open and edit these files is stripped away. You can also protect externally stored casts using the same process. These protected casts files are saved with a .cxt extension (Figure 9-21). When using a Lingo call to open up another movie after you have protected it, be sure to specify the exact file name and extension. Director will not differentiate if you want to open a .dir, but only have a .dcr file saved.

Protected files are uncompressed and therefore open faster than files saved as Shockwave movies.

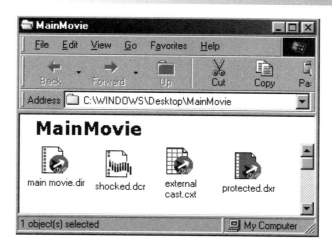

Figure 9-21   Protected files are saved with their own unique file extension.

SAVING AS SHOCKWAVE MOVIES

One way to distribute your movie is to save it as a Shockwave file. Shockwave movies are saved with a .dcr extension. There are both advantages and disadvantages associated with saving your movie this way. One reason to save it as a Shockwave file, commonly referred to as "Shocking" your movie, is to compress the overall file size of movies for distribution over the Internet or on floppy disk (Figure 9-22). Another reason is to protect the movie so that end users will not be able to open it up and make any alterations to your original files. The down side is that Shockwave movies are compressed to reduce the overall size of the file and will take a bit longer to initially open the file. To learn more about working with movies using Shockwave, see Chapter 10, Shock It For The Web.

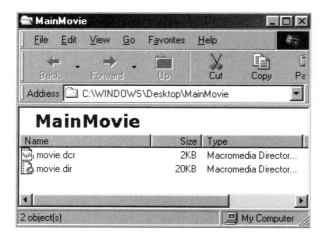

Figure 9-22   Shockwave movies are much smaller in file size compared to the original Director movies from which they were created.

WHICH FILES TO INCLUDE

When you begin to distribute your movies, depending on how you have created them, you will probably need to include more than just the projector file. Distributing a series of files is typical, especially when your movies become more complex (Figure 9-23).

When you go to package your finished movie, you must be aware of which files are necessary to distribute to the end user. Some projects require that you only provide a projector while other projects require a whole slew of files in addition to the projector.

Figure 9-23   Complex Director applications will require many supporting files to be
distributed in order to run properly on the user's system.

If you are creating applications for stand-alone purposes (CD-ROMs and Kiosks), one
thing that you will almost always need to include is a projector file, the executable
application that runs your program. You must also include any linked media files. This
includes all files that were stored externally from your Director movie, whether it was
graphics, audio files, or digital video files. All external movies should be kept in the
same folder as the projector or in a folder inside the folder that the projector is in (Figure 9-24). If any one of these external links is changed or broken, the user will be
prompted with a "where is...," the particular file dialog window when they go to play
the movie for the first time trying to recreate the link (Figure 9-25). If your project
includes external casts, these files must also be included in the packaged version.
Depending on the complex features used during the development of your movie, the
Xtras folder is automatically bundled internally into the projector. If you use any third-
party Xtras, you will need to include a copy of the Xtras folder with the rest of the
movie's files in order to have the movie play back properly. One of the main things to
make sure gets included is any external Director movies being called from the main
Director movie.

Figure 9-24   All external movies should be saved in the same folder as the projector.

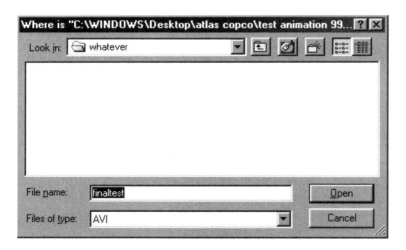

Figure 9-25   The "Where Is..." dialog box indicates a broken link to an external file.

Another file to make sure gets included for Windows platform projectors is the Lingo.ini file. The Lingo.ini file is a type of text file that contains the information about which Xtras, XObjects, and DLL files need to be loaded in order to play back this projector on a Windows system. Therefore, it is important to include this file in the same folder with your projector.

Including externally linked files is crucial, whether they have been compressed, protected, or left in their original state.

XTRAS

Every time you create a sprite that requires the use of an Xtra, Director automatically adds it to the list of necessary Xtras in the Movie Dialog window. If you use any Xtras during the development of your movie, it is important to include the Xtras with your projector. The end user must have these Xtras present on his system in order to view the movie properly, if at all. If you do not distribute a copy of the Xtras along with the projector file, your movie will not play back the way you had intended it to play. To see which Xtras you used during the development of your movie:

1. Open a Director movie.
2. Select Movie from the Modify menu.
3. Select Xtras.

The Movie Xtras dialog box appears (Figure 9-26). This window shows a listing of all the Xtras that are used by Director movies. The easiest thing to do is to automatically have Director create an Xtras folder for you that includes these Xtras. Having all of these files assures that your movie will play back without any problems. On the other hand, having all of these Xtras available increases the size of your projector. Obviously, you may not need all of these Xtras for your movie. To minimize the projector's file size:

1. Select the unnecessary Xtras from the Movie Xtras dialog window (Xtras not being used in the current movie).
2. Click the Remove button to remove these from the list of Xtras you want to distribute.

To have Director analyze your movie for required Xtras when you are finished building your program:

1. Choose Create Projector from the File menu.
2. Open up the Projector Options window.
3. Select Check Movie for Xtras.

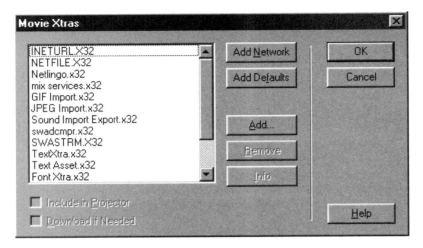

Figure 9-26   The Movie Xtras dialog box lists all the extras used in a Director movie.

When creating ShockWave movies, choose to have the required movie's Xtras downloaded when decompressing the application from the Web.

INSTALLATION PROGRAMS

When you are finished creating your Director movie, projector, and protected files, its time to distribute the program to your end users. Generally, you will not want to send out a CD-ROM containing a folder of the files and make the user copy it onto his system. Like most CD-ROMs you purchase, the program contains some type of setup or install application. Director does not have the capability to create one. You must use a third-party program to create this setup file that will automatically install all of the required files onto the end user's system. One program that I use to create installation programs for Windows-based applications is a program called Setup Factory 4.0 by Indigo Rose Corporation. To find out more information about this product, check out their web site at www.indigorose.com.

Most third-party installation programs can create a guided wizard that will help the end user properly install your program on their system with just a few clicks of the mouse. You can set up the wizard's screens to give your program a customized look and feel (Figure 9-27). To create an installation program for your Director project:

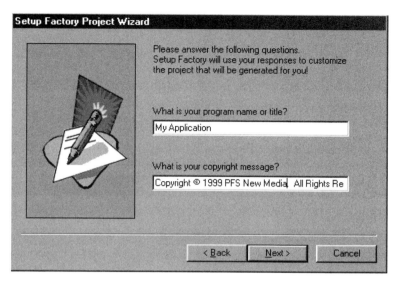

Figure 9-27   Installation Wizard screen.

1. Open Setup Factory or equivalent program.

2. Select the name for your program.

3. Choose the file or folder you want to add to the installation program (Figure 9-28).

4. Select the destination where you want the application to be installed on the end user's system.

5. Customize the appearance of the wizard by choosing which screens appear during the installation process and how they look.

6. Compile all of the selected files to create the actual installation file (setup.exe; Figure 9-29).

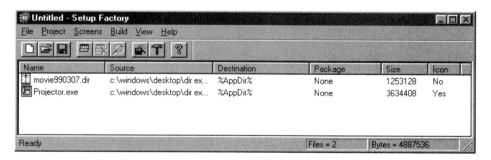

Figure 9-28   Select the files that will be included in the installation program.

Figure 9-29   Double-click the setup.exe icon to install the program.

CREATING SCREEN SAVERS

One of the more creative and interesting ways to distribute your Director movies is in the form of a screen saver. There are third-party programs that allow you to convert your normal Director movie into a saver format. Programs such as CineMac Screen Saver Factory by MacSourcery take your movie and convert the files into the proper structure necessary for creating a screen saver application. Director comes with a demo version of CineMac on the Director CD-ROM. For more information about this program, check out the MacSourcery web site at www.macsourcery.com. CineMac does all the work for you behind the scenes. Use its wizard to walk you step by step through the process of how to turn your movie into a screen saver file (Figure 9-30).

To create a screen saver to run on a Windows platform, just like Director, you need to use the CineMac version for Windows. To create a version to run on a Macintosh system, you need to convert your file using the CineMac version for Macintosh.

Figure 9-30   CineMac Screen Saver Wizard.

1. Launch the program.
2. Select Convert Projector from the File menu.
3. Select which projector you want to make into a screen saver program.
4. Hit OK. A window will appear indicating that the screen saver file has been created successfully.

There are several options to consider when designing an application to be used as a screen saver. The most common screen savers play a noninteractive movie that animates on your screen when the computer is not being used for a period of time. The screen saver is disabled when the user moves his mouse or hits any key on the keyboard. To create this option, you need to set a few script commands back in your Director movie.

Enter the following movie script to have the program quit when the mouse is activated or a key is pressed:

```
Global gMouseH, gMouseV - position of mouse at
      --movie start
on startmovie
   put the mouseH into gMouseH
   put the mouseV into gMouseV
   set the keyDownScript to "quit"
   set the mouseDownScript to "quit"
end startMovie


on enterframe
    if (the mouseH <> gMouseH or the mouseV <> gMouseV) then
    quit
    end if
end enterframe
```

To have your cursor disappear while the screen saver is running, use the Lingo command to hide a cursor:

```
on startMovie
    set cursor = 200

end
```

This Lingo code will make your Director movie quit any time you move your mouse or press any key on the keyboard. It is very hard to develop programs when they are set up to keep quitting on you as you are playing your movie. Therefore, do not add these Lingo scripts until after you have designed the content of your movie. When you are satisfied, add the script just before creating a projector.

Follow the specific instructions that come with the screen saver conversion software you choose on how and where to install your screen saver application. Keep the file size of your screen saver movies small so that any system will be able to play the application smoothly. Small file sizes will also help with distribution methods, either on floppy disk or downloadable from a web site.

INTERACTIVE SCREEN SAVERS

You can also add interactivity to your screen saver, but then you will need to add a quit or exit button in order for the user to leave the screen saver and return to their regular program. To create a screen saver with interactive options:

1. Create an interactive movie as normal.
2. Add a quit or exit feature using either a behavior or Lingo script (Figure 9-31).

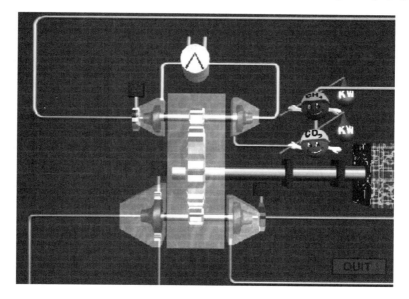

Figure 9-31   Add a quit button to any screen saver that allows user interactivity.

To use a behavior:

A. Select a sprite.

B. Open the Behavior Inspector.

C. Create a new behavior.

D. Select on mouseUp in the Event column.

E. Select Exit from the Action column.

OR

To use a Lingo script:

A. Create a movie script.

B. Type in the following command:

```
on mouseUp
   quit
end
```

C. Create a projector.

D. Use CineMac or other application to convert your movie into the screen saver format.

WEB PAGE LINKS FROM SCREEN SAVERS

Another screen saver option becoming popular as a tool for promotional and advertising applications is for a company to create and distribute a screen saver that links to their website when a certain action takes place (i.e., the logo on screen is clicked; Figure 9-32). To add this feature into your screen saver:

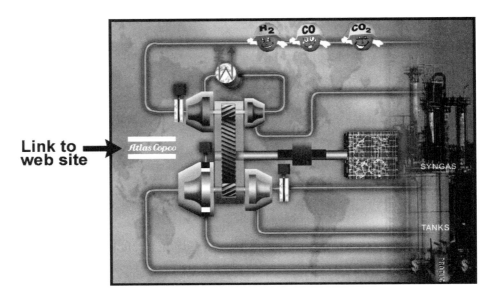

Figure 9-32   Use any object or image on the screen, such as a logo, as links to the Web.

1. Create an interactive movie as normal.

2. Add the following Lingo script:

```
on mouseUp
    go to netPage "URL"
    -- example: "http://www.fullscope.com"
end
```

3. Create a projector.

4. Use CineMac or other screen saver application to convert your movie into a screen saver format.

EXPORTING DIRECTOR MOVIES AS QUICKTIME MOVIES

When you choose QuickTime as your format from the Export Options window, you have a number of choices to select in order to customize the playback quality and other characteristics from the different parameters available. To access these parameters, click on the Options button from the main export window (Figure 9-33).

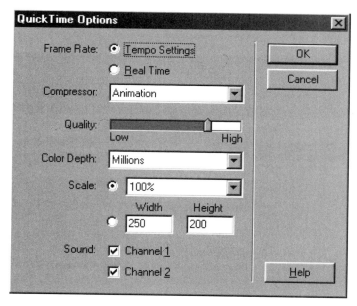

Figure 9-33   Export Director movie options as QuickTime movie.

The Tempo Setting exports your movie using the frame rate you had set for the correct movie in the tempo channel to a QuickTime movie setting. The tempo setting determines the number of fps in the QuickTime movie. The faster the tempo, the more fps, and vice versa. Therefore, the final size of the QuickTime movie is ultimately determined by the:

1. Tempo settings
2. Transition speeds
3. Palette transitions

The Real Time setting exports your movie as a QuickTime file at the same rate that matches the performance of your Director movie. Each frame in your Director movie becomes one frame in the QuickTime movie. Playback problems can occur with how your movie was initially intended to look due to Lingo scripts. Test your movie with all Lingo scripts off to see how your movie will perform before choosing the Real Time setting option.

Whichever setting you choose, you will still want to select a compression format to help reduce the file size of your movie. The compression format you choose will determine the playback quality of the movie. Use one of the standard compressors to set the different playback options including size, sound track, and image quality of your movie. See Chapter 8 to get a more detailed explanation of digital video compressors and decompressors (codecs).

Externally linked files are not included in the exporting process to QuickTime. Sound files set to loop will not loop when exporting to QuickTime.

MADE WITH MACROMEDIA LOGO

Macromedia's licensing agreement allows you to freely distribute a projector (a file that allows a movie to run without Director) to the end user as long as you are not selling your applications. If you begin charging a fee for your programs, then you must follow the terms and conditions listed in the Macromedia Licensing agreement:

1. Every project you create and distribute must contain the Made With Macromedia logo somewhere in your movie and on the exterior packaging (Figure 9-34).
2. You must sign a Macromedia licensing agreement for distribution.
3. Send two copies of your final project (packaging and all) to Macromedia.

Figure 9-34   *Made With Macromedia logo.*

If you have any questions regarding the Made with Macromedia distribution requirements, check out their website for the latest information at www.macromedia.com or call the Made with Macromedia FAQ hotline at 415-252-2171.

EXPORTING YOUR MOVIE AS A DIGITAL VIDEO FILE OR BITMAPPED FILE

Director allows you to export your movie, in whole or in part, as a digital video file. If you are working on a Macintosh system, you can export your Director movie as a QuickTime movie (.mov). If you are working on a Windows system, export your movie as a QuickTime movie (.mov) or a Video for Windows file (.avi). This is useful so that you can import your current digital video movie into other applications or back into Director as a single cast member. There are, however, several drawbacks with this feature:

1. You lose all interactivity.
2. You lose all sound when exporting as a Video for Windows file.
3. You cannot control the frame rate for playback any more.
4. Sprite animating by Lingo commands are lost.

You can also choose to export a series of frames or an individual frame from your Director movie. Director will output a BMP file on a Windows system and a PICS, PICT, or Scrapbook file on a Macintosh system.

Director takes snapshots of the stage, frame by frame, and puts them together forming the video file. This is why the Lingo activated sprites are not exported.

To export a Director movie as a digital video file or as a series of bitmapped files:

1. Open a movie in Director.
2. Select Export from the File menu. The Export window appears (Figure 9-35).

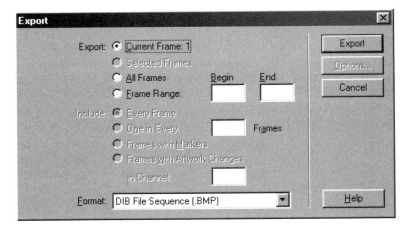

Figure 9-35   Export window.

3. Choose one of the export options:

   A. Current Frame—exports the current frame displayed on the stage.

   B. Selected Frames—exports a series of frames that are selected in the score (Figure 9-36).

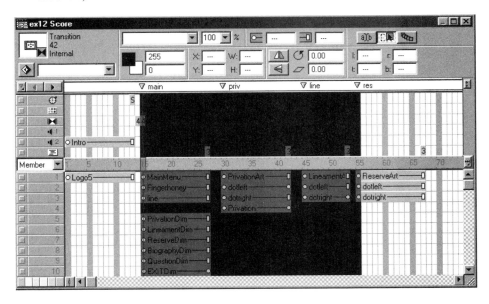

Figure 9-36   Highlighting selected frames to export.

C. All Frames—exports the entire movie.

D. Frame Range—exports a series of frames between a beginning frame number and ending frame number that you enter.

4. Select one of the following options if you chose Selected Frames, All Frames, or Frame Range as your export choice (Note: These options do not apply to digital video files):

A. Every Frame—exports all the frames in a selected area.

B. One in Every ___ Frames—exports only one frame per interval you set.

Example: One in Every 5 Frames.

C. Frames with Markers—exports only the frames indicated with a marker (Figure 9-37).

D. Frames with Artwork Changes in Channel—exports a frame for each time a sprite changes in a given channel. (Figure 9-38).

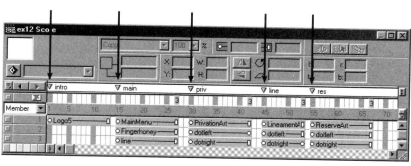

Figure 9-37   Export a bitmapped image for each frame identified by a marker.

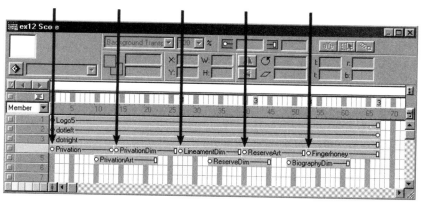

Figure 9-38   Export a bitmapped image for each time a sprite changes in a given channel.

1. Select the type of file format from the popup menu located at the bottom of the Export window. The choices depend on which platform you are working on: BMP (Windows), Video for Window (Windows), QuickTime (Windows and Macintosh), PICT (Macintosh), PICS (Macintosh), and Scrapbook (Macintosh).

2. If you are exporting QuickTime digital video files, click on the Options button to set the parameters for the video file (see Setting QuickTime Export Options later.)

3. Once everything is set, click Export. If you have not previously saved the movie, a dialog box will appear, prompting you to name and save the file.

 When exporting BMP or PICT file formats, Director automatically adds the corresponding frame number as it creates a new file for each frame being exported. The first frame would have a 0001 attached to the end of the file name and so on. (Figure 9-39).

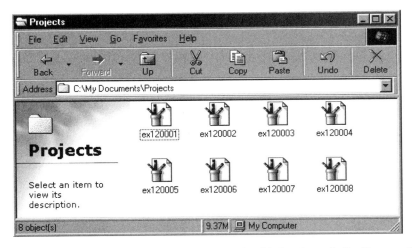

Figure 9-39   *A sequential numbering system is added at the end of a file name for images exported from director.*

S U M M A R Y

This chapter points out the many different alternatives available to you as a developer for preparing your Director movies. As new technologies emerge, I'm quite sure Director will change to meet the distribution needs of those platforms and formats. Be patient when finalizing your project. Trying to rush through it can lead to disaster. Failing to set one or two options can cause your movie to play incorrectly on the end user's system. Good luck and take pride in your finished masterpiece.

chapter 10

SHOCK IT
FOR THE WEB

The overwhelming growth of the World Wide Web has opened the doors for new ways companies (and individuals) can advertise, educate, and entertain people on a global level. Today, web addresses are more prevalent than street addresses. This new way of doing business has given birth to a new breed of programmers. Multimedia, although in its infancy itself, is expanding into a whole new platform capable of reaching millions of people around the world through the Internet. Programs like Director allow you to turn static web pages into highly interactive applications while incorporating layered graphics and animations that blow simple animated gifs out of the water. Even though movies were able to be used on the Web before, the latest versions of Director have really taken the Internet by storm. These releases allow you to save your projects as Shockwave movies, create Java applets, and write HTML documents directly from inside Director. Director 7 Shockwave Internet Studio comes with all the tools you need to develop fully loaded applications geared for the Web.

Afterburner has now been incorporated into Director. Use the Save as Shockwave option to turn your movie into a Shockwave document. There is no need to compress your movies outside of Director.

333

MULTIMEDIA'S EVOLUTION ON THE WEB

In the early days of the Internet (when buffalo roamed wild across the great prairies … well) multimedia applications were not able to run within a website browser as they do today. At best, most browsers supported animated .GIF files as a means of impressing viewers. As the limits of the Web were expanded, external applications and media-type players allowed you to download a file and view it in a separate window. Movie Player was used to display QuickTime digital video files. Today, the boundaries of the Web have been once again broadened. The use of small plug-ins and extensions allows you to incorporate interactive multimedia within the same browser window as the rest of the content of the page (Figure 10-1).

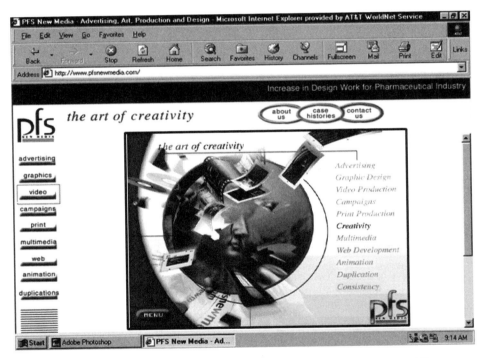

Figure 10-1   Shockwave movie running inside a web browser (see Color Figure 27).

PREPARING A MOVIE FOR THE WEB

When starting from scratch, you should consider a different development process when designing an interactive movie for the Internet as opposed to your standard stand-alone media formats. Keep in mind that the bandwidth, or speed at which information travels over the Internet to your computer, is typically much slower than any other platform you currently use to store or distribute interactive applications. The biggest complaint from viewers trying to access a website or intranet site is the user experiencing extremely slow connection speeds and long download times. There are a number of techniques you can incorporate into your development techniques to improve the way your movie looks and functions and decrease the time it takes to download your program.

◆ Stage Size—the physical dimensions of your stage greatly affect the overall size of your movie. Try to keep the stage size down as much as possible for applications that will be accessible from the Web.

◆ Cast Members—delete any unused cast members from your movie. These files only add to the overall file size and increase the time it takes to download your movie.

◆ Vector Images—when possible, use vector-based images over bitmapped graphics to reduce the size of the file. Vector images are computer-calculated images, not a series of pixels, which can be resized and reshaped without changing the quality of the image.

 Having vector shapes animate in Director can actually slow down the playback of your movie. Use vector shapes created in Director for static images. Macromedia Flash is designed to animate vector images quickly, maintaining its small file size.

◆ Reduce Color Depth—there is very little reason to use 24-bit images on the Web. The sheer lack of widely available high-speed Internet connections means that most users have to wait ungodly amounts of extra time to see a higher quality image. There are a number of techniques, including transforming bitmaps and applying custom palettes that can be used to get lower bit-depth images to look exactly like the same as their higher file sized counterparts.

◆ Audio Quality—audio is a growing part of Internet and intranet sites today. However, using lower sample rates for basic narration and musical pieces without a wide range of frequencies can dramatically reduce the file size of a clip without sacrificing too much quality.

◆ Video Compression—Currently, Shockwave movies do not run digital video files. You must work with externally linked files. Due to the increasing demand for video on the Web, this drawback will quickly be changing, allowing you to include digital video files in your Shockwave movies. Digital video files for the Web require more compression and formatting than what is normally applied for CD-ROMs and kiosks (see Streaming Media on the Web for more alternatives).

◆ Streaming Media—with the demand for faster access time to files, new technologies are emerging allowing the user to either begin listening or viewing the content immediately or have it start playing even before the entire file is downloaded.

WHAT IS SHOCKWAVE?

Shockwave is a type of technology that allows you to view Director and other applications through the Internet in your web browser. The ability to create Shockwave movies is commonly referred to as "Shocking" a movie. Once the movie is shocked and posted online, web users can than interact with the movie the same way as you would off of a CD-ROM. Shockwave technology started off as an independent player that allowed you to view Director movies in a separate window. Like most things, Shockwave has become even more powerful yet compacted to a simple plug-in that allows you to run a Director movie in the same browser as the rest of the web page. This is the same type of compression formerly used by the AfterBurner Xtra in previous versions of Director, now incorporated as a part of Director's internal features. Shockwave is a type of application that allows you to play compressed movies (created with the Save as Shockwave Movie option in the File menu) from both stand-alone media formats or through the Web. Shockwave technology is so powerful, it is being incorporated into other programs for content distribution on the Web including Freehand, Flash, Authorware, and xRes.

Compressed Shockwave movies and uncompressed Director movies are cross-platform. Uncompressed projectors are platform specific. Windows projectors can only be played on a Windows system and vice versa for Macintosh systems.

CREATING A SHOCKWAVE MOVIE

This will probably be the shortest section of this book. Director has made saving and creating Shockwave movies extremely simple. To create a Shockwave movie:

1. Open a Director movie.
2. Save the movie. Director will prompt you if you try to save a movie as a Shockwave movie without saving any changes made to your original movie (Figure 10-2).
3. Once the Director movie has been saved, select Save as Shockwave Movie from the File menu.
4. Name the movie and hit OK. Director will compress and compact the movie into the proper format, displayed on your system as a shocked icon instead of a regular movie icon (Figure 10-3).

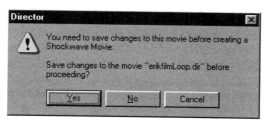

Figure 10-2   Warning to save original Director movie before being able to save it as a Shockwave movie.

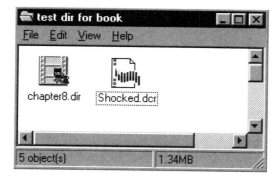

Figure 10-3   Shockwave icon.

Come up with some type of naming convention to help you easily identify Shockwave movies when viewing a list display. One suggestion is to add an "S" at the end of the file name. Make up your own naming procedure for all your types of files.

DIRECTOR ON THE WEB: THE PROS AND CONS

As you begin to develop a project, it is important to consider a number of factors that will make a difference on whether or not you can develop your Director application for distribution via the Internet. Depending on the type of project you are working on, some of the following factors might affect your decision to develop a web-based multimedia project:

Advantages

◆ Movies are accessable 24 hours a day.

◆ Cross-platform compatible.

◆ Easy access from around the world (provided you are connected to the Internet).

◆ More interactivity capabilities and animated content than regular style websites.

◆ Easy to update on a regular basis (at a fraction of the cost of re-burning new CD-ROMs for each time changes are made).

◆ Multiple user accessibility at the same time.

Disadvantages

◆ Slow connection and access speeds.

◆ Bottlenecking and other bandwidth limitations.

◆ Interactivity and multimedia support limited compared to other types of media, such as CD-ROM and Kiosks.

◆ File sizes need to be kept as small as possible, such as physical movie dimensions, digital media limitations, color issues (palettes), and quality of images.

◆ End user may need to download plug-ins for browser.

SETTING YOUR SYSTEM'S DEFAULT BROWSER

Most computers today have at least one browser installed on the system. Whether you prefer to use Netscape Navigator, Microsoft Internet Explorer, or another browser, check with each manufacturer to find out about any limitations that may exist with viewing Shockwave movies, especially with older versions of the browser software. If you have multiple browsers installed on your system, the first thing you should do is check to see which one Director recognizes as the system's registered browser. To check the path and application Director tries to open:

1. Select Message from the Window menu.

2. Type the command:

```
put browserName()
```

Director should return a new line indicating the drive, path, and file name that it will use when it encounters a Net Lingo command (Figure 10-4).

To change the default browser or set a new path:

1. Select Preferences from the File menu.

2. Choose Network from the popup menu. The Network Preferences window appears (Figure 10-5).

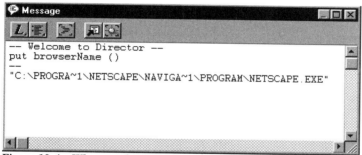

Figure 10-4   *When you key* **put browsername** *in message window it displays drive and path name to default browser.*

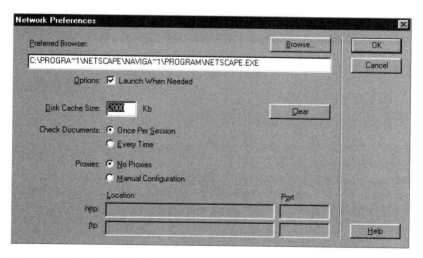

Figure 10-5   *Network Preferences window.*

3. Enter a path string in the Prefered Browser field.

   Windows Example:

   `C:\programs\netscape\navigator.exe`

   Macintosh Example:

   `Macintosh HD:Programs Folder:Netscape:Navigator`

   By setting the exact path for Director to follow from the drive name or partition to the exact executable application, Director can access that program as the default browser.

Be sure to check the Launch When Needed option in order for Director to effortlessly locate a web browser.

EMBEDDING MOVIES WITH HTML

Save your movie as a Shockwave movie to run your application in a browser. The shocked file must first be embedded into the HTML document that is used to run the particular page being displayed. Director can even create the HTML page for you if you are unfamiliar with how to create an HTML document (Figure 10-6). To create a Shockwave movie and the HTML document in complete form:

1. Open the Director movie you want to compress into a Shockwave movie.
2. Select Save as Shockwave Movie from the File menu.
3. Enter the name and location for where you want to save the Shockwave movie. You can keep the same name as your original movie because Director automatically adds the .DCR extension onto the file name.
4. Select the Generate HTML option to have Director create the HTML script needed to run your movie in a browser (Figure 10-7).

If you are familiar with HTML coding and want to write out your own HTML script, all you need to include is the following line to have your Shockwave movie appear in your browser when you launch that specific URL address:

`<embed src="NameOf Movie.dcr"`

Save your Shockwave movie in the same location as the original .DIR movie. This will help if you are linking to any external files.

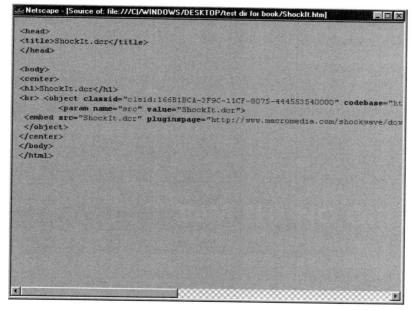

Figure 10-6   HTML document created by Director.

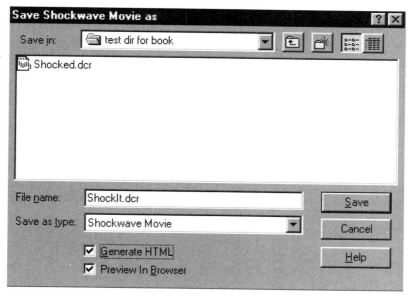

Figure 10-7   Generate HTML option in the Save As Shockwave Movie As window.

NAVIGATING TO A WEBSITE

Just like Director can navigate to different sections within the same movie or open up a completely separate application, you can also give your movie the capability of linking to specific websites. You can add this functionality to any Director movie, projector, or Shockwave movie. Through some simple Lingo commands or the use of Behaviors, linking to a website is as easy as typing in the URL. For this feature to work, you must be online and connected to the Internet. Setting up this command will automatically open the browser that is installed on your system. If you are accessing the browser from a stand-alone application, you will automatically return to your Director movie once you close out of the browser. To open a URL in the user's browser:

Using Lingo, enter the following sprite or frame script:

```
on mouseUp
    --enter any appropriate handler to activate the command
    gotoNetPage "URL address"
end
```

Using Behaviors:

1. Open the Behavior Library (Version 6) or the Library List (Version 7).
2. Select the Go To Net Page (Version 6) or Go To URL (Version 7) behavior.
3. Enter the appropriate URL in the popup menu in the Parameters window (Figure 10-8).

If you have more than one browser installed on your computer, you can define which browser becomes the system-preferred default browser (see Setting Your Systems Default Browser).

Figure 10-8   Use the "Go To Net Page" behavior to select a specific URL address to link to and from.

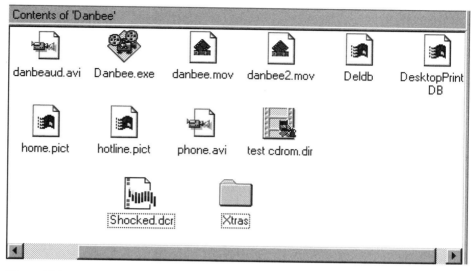

Figure 10-9   Include a folder containing any Xtras used in your project.

You will also need to include the Director Net Support Xtras if you are using Net Lingo in your movie. To make the appropriate Xtras available for your end users:

1. Create a new folder in the same folder as your project.
2. Name it "Xtras" (Figure 10-9).
3. Copy any Xtras in your movie into this folder.

Do not use the projector options Include Network Xtras or Check Movie for Xtras. This will not perform the same function and may not allow the user to view your movie.

Linking to a website can be of great use for many situations. One common feature is to have users access up-to-date help from the website. From the site, there might even be an e-mail link to contact someone for further assistance.

RETRIEVING SHOCKWAVE MOVIES FROM THE NET

While playing a Director movie, you may want to open up and play a new Shockwave movie from the Internet. Using the `goToNetMovie` command allows you to play a new Shockwave movie in the same display area as the initial movie. You can use this command to access movies from either an HTTP or FTP server. To retrieve a Shockwave movie from a URL address:

Using Lingo, enter the following sprite or frame script:

```
on exitFrame
    --enter any appropriate handler to activate the command
    gotoNetMovie "http://www.thePageName.com/movies/movie1.dcr"
end
```

You can even choose to locate a marker within a given movie:

```
gotoNetMovie"http://www. PageName.com¬
/movies/movieName.dcr#markerName"
```

You must be connected through an ISP (Internet Service Provider) or have movies saved in a directory named DSWMedia on your local hard drive for testing purposes.

AUDIO ON THE WEB

In addition to adding interactive programs with animated scenes you could also add audio to your Shockwave movie to give it more flare. For entertainment purposes, music and sound effects bring a silent screen to life. Narrative instructions make any training application that much easier to learn and comprehend the material. Director uses the Shockwave for Audio Xtra to compress internal sound files and store them as external audio files. As with all types of compression, the higher the ratio the lower the quality. Shockwave Audio (SWA) compression technology makes audio files smaller to access them faster from both stand-alone media or off the Internet. To add shocked audio to your movie:

1. Select Shockwave for Audio from the Xtras menu.
2. Select the Enabled check box in the Shockwave for Audio Settings window to activate the Shockwave compression (Figure 10-10).

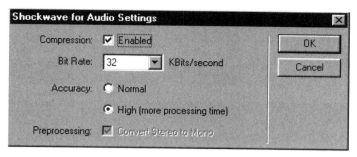

Figure 10-10   Shockwave for Audio Settings window.

3. Select one of the Bit Rate choices from the pulldown menu.

4. Set the parameters for accuracy and preprocessing as desired.

5. Click OK.

Setting a bit rate of 48 Kbits/sec and lower automatically converts your sound file into mono.

You cannot test Shockwave audio inside your original Director movie. Audio clips are not actually compressed until a projector or Shockwave movie is made.

SHORTER WAIT TIMES WITH STREAMING MEDIA

One topic that is sure to come up during a discussion of throughput of the Web is the limitations and lag times that come when trying to move larger media files, such as digital video and audio files, over the net. The solution to this problem (besides everyone getting ISDN lines in their homes) is to use the technology known as streaming. Streaming media basically works by playing files before the entire file has been downloaded. Streaming gives the user the impression of instantaneous downloads by either displaying the first frames of the file or using a placeholder image. In other words, the media will start playing when the file has downloaded enough of the information to begin playing in an uninterrupted manner while the remainder of the file downloads. Director allows you to incorporate streaming audio files into your movie. On the Windows platform, Director uses the Create Shockwave Audio File Xtra to compress external audio files for streaming. This is not the case for Macintosh users. You must use SoundEdit 16 to turn externally linked audio files into streaming media on the Mac.

VIDEO ON THE WEB

Unlike audio files, downloading digital video files from the Web can take a good deal of time due to the size of the files. That's not to say that there are not ways of reducing file sizes to be optimized for web distribution. Whichever compression settings you pick for your videos, streaming them can greatly reduce the long download times. To set up the streaming digital video file options with your Shockwave movies:

1. Select Movie from the Modify menu.

2. Select Playback from the popup menu. The Movie Playback Properties window appears.

3. Click on the Use Media As Available (Version 6) or Play While Downloading Movie (Version 7) in the Streaming options (Figure 10-11).

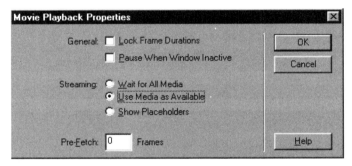

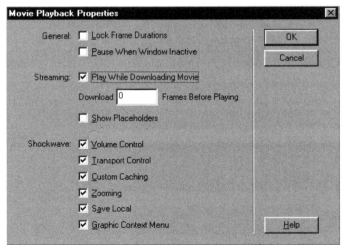

Figure 10-11   Movie Playback Properties window for Version 6 and Version 7.

4. Enter in the number of frames to download before displaying those images and begin playing your movie in the Pre-Fetch field (Version 6) or the Download __ Frames Before Playing (Version 7).

5. Click OK.

Selecting Wait for All Media disables streaming and forces your movie to be completely downloaded in order to begin viewing the digital video clip.

This will now cause your movie to be displayed almost instantly and begin to play while the remainder of the file downloads from the hosting server. The length and complexity of the movie and the speed of the modem at which you are connected with will determine what percentage of the movie needs to be downloaded in order to play the movie without getting hung up during the download.

Currently only QuickTime movies are supported through Shockwave. Video for Windows media files can be downloaded and then viewed but cannot be not shocked.

Due to slow download times with the Web, digital video files should be compressed down as much as possible. You will not be able to get playback of video at 15 fps, unless the physical size of the file is smaller than a postage stamp. Programs like Media Cleaner Pro by Terran Interactive are a great tool to have if you plan to incorporate digital media in your website. Some tips to remember when working with digital video files for the Internet:

◆ Determine the average access rate of your user. Keep in mind that video will not look great coming over a 28.8k modem. A 56k modem is really the minimal speed to view a digital video file and still have it look like a digital video file (not a slide show).

◆ Reduce the number of fps in your clip. Standard video in the United States plays at a rate of 30 fps. Most CD-ROMs work at 15 fps. Web-based video clips probably run best at 5 to 10 fps.

◆ Reduce the physical size of your movie. Instead of working with a dimension of 320 pixels wide by 240 pixels high, drop down to 160x120 or smaller for better performance.

◆ Keep your clips short. Use only 10 to 15 seconds worth of footage to keep download time to a minimum. If you really want to show more footage, provide a quick sample version (10 seconds long in a 120x90 pixel window) to view and then offer a larger version (30 seconds long in a 200x150 pixel window).

◆ Have all of your videos set for QuickStart or Streaming options. This will display the first several images much more quickly than letting the user wait for the entire file to be downloaded.

DON'T FORGET THE PLUG-INS

You are probably already familiar with the term plug-ins from working with Director's Xtras or other programs like Photoshop filter plug-ins. Plug-ins are a group of players (or similar type application) required to be installed on the user's system in order to take advantage of viewing certain types of files in a web browser. In essence, they add more functionality to a program allowing a developer to expand the features available beyond the scope of the original program's capabilities. Plug-ins are also used for the Web to allow more complex applications and files to be accessible and functional. These types of plug-ins on the Web allow the viewer to experience QuickTime movies, VRML, Director movies, Authorware applications, Flash animations, Acrobat files, and more from the Internet. Some plug-ins now come standard with the latest browsers, while others need to be downloaded and installed on the user's system before being able to view these types of files. If you are adding a Shockwave Director movie to your website, you might want to provide a link to the Macromedia website (www.macrome-dia.com) so the user can quickly and easily download the required plug-in. The following are a few suggestions to help the user get the proper plug-ins and view your sight without any problems:

1. Create your web page with a hypertext link to the plug-ins page to each company's website (Figure 10-12).

2. Provide instructions on your site about the steps the user should follow to download and install the proper plug-in.

3. Provide a copy of the plug-ins if you are distributing a copy of your application on a CD-ROM or other stand-alone media. (Check with the licensing agreements for permission first before distributing copies of the plug-ins.)

Because Shockwave has become such a popular and heavily used tool on the Internet, the Shockwave plug-ins come as a standard feature when you install Netscape Communicator 4 and Microsoft Internet Explorer on your system.

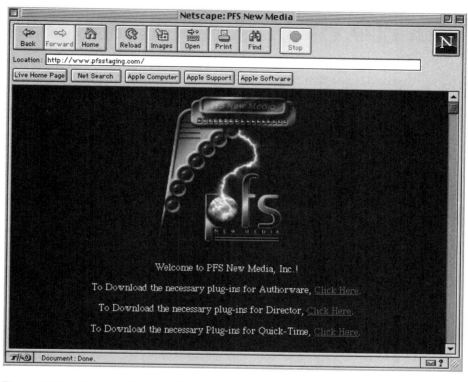

Figure 10-12   Hypertext links to other websites in order to download the necessary plug-ins (see Color Figure 28).

If you provide a link to another company's site, I recommend you have it open in a new browser window. The advantage for this is that if the user begins hunting around or venturing off into new sites, no matter where they go, your browser window will still be open in a separate window when they close out of the second browser window.

A CUP OF JAVA TO GET YOU GOING

Java applets are small codes or applications written in a cross-platform programming language that adds functionality to programs. Director offers the option to create a Java applet by saving your movies using the Save As Java feature. Once you choose this option, your Director movie is converted into a "Java movie." The advantage of saving your movies as Java allows you to play simple movies on the Web without needing the Shockwave plug-in. This may be advantageous for intranet projects and websites where plug-ins are not allowed. To save your movie as Java:

1. Open the Director movie that you want to convert to Java.

2. Save your movie with a single-word name. You cannot have any spaces in the file name or Director will prompt you of the error (Figure 10-13).

3. Select Save as Java from the File menu. The Save As Java window appears (Figure 10-14).

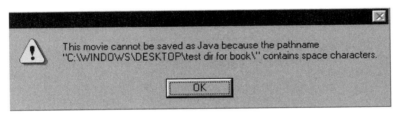

This movie cannot be saved as Java because the pathname "C:\WINDOWS\DESKTOP\test dir for book\" contains space characters.

OK

Figure 10-13   Warning prompt indicating that you must save Java applications using a one-word naming structure.

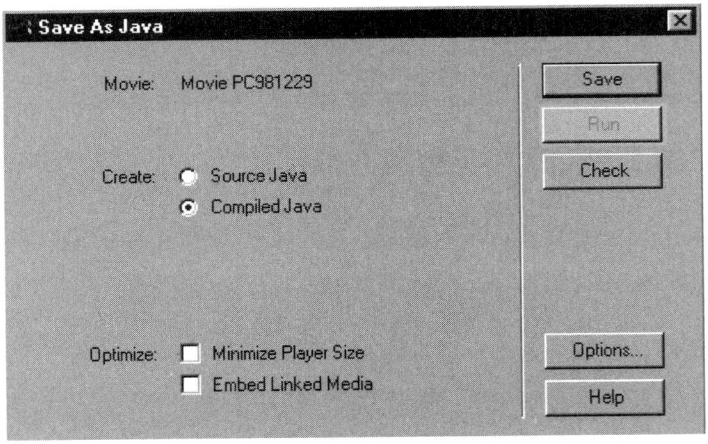

Save As Java

Movie: Movie PC981229

Create: ○ Source Java
          ⊙ Compiled Java

Optimize: ☐ Minimize Player Size
           ☐ Embed Linked Media

Save
Run
Check
Options...
Help

Figure 10-14   Save As Java window.

4. Click on the Options button to optimize your movie settings in the Save As Java Options window (Figure 10-15). This window allows you to customize the quality and playback performance of your movie.

5. Click Save. Director saves the movie with a .DJR file extension.

Not all Director options are available in Java. Test your application to find out which features work and which ones do not.

Java movies are protected and cannot be re-opened in Director. Be sure to save a copy of your original Director movie in case you have to make any changes.

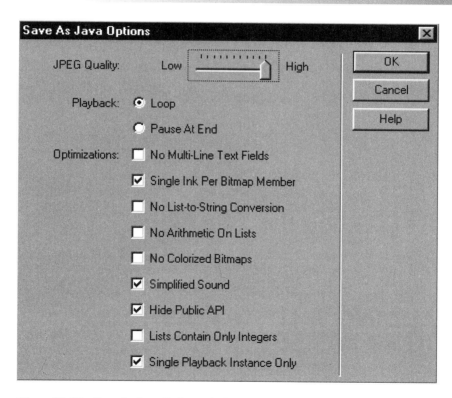

Figure 10-15   Save As Java Options window.

MIME'S ROLL IN ALL THIS

MIME is an acronym for Multipurpose Internet Mail Extensions originally developed for sending and receiving multimedia formats via e-mail. This technology has been incorporated into the standard HTTP communication protocol used for most web-based servers. This means that a browser is now capable of reading the content of a file and determining whether the browser will be able to play or display it in its native format or whether it will require the support of a plug-in. This is important for you to know if you plan to distribute Director movies on the Web. A Shockwave MIME type must be set up on your web server in order to recognize the Shockwave files. To set up this functionality in Director, use the following netMIME commands:

```
on checkNetOperations the URL
   if netDone (the URL) then
   set myMimeType = netMIME ()
   case myMimeType of
      "image/jpeg": go frame "jpeg info"
      "image/gif": go frame "gif info"
      "application/x-director": goToNetMovie the URL
      "text/html": goToNetPage theURL
      otherwise: alert "Please choose a different item."
   end case
   else
      go the frame
   end if
end
```

The case in this Lingo command checks what type of information is being downloaded and tells Director how to respond.

ADDING A LITTLE FLASH TO YOUR WEBSITE

Director now allows you to incorporate vector-based Flash animations into your movies, whether you package them as stand-alone projectors or Shockwave movies. The advantage to using Flash for movies geared toward website applications is that you can include some elaborate animations while keeping the overall file size down to a mini-

mum. This makes it possible so you do not have to sacrifice imagery to save on download time. There are two ways to import a Flash animation into Director:
   Build your animation in Flash and save it.

1. Open Director.
2. Select Import from the File menu. Import the Flash movie as you would any other file.
3. Select Cast Member from the Modify menu.
4. Select Properties from the popup menu.
5. Set the property values for the given Flash movie.
   OR
6. Build your animation in Flash and save it.
7. Open Director.
8. Select Media Element from the Insert menu.
9. Select Flash Movie from the popup menu (Figure 10-16).

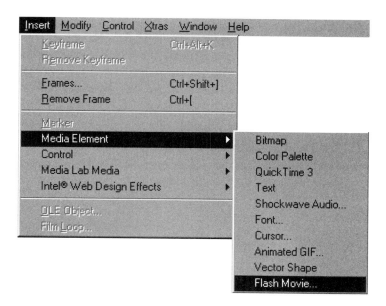

Figure 10-16   Incorporating Flash movies into your Director movies.

10. Click on the Browse button in the Flash Asset Properties window to select the Flash movie you want to import from a fixed disk or click Internet to type in the URL address of the site you want to link (Figure 10-17).

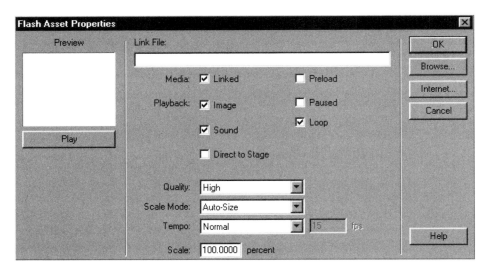

Figure 10-17   Flash Asset Properties window.

11. Set the other parameters in the Flash Asset Properties window.

12. Click OK.

The variables that appear in the Flash Asset Properties window perform the following functions:

♦   The Linked media option stores the actual Flash movie as an external file. Deselecting this check box tells Director to make a copy of the movie and add it into the movie as an internal cast member.

♦   Preload tells Director to load the entire movie into memory before beginning to play it. Otherwise Director will begin playing the Flash animations as it is streaming the rest of the file.

♦   Image determines whether or not the movie is visible on stage.

♦   Pause determines whether the movie starts out paused on the first frame or automatically begins playing when the playback head reaches the first frame of the sprite.

♦   Sound toggles any sound on and off that was added in Flash.

♦   Loop makes the movie start again from Frame 1 after it reaches the last frame. Deselecting Loop makes the movie play only once.

♦   Direct to Stage makes the Flash movie function like digital video clips. If Direct to Stage is selected, your Flash animation will be displayed on top of all other images, regardless of which channel is placed in the score. If Direct to Stage is deselected, your Flash animation will have the same type of layering capabilities as any other sprite.

◆ Quality determines the appearance of your images. Setting the value to high will turn anti-aliasing on. Setting the value to low will turn anti-aliasing off. Using one of the auto settings will try to present the best quality image, but automatically switch to the other setting if Director cannot handle the frame rate at that quality (Figure 10-18).

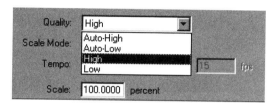

Figure 10-18   Quality pulldown menu.

◆ Scale Mode determines how the movie is displayed on the stage.

1. Show All keeps the aspect ratio of the movie and fills in any gaps with the movie's background color.

2. No Border keeps the aspect ratio of the movie but crops the image as necessary so as not to leave any borders.

3. Exact Fit stretches the image to fill the dimensions of the sprite.

4. Auto Size alters the sprite's bounding box to always fit the movie if the sprite is rotated or skewed.

5. No Scale does not allow you to resize the sprite.

◆ Tempo allows you to control the rate at which your Flash movie plays back in correlation to your Director movie.

◆ Scale displays the size of the movie in percentages of its original size.

The preload feature is only available if you select Link media.

Flash animations only play for as long as the sprite is in the score. This is similar to how digital video files work. Stretch the sprite to span more frames or use Wait for Cue Point to have Director play through the entire Flash animation before continuing playing the rest of the movie.

TIPS FOR OPTIMIZING YOUR WEB-BOUND MOVIES

There are always a few techniques that you can use to get faster download times, crisper images, and optimal results with your Shockwave movies. I encourage you to tell others about the tips you have discovered that make programming happen a lot smoother. (After all, we are all part of the same big happy family of Director developers.) The following is a brief list of suggestions, but there are many more:

◆   Reduce the color depth of your movie to 8-bit or lower.

◆   Design one optimal color palette or use as few palettes as possible.

◆   Reduce the size of your stage. Most web-based movies do not need to run at 640x480.

◆   Keep the number of cast members down to a minimum. (Delete unused cast members from the movie.)

◆   For streaming movies, put your cast members in the order they appear so the Shockwave movie can download the cast members it needs to display first.

◆   Use short audio clips that loop (when possible) instead of long musical selections. Larger audio files lead to longer download times.

TESTING YOUR "INTERNET" MOVIE

The most important process you can do before advertising your site to the public is to test that the Shockwave movie functions correctly. To test the movie before going online:

1. Create an HTML document with the `embed src` tag referencing the Shockwave movie.

2. Place the HTML document, Shockwave movie, and all related files into the same folder on your hard drive.

3. Launch any browser on your system.

4. Drag the HTML document into the web browser. This should display whatever was set up in the HTML page and begin to play the Shockwave movie immediately.

The next real test, once everything works well off your desktop computer, is to post it up on a server and view it off of the Internet. From here you will be able to tell whether all of your files are present and have been uploaded onto the server correctly.

 Test downloading your movie from different modems to see the actual download times at the different data rates.

SUMMARY

There's no question that the Web is going to be the way information and entertainment will be channeled to millions of people worldwide over any other source available today. The surge of popularity leads me to believe that people developing applications using Director will be able transition into web-based programming without any problems. Each version of Director that has been released has added more features and controls for developing for the Web. I'll bet that the next version of Director includes even more features geared for seamless web integration.

ENHANCING

YOUR MOVIE

The basis behind this book is to give you the opportunity to jump right into any chapter, find the answers to your development questions, and jump back out without requiring you to read the book cover to cover. This chapter takes that same approach and brings it one step further. You will find many advanced examples covering a variety of topics that you can integrate into your next Director project. These topics assume you have the basics of Director firmly under your belt. If you are ready, let's start adding some improvements to your applications.

UPGRADING FROM POWERPOINT

The majority of corporate presentations are created in or derived from some type of PowerPoint presentation. PowerPoint has a very easy learning curve, allowing beginners to start right off and begin building a presentation in no time. Although it has taken major steps forward with the addition of some more interesting features, PowerPoint is really designed as an application for novice programmers who like to work with the program's generic screen templates (Figure 11-1). But with limited interactivity, minimal web integration, and inadequate means of handling digital video, audio, and animations, PowerPoint leaves a lot to be desired for the more advanced programmer. The good news is that a typical PowerPoint presentation can be the building block for a more advanced Director movie. Director puts together the same type of presentations that PowerPoint can, but includes many more sophisticated features that PowerPoint just cannot touch.

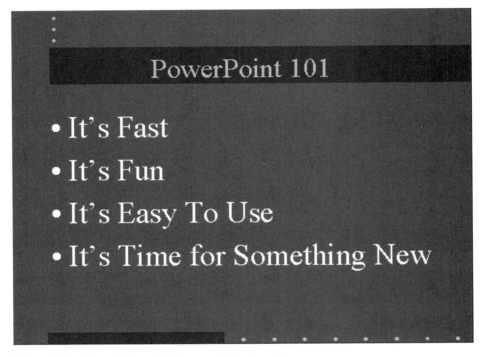

Figure 11-1   Generic PowerPoint presentation template.

There is no reason that you have to throw out your old PowerPoint presentations. You can import your PowerPoint files into Director quickly and easily and begin to expand on them immediately. Director will create a new cast member for each screen of your presentation (Figure 11-2). Director will also auto compile the score for you based on the order that you built your presentation (Figure 11-3). This includes your basic navigation and transitions. To bring your existing PowerPoint presentation into Director:

1. In PowerPoint, finish building your slideshow.
2. Select Save As from the File menu.
3. Name the File.
4. Select PowerPoint 4.0 from the Save As Type pulldown menu (Figure 11-4).
5. Select a destination folder and click OK.
6. In Director, select the cast where you want Director to store your slides from PowerPoint.
7. Select Import PowerPoint File from the Xtras menu.

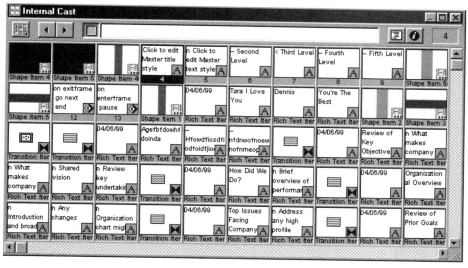

Figure 11-2 *Director automatically creates a cast member for each element used in PowerPoint.*

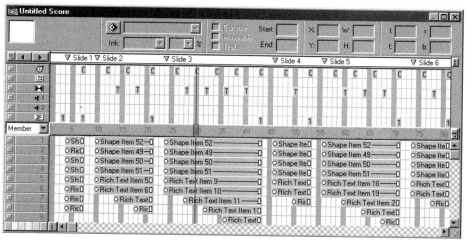

Figure 11-3 *Director automatically builds a score to deliver the same functionality that existed in PowerPoint.*

8. Select the PowerPoint file (.PPT) you saved in Step 5.

9. Enter the settings for optimizing the presentation in the PowerPoint Import Options window (Figure 11-5).

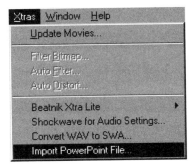

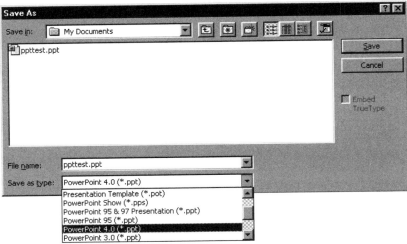

Figure 11-4   Director imports PowerPoint 4.0 presentations.

Figure 11-5   PowerPoint Import Options window.

10. Click Import. A progress bar appears indicating that the slides are being transferred into Director and the programming is being written to the score.

11. Click OK in the Import Results window when your presentation has successfully imported into Director (Figure 11-6). Depending on the type of presentation you create, your Cast will be filled with various types of graphic, text, navigation, and transition cast members. The Score data will also be automatically constructed with all the properly layered sprites, transitions, and interactive commands.

Test your presentation thoroughly after you import your PowerPoint file into Director. There are some features and commands that do not translate into Director's formatting. These inconsistencies are just stripped out by Director.

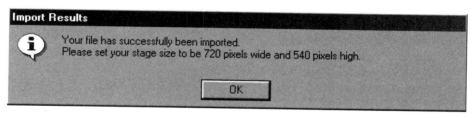

Figure 11-6   Import Results window.

CREATING HYPERLINK TEXT IN DIRECTOR

Just like on the Web, you can add hyperlink text to your Director movie, as shown at the bottom of Figure 11-7. This hypertext can provide just about any type of link or other interactive aspect normally associated with navigational commands. Use the hyperlink to navigate to a specific URL on the Web or have it jump to another section of your movie.

To create hyperlink text:

1. Select Text from the Window menu or click the Text Window shortcut button in the Toolbar (Figure 11-8).

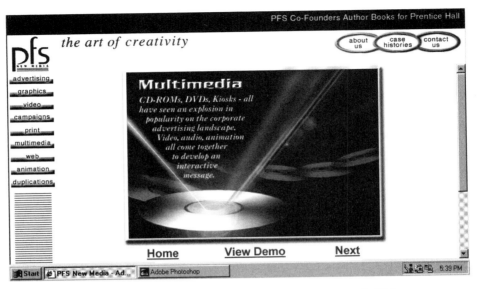

Figure 11-7   Hypertext links created in Director work the same as on the Web.

Figure 11-8   Click the Text Window shortcut button to open the Text Window.

2. Type in the desired word or phrase that you want to have hyperlink characteristics. If you only want a portion of the phrase to be hypertext, highlight only that text (Figure 11-9).

3. Select Inspector from the Window menu.

4. Select Text from the submenu. The Text Inspector window will appear.

5. Enter the URL in the Hyperlink box for where you want to link or any message you want to send to the `hyperlinkClicked` handler.

6. Close the Text window.

7. Select the Text cast member in the Cast.

8. Open a new script.

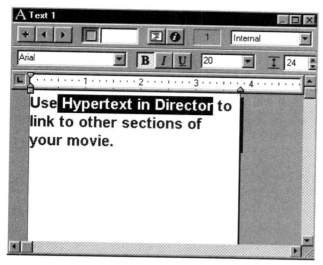

Figure 11-9   Highlight the text to be hyperlinked.

9. Enter the following script:

```
on hyperlinkedClicked
     go to frame "markerName"
     --enter any type of navigational or control command
end
```

10. Rewind and play your movie.

> **Director's default hyperlink settings include displaying the hypertext in a blue underlined font that changes to purple once it has been selected.**

SETTING A TIME LIMIT

I'm sure most of you have taken a test at least once in your life where you were given a certain amount of time to complete a task. A proctor sat in the front of the room whose only job was to announce "pencils down" at the end of the session. Why not continue the tradition in the Computer Based Training applications (CBT) you create in Director (Version 7). This can be a very useful feature for training programs where speed or reaction time are important factors in the training process. You can develop your application to display a countdown clock on which you can set a specific time interval from where it will begin counting down. This can run in units of days, hours, minutes, seconds, and hundredths of a second (Figure 11-10). I generally add a few functions to the training application itself, which tends to make programming the links a pretty complicated matrix to follow. A typical example of how to utilize a countdown in a program is to provide a link that navigates to the next section of the program if the user responds correctly to the situation within the alloted time. If time expires, the user is usually sent to another location, either to review the materials or try the question again.

When developing any movie that involves complex interactive navigational aspects, be sure to map out your links on paper before you begin to program the movie in Director. See Chapter 2, Planning Projects from the Ground Up.

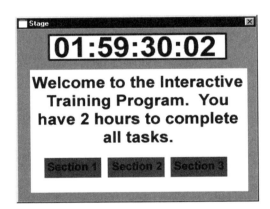

Figure 11-10   Countdown clock created from the Countdown Timer Behavior being applied to a field text box.

To add a countdown clock to your application:

1. Add a text or field box on the stage.
2. Select Library Palette from the Window menu.
3. Select Text from the Library List pulldown menu.
4. Drag the Countdown Timer Behavior from the Library window and apply it to the text or field box. The Parameters for "Countdown Timer" window appears (Figure 11-11).
5. Use the menus and sliders to customize how you would like the timer displayed and from what starting point.

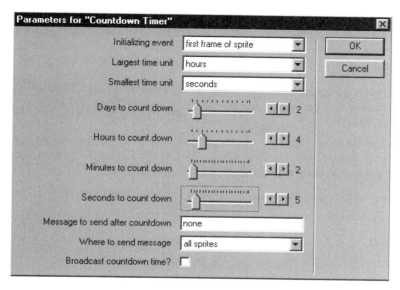

Figure 11-11   Parameters for Countdown Timer window.

6. Enter the message (function to take place) in the Message To Send After Countdown field for what the program should do once the countdown reaches zero.

You must remember to define your message with the proper handlers and commands (such as a keyDownScript) in order for the function to operate or else the countdown will reach zero and do nothing.

ACCESSING MEDIA ON CD-ROM FROM DESKTOP PROJECTOR

One of the more complex features in Director allows you to access external media files from a CD-ROM while running the projector from the hard drive of the computer. One reason for going through this process is to allow yourself the opportunity of updating movie files and just redistributing the new disk. Also, if your system's hard disk space does not have a lot of available storage space on it, keeping all of the linked media on a CD-ROM frees up that amount of drive space on the system. Although you might not think about it, software theft does happen quite frequently. Keeping media on a CD-ROM is a good way to deter people from stealing unauthorized copies of the program off your computer. By storing all the media files on a separate disk, no one can take a fully functioning copy of your work. This is especially valuable if you are selling your programs or demonstrating a prototype application.

To set up this option:

◆ Use a movie script to determine the drive letter of the CD-ROM on a Windows system (see the section below "Determining CD-ROM Drive Letters for Windows Systems").

◆ Use the searchPaths command to have Lingo track down the appropriate file path and destination. This allows Director to follow the system files's hierarchy where the movie was saved.

```
set the searchPaths = ["c:\mainDirectory\folder\ &
  d:\cdrom\source\"]
```

OR

```
set the searchPaths, 1, myCDROM & "\myFiles"
  --where the number represents the sprite, myCDROM
  represents the CD-ROM drive, and myFiles represent the
  exact location of the required media files.
```

If you know that all the external files are coming off the CD-ROM, there is no reason to have your system check through the folder from where your projector file is launching:

```
set the searchCurrentFolder = False
```

When redistributing updated movie files, remember to use the same file names and directory structure or the paths will not be able to correctly identify the linked media.

DETERMINING CD-ROM DRIVE LETTERS FOR WINDOWS SYSTEMS

The previous section discussed running a projector from the hard drive of a system while accessing media stored on a CD-ROM. If you are distributing your applications to different users, their CD-ROM drive letters might vary from system to system. For this to work properly on the Windows platform, your application must be able to reference the letter of your CD-ROM drive on your system (Figure 11-12). If you or the end

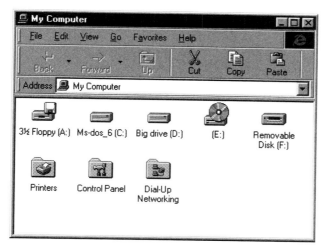

Figure 11-12   *CD-ROM drive letters vary from system to system, depending on the number of devices and partitions dedicated to that particular system.*

user receives an error message stating that the linked media cannot be found on the CD-ROM, it was probably assigned to a different drive letter than the drive letter used during authoring. Make the following changes to your program:

◆ You must have a version of FileIO Xtra installed on your hard drive.

◆ Use the searchPath command described in the previous section.

◆ Use the following movie scripts:

```
on startMovie
   put CheckDrive ("fileName.mov") into myCD
   --type in the correct file name and extension here
   append the searchPath, myCD & "\folderName"
end

on CheckDrive findFile
   --where findFind is defined as a local variable
   repeat with I = 67 to 90
   set drive = numToChar ( i )
   set thisPath = string(drive & ":\"&findFile)
   set myFile = new(xtra "fileio")
   openFile (myFile, thisPath, 1)
      if status(myFile) = 0 then
```

```
set myFile = 0
return drive & ":"
exit
  ·end if
end repeat
set myFile = 0
alert "Please check the file "fileName" is on your CD-ROM"
end
```

These combinations will search for the file by the name specified in the `search-Path` command on the root level for each drive and device mounted to the system. The call will return the letter name for the CD-ROM drive it finds containing that specific file name.

This technique for determining the drive letter only applies for Windows systems. Use the following path example for Macintosh systems: "MyCD:Folder:MovieName." Any Macintosh-mounted drive with that name and path will recognize and play that file automatically.

There are other third-party Xtras and applications that can also be used to determine the drive letter of your CD-ROM drive. Check out MasterApp from UpdateStage at www.updatestage.com.

ROLLOVER WORKAROUNDS

If your application includes rollovers and you are experiencing some strange behaviors with them when you first link to a new page, there may be a simple fix. The reason for some of your strange rollover occurrences could be related to the fact that a sprite can receive a mouseEnter event (Event used for controlling rollover functionality) only once it has been drawn to the stage. The user may experience a problem if his mouse is already over the area of the sprite that contains the rollover properties, but it has not been drawn yet. When the sprite becomes visible and the mouse is already over it, the sprite does not receive the command that the mouse is over the sprite until it is rolled off the sprite and then back on to it again. This can actually lead to a number of misbehaviors and inconsistencies with your programming.

To demonstrate this problem, the examples in Figure 11-13 are to have a graphic change when the mouse is rolled over the sprite and navigate to a new section when it is

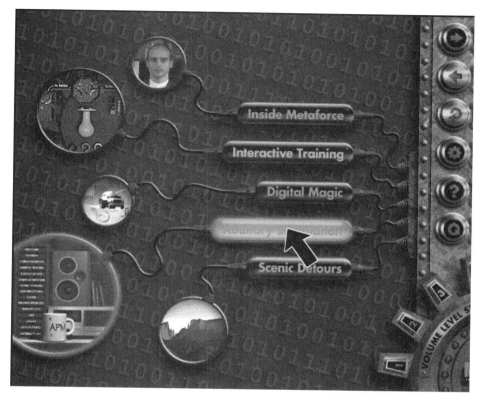

Figure 11-13   Rollover actions control the appearance and functionality of the sprites on stage.

clicked. If the user clicks the button (before rolling off and back on to the sprite), the button does not remain in its "toned-up" state when it navigates to the new section. In fact the button will not "tone-up" again until the user rolls off and back on to the sprite again. The solution is to use a custom Lingo script that will test the rollover state before drawing the sprite to the stage.

The Rollover Script Fix for Director 6:

```
property mySprite, myOrigMem, myRollMem
on beginSprite me
    set mySprite to the spriteNum of me
    set myOrigMem to the member of sprite mySprite
    set myRollMem to member (the memberNum of Sprite
        mySprite + 1)
```

```
      if the rollover = mySprite then
          set the member of sprite mySprite to myRollMem
      end if
end


on mouseEnter me
    set the member of sprite mySprite to myRollMem
end


on mouseLeave me
    set the member of sprite mySprite to myOrigMem
end


on mouseUp
    go marker (1)
end
```

The Rollover Script Fix for Director 7:

```
property spriteNum
property mySprite
property myOrigMem
property myRollMem


on beginSprite me
    mySprite = sprite (me.spriteNum)
    myOrigMem = mySprite.member
    myRollMem = member (mySprite.memberNum + 1)
    if the rollover = spriteNum then
    mySprite.member = myRollMem
    end if
end


on mouseEnter me
    mySprite.member = myRollMem
end
```

```
on mouseLeave me
   mySprite.member = myOrigMem
end


on mouseUp me
   go marker(1)
end
```

Using this script will fix the rollover problem. This test checks to see if the mouse is over the sprite as soon as the sprite exists. If the mouse is over the sprite, the state of that sprite is changed to the rollover property before it is drawn to the stage.

SUPPORTING FILES WITH THIRD-PARTY APPLICATIONS AND XTRAS

As with many applications you create, you will need to add different types of file formats that require additional programs to run or view the given files. Director has the ability to automatically launch the required applications through Lingo scripts and Xtras, as long as the required applications are installed on your hard drive. There are many different types of small applications and Xtras that can be used to open, view, or work with a wide variety of files and documents. Some applications can be distributed along with your movie, others are downloadable from the Web.

Before including or distributing any Xtras or other programs, check with the developers of those applications for any licensing or copyright issues.

A common request is to include .PDF files in the electronic programs you create. PDF files require Adobe Acrobat Reader or Viewer in order to open and view these compressed documents (Figure 11-14). Director now has the ability to work with .PDF files packaged within your movie by using such Xtras as the AcroViewer Xtra by Xtra-Media. The advantage is that you can now have cross-platform electronic files, catalogs, presentations, and tutorials all controlled from your Director movie. Check out AcroViewer on the Web at www.xtramedia.com/AcroViewer.html.

Another type of application used to support integrated multimedia files is a small executable application known as Whip reader. To view CAD drawings in your Director or Shockwave movies through a web browser, install this application onto your system. This reader gives your viewers full access to CAD drawings, including the ability to

Figure 11-14   PDF files in Adobe Acrobat Reader.

zoom in and out and pan left and right without losing any quality in the image (Figure 11-15). You can download this application from the Autodesk website at `www.autodesk.com/products/whip/index.htm`.

Using custom Xtras with your Director movie instead of just trying to rely on the application itself can help minimize potential conflicts trying to launch and execute these other programs.

As technology grows, clients are demanding more complex functions be added into the software you design for them. Look around to find out which Xtras developers have used or created in order to allow for these complex features to be easily added into your Director applications. You can find a list of custom third-party Xtras, a description of their function, and a link to the companies that created them off the Macromedia website at www.macromedia.com/software/xtras/director.

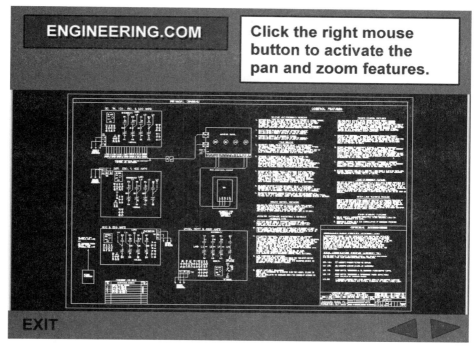

Figure 11-15   AutoCAD drawings can be accessed through a Director movie.

ADVANCED LINGO TECHNIQUES: CREATING CUSTOM CODES

One of the most valuable features in Director is its ability to use its own internal programming capabilities to create your own development tools. Director is one of the unique programs that allows you to extend its functionality and create these tools to customize and simplify the way you develop your movies. One example that advanced developers use often to save themselves time is to write movie scripts that will eliminate certain repetitive tasks. When you need to perform the given task, you can invoke the script from the message window.

One such utility allows you to create custom handlers called "generateMembers." During the authoring process of a project, you may need to create multiple copies of a specific cast member. Director allows you to build small utility applications that will do the time-consuming work for you.

To initiate the utility:

1. Open the Message window from the Window menu.

2. Type: `generateMembers(baseMem,howMany)`

This command states that baseMem is the member name or number of the member that you want to duplicate and howMany tells Director how many copies of that cast member to make.

To use the utility during development, enter the following Lingo script:

```
onGenerateMembers baseMem,howMany
```

```
set memType to the type of member(member baseMem)
```

—This line stores the type of member to be generated.

```
if memType = #empty then
    alert "You need to specify a non-empty cast member."
    return
end if
```

—These lines perform an error checking process for non-existent cast members.

```
set nextMem to (the number of members of castLib 1) + 1
```

—This statement functions if the cast member is valid. This will look at the number of the last cast member (number of members) and place the new cast members after the last one, calculating that number, adding that value to the variable "nextMem," and increasing that number by one.

```
set nameIndex to 1
```

—This line creates the variable used for indexing the newly created cast member's name.

```
set baseName to the name of member(member baseMem)
```

—This value will be used with the "nameIndex" variable to create the names for the newly generated cast members.

```
repeat with i = 1 to howMany
```

—Where i represents the number of duplicates.

```
set newMem to new(memType,member nextMem of castlib 1)
set the name of member(member newMem) to baseName & nameIndex
set the media of member (member newMem) to newMedia
```

—These lines set the new cast member in cast position "nextMem" of castlib 1, and stores the member reference in a variable "newMem." This command sets the name and media of the newly created cast member "newMem." The new name is based on the original member's name with the index number appended to the end of the name "1," "2," "3," and so forth.

```
set nameIndex to nameIndex +1
    --increment the naming index
set nextMem to nextMem + 1
    --increment the member number index
end repeat

end
```

Each time you build one of these types of utilities, store them in an external cast so you can use them for other movies. Link them during the authoring phase, but unlink these utility casts before making your final projector in order to reduce the overall file size of your movie.

INTEGRATING QUICKTIME VR

The days of merely adding still graphics to a presentation are quickly fading. Users today want more, they want the ability to interact with their movie and choose for themselves what they are looking at on the screen. The answer to this desire is the use of QuickTime VR (QTVR; Figure 11-16). QTVR is a unique type of digital video file that allows the user to pan and zoom within the file to view different aspects of the movie. This feature gives the user full control of what is being displayed while providing the illusion of viewing a 3D world. There are basically two types of QTVR movies (Figure 11-17):

1. Panoramic scenes—where you view an image wrapped around you in a full 360 degree display.
2. Objects—where you can view all possible angles of an object by rotating it in front of you.

QTVR files work on both Macintosh and Windows platforms and can easily be imported into your Director movies. These files work like most other digital video files, imported into Director as linked cast members and can be integrated as a part of your movie as a regular sprite. You must have the proper Xtras (such as the QTVR Xtra) installed on your system in order to view these files in your Director movie.

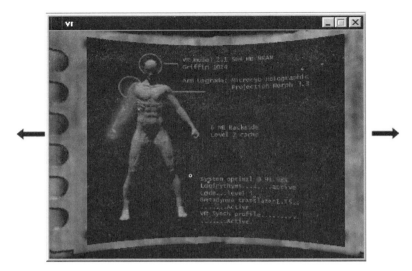

Figure 11-16   Sample QTVR files (see Color Figure 29).

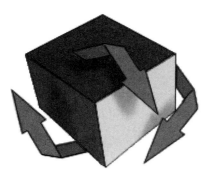

Figure 11-17   Panoramic vs. objects virtual reality is determined by the viewer's position relative to the image (see Color Figure 30).

It is a good idea to include the required Xtras when distributing your movie or provide instructions on how the user can obtain these applications from the Web in order to properly view your movie. Check with the makers of any Xtras you plan to distribute to see if there are any licensing agreements that you need to secure before passing out the required Xtras.

There are three basic steps required to use QuickTime VR files in your Director movie:

◆ Setup—registers the QuickTime VR components that will recognize the QTVR Xtra.

◆ Open—opens the movie.

◆ Display—shows the movie onscreen, constantly updating the screen based on the user's interactions.

It is important to understand that opening a QTVR movie does not display your movie. These are two distinct commands in which both must be included.

The following are some of the basic scripts you need to implement to run a QTVR file in your Director movie:

```
on startMovie
    global gQTVRObj

    QTVREnter(xtra "QTVRXtra")

    set gQTVRObj = new(xtra "QTVRXtra")
    --creates a new instance of the xtra
end

on stopMovie
    global gQTVRObj

    QTVRClose(gQTVRObj)
    --closes any open QTVR movies

    QTVRExit(xtra "QTVRXtra"
end
```

To open and display the QTVR file and convert Lingo variables to strings for use by the Xtras:

Example: `QTVROpen(gQTVRObj,"Hard  Disk:folder:Pano.mov", "0,0,300,150","visible"`

```
on openQTVRMovie, pMovieName, pSprite
    --where pMovieName = full system path name
    --pSprite = sprite place holder with size and location
    global gQTVRObj

    set tRect = rectToStr(the rect of sprite pSprite)
    put QTVROpen(gQTVRObj, pMovieName, tRect, "visible")
```

```
   end


on rectToStr myRect
   set myString = string(myPoint)
   delete char 1 to 5 of myString
   delete char (the length of myString) of myString
   return myString
end


on pointToStr myPoint
   set myString = strig(myPoint)
   delete char 1 to 6 of myString
   delete char (the length of myString) of myString
   return myString
end


on exitFrame
   --Displaying the Movie
   global gQTVRObj

   if isQTVRMovie(gQTVRObj) then
      if rollover(10) then --the QTVR movie
         QTVRMouseOver(gQTVRObj)
   --have QTVR controls take over
   --allows the user to interact via mouse
   else
         QTVRIdle(gQTVRObj)
         cursor 200
         cursor -1
      end if
end
```

Keep in mind that QTVR files are brought up as "direct-to-stage" movies. They are displayed as the highest in priority on your screen; often, Director cannot even recognize these files on its own. You must tell the Xtra when to recognize and respond to the user's interaction towards the QTVR movie.

There are many other Lingo codes that may be required depending on the exact application for which you plan to use your QTVR file. To find out more information about using QTVR, check out the QuickTime VR website at www.apple.com/quicktime.

A CUSTOM TAILORED LOOK THROUGH LOCALIZATION

Director's ability to incorporate database fuctionalities allows you to develop programs that can look like they are being custom designed for the end user without having to create a separate application for each. This is possible through a process known as localization. Localization within an application generally refers to the software's ability to be tailored for a particular group or individual through an alteration of text and graphics (Figure 11-18).

Figure 11-18   Customizing presentations using localization.

The trick to avoiding creating multiple versions of the same software is to build one application that uses external cast libraries. The portions of the applications that will be changing from situation to situation are placed into these external cast libraries.

To change the Localization Library with Lingo:

1. Open your Director movie that contains your Localization Library Cast (Figure 11-19).
2. Choose Cast Properties from the Modify menu.
3. In the Find File dialog box, select the name of the initial cast to localize (Figure 11-20).

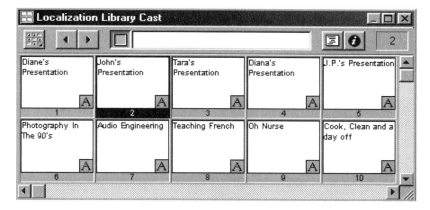

Figure 11-19   Localization Library Cast.

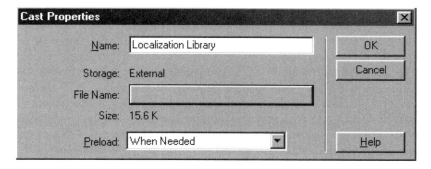

Figure 11-20   Find File dialog box.

4. Click OK.

5. Enter the following movie script:

```
On localize castLibrary
   If the machineType = 256 then
   Set dirchar = "/"
   Else
      Set dirchar = ":"
   End if
   Set the filename of castlib "localization" = the
 pathname & "localize"&dirchar&castlibrary
 end
```

6. Select Message from the Window menu.

7. Enter in the line:

```
Localize "name2"
```

8. Close the Message window.

The handler outlined in Step 5 takes the name you insert and looks in the Localize directory for that particular cast library. It then sets that name as the Localization cast library. You should be able to see how your now-templated program becomes customized for the particular end user without having to create multiple movies from scratch.

SUMMARY

This chapter went into detail showing you various examples that you can include in your movie to bring it up to a more advanced program—one that is a few steps ahead of the competition. This chapter assumes that you are familiar with some of the more intricate details of Director programming, especially with setting up Lingo Scripts. Take these ideas and expand on them to add even more power and excitement to your Director movies. Whatever the future holds, learning how to improve your Director skills can only make your projects that much more exciting (and hopefully a few more dollars). Stick with it and constantly experiment. You'll never know what you can develop unless you push past your limits and venture into bold new territories. If you come up with a winner, let me know how you did it. Good luck as you journey beyond the multimedia world as we know it.

INDEX